INDIVIDUAL
VOLUNTARY
ARRANGEMENTS

INDIVIDUAL VOLUNTARY ARRANGEMENTS

Stephen A Lawson, Solicitor,
Partner, Anstey Sargent & Probert

jORDANS

1992

Published by
Jordan & Sons Limited
21 St Thomas Street
Bristol BS1 6JS

© Jordan & Sons Limited 1992

British Library Cataloguing in Publication Data
A catalogue record for this book is available from the British Library.

ISBN 0 85308 180 8

Typeset by Rowland Phototypesetting Limited
Bury St Edmunds, Suffolk

Printed at The Bath Press Limited, Bath

PREFACE

Innovations in the law may widely be regarded as a mixed blessing. When one is used to a 'state of affairs', radical changes are sometimes unwelcome. Nevertheless, reform is to be welcomed when it really is reform.

The law relating to personal insolvency had remained largely unchanged since the passing of the Deeds of Arrangement Act and Bankruptcy Act of 1914. It was extremely difficult, if not impossible, for a debtor to enter into a legally binding voluntary agreement with his creditors and, whilst deeds of arrangement and compositions under the 1914 Act had their place, they were often found to be creatures of limited scope or value.

The introduction of the concept of an individual voluntary arrangement allowing a debtor to come to such an agreement with his creditors was therefore a timely innovation.

It is nearly six years since the Insolvency Act 1986 came into force and, accordingly, insolvency practitioners, whether accountants or solicitors, have had time to gain experience as to the working of the Act and Rules. Whilst learning and experience will continue, and notwithstanding the fact that to date there is little established case law, many lessons have nevertheless been learnt and much practical experience gained. This book does not set out to be a weighty legal commentary, nor does it seek to set itself up as being a rival to those eminent legal textbooks associated with the names of pre-eminent lawyers. Its purpose is to look at voluntary arrangements essentially from a practical point of view in relation to the questions: 'What are they?', 'How do they work?', 'What are their essentials?' and 'What are the problems and pitfalls?'.

Whilst this book is aimed at accountants and solicitors dealing with insolvency matters, it is also intended to be of assistance to professional advisers generally who, although not professing any expertise in insolvency, from time to time come across voluntary arrangements and need to know how they work.

The Act and the Rules are deficient in their lack of any real 'meat' as regards the implementation and actual supervision of an arrangement. Accordingly, much of this book is devoted to the preparation of the proposal on which the success or failure of the arrangement will depend.

Amendment of legislation in the foreseeable future is unlikely. The judges may have their say but, at least for a while, it seems that many points may remain uncertain: these include the concept of failure, the effect of a supervening bankruptcy order and the whole question of the termination of an arrangement.

Inevitably, in the absence of statutory or judicial authority, on many points dealt with in this book I have personal views and opinions; with the passage of time, I may be proved right or wrong.

It is undoubtedly true that, in many proper cases, individual voluntary arrangements can work. Professionals concerned with insolvency now have greater experience and confidence. However, arrangements will never replace bankruptcy entirely, and they will not succeed where there are not the funds available to set them up, where the assets available either immediately or at some time in the future are insufficient to lead to a realistic offer to the creditors, or where the debtor is unco-operative. Nevertheless, there are many instances where arrangements can and will work. It is surely incumbent on all those who are called on to advise those unfortunate enough to find themselves caught up in the raging torrent of debt to be aware of the existence of such arrangements, and to have some idea of how they can work and what their implications are. Too many people have bankruptcy orders made against them where, if perhaps some thought had been given at an earlier stage or the person had taken advice at an earlier stage, the new alternative could have been implemented.

It is hoped that this book will be of some assistance to those called on to advise and also to those who find themselves classed as either debtor or creditor in the great divide of debt.

My unfailing thanks go to my colleague and partner, Mrs Gillian Smith, Licensed Insolvency Practitioner, for her contribution to this work and for her support and encouragement. All omissions and deficiencies are, however, entirely my responsibility.

A debt is owed which words cannot adequately express to my secretaries, Mrs Frances Seabourne and Mrs Ann Sanford, who have had to cope with drafts and manuscripts which at times must not only have sorely tried them, but have reminded them of the fallibility of all humanity. I express my appreciation too to my family, who on many evenings have left me alone with 'The Book', wondering sometimes perhaps if individual voluntary arrangements had wholly taken over my life.

Finally, I express my appreciation to those many friends and colleagues from the accountancy world for their pieces of helpful assistance: in a very real sense, this book is aimed at, and informally dedicated to, those people. In particular, my special thanks to Stephen Peters and Bruce Lockhart of Messrs Ernst and Young, Exeter.

S A Lawson
Exeter   June 1992

CONTENTS

PREFACE   v
TABLE OF CASES   xi
TABLE OF STATUTES   xiii
TABLE OF STATUTORY INSTRUMENTS   xvii

Chapter 1 – AN INTRODUCTION   1

1.1   The Innovation   1
1.2   The Position prior to 1986   1
1.3   The New Provision   3
1.4   The Basic Procedure   3
1.5   The Nominee and Supervisor   4
1.6   The Nature of an Individual Voluntary Arrangement   4
1.7   Flow Chart: Individual Voluntary Arrangement   5

Chapter 2 – FORMATION OF THE INDIVIDUAL VOLUNTARY
            ARRANGEMENT   7

2.1   Sources of Law   7
2.2   Jurisdiction   7
2.3   Capacity   8
2.4   First Approach to the Nominee   9
2.5   Desirability of an Individual Voluntary Arrangement   10
2.6   Costs and Legal Aid   12
2.7   Case 1 and Case 2   13
2.8   Partnership as Debtor   13

Chapter 3 – THE PROPOSAL   15

3.1   Requirements of the Act and Rules   15
3.2   Particular Assets and Liabilities   28
3.3   Specific Considerations   33

Chapter 4 – PROCEEDINGS FOR THE INTERIM ORDER   43

4.1   Introduction   43
4.2   Purpose of the Interim Order   43
4.3   Involvement of the Nominee   44
4.4   The Application   44
4.5   Who May Apply?   45
4.6   Effect of Application   45
4.7   Cases in which an Interim Order can be Made   46

4.8   Service   47
4.9   Hearing of the Application   47
4.10 Where Debtor is an Undischarged Bankrupt   48
4.11 Where Debtor dies before the Court has made an Interim Order   49
4.12 Where Debtor dies after the Court has made an Interim Order   49
4.13 Official Receiver/Trustee   49
4.14 Duration of Interim Order   50
4.15 Form of Order and Service   50
4.16 Practice Direction (Bankruptcy: Voluntary Arrangements)   51

Chapter 5 – ROLE OF THE NOMINEE AND NOMINEE'S
  REPORT   53

5.1   Introduction   53
5.2   Nominee's Report   53
5.3   Form and Purpose of the Report   54
5.4   Nominee's Powers   54
5.5   Consideration of the Report   55
5.6   Effect of Death of Debtor   56
5.7   Replacement of Nominee   56
5.8   Form of Order   57
5.9   One-stage Procedure ('Concertina Order')   57

Chapter 6 – CREDITORS' MEETING   59

6.1   General   59
6.2   Effect of Approval   69
6.3   Challenge of the Meeting's Decision   72

Chapter 7 – IMPLEMENTATION AND SUPERVISION OF THE
  ARRANGEMENT   79

7.1   Requirements of the Act and Rules   79
7.2   General Considerations   84
7.3   Specific Considerations   86

Chapter 8 – DEFAULT AND FAILURE   93

8.1   Introduction   93
8.2   Default   93
8.3   Statutory Considerations   93
8.4   Effect of Bankruptcy Order on Arrangement   96
8.5   Failure   96
8.6   Completion of Arrangement   96
8.7   Setting Aside   97
8.8   Frustration   97
8.9   Criminal Liability   97

Chapter 9 – SPECIAL CONSIDERATIONS WHERE THE DEBTOR
   IS AN UNDISCHARGED BANKRUPT   99

9.1 Introduction   99
9.2 Application for Interim Order   99
9.3 The Interim Order   99
9.4 Declaration as to Existence of Bankruptcy   99
9.5 Further Provision in Interim Order   100
9.6 Effect of Approval   100
9.7 Annulment   101
9.8 Directions   101
9.9 Specific Provisions in the Rules   101
9.10 Categories of Creditor   102
9.11 Hand-over of Property   102
9.12 Opposition to Application for Interim Order by Official Receiver
     or Trustee   103
9.13 Pending Bankruptcy Petition   103

Chapter 10 – EFFECT OF BANKRUPTCY PROCEEDINGS   105

10.1 Introduction   105
10.2 Void Transactions   105
10.3 Effect of Bankruptcy Order on the Arrangement   106
10.4 Bankrupt's Estate   107
10.5 Preferential Creditors   107
10.6 Unsecured Creditors   108
10.7 Appointment of Trustee   108
10.8 Proceedings on a Debtor's Petition for Bankruptcy   108

Chapter 11 – MATRIMONIAL CONSIDERATIONS   111

11.1 Introduction   111
11.2 Position of the Spouse Generally   111
11.3 Matrimonial Proceedings Pending at the Time of Preparation of
     the Proposal and Application for the Interim Order   112
11.4 Matrimonial Proceedings Arising after an Arrangement has been
     Approved   112
11.5 Matrimonial Home   113
11.6 Other Considerations as regards the Spouse   115
11.7 Debts due to Spouses   116
11.8 Provable Claims   116

Chapter 12 – VALUE ADDED TAX AND OTHER TAX
   CONSIDERATIONS   117

12.1 Introduction   117
12.2 Status as Preferential Creditors   117
12.3 Attitude of the Taxation Authorities   117
12.4 VAT considerations   118
12.5 Other Tax Considerations   119

Appendix 1 – DRAFT PROPOSAL AND RELATED MATERIALS   123

Appendix 2 – FORMS AND DRAFT LETTERS   163

Appendix 3 – EXTRACTS FROM INSOLVENCY ACT 1986   211

Appendix 4 – EXTRACTS FROM INSOLVENCY RULES 1986   229

Appendix 5 – SOCIETY OF PRACTITIONERS OF INSOLVENCY
    GUIDELINES   243

INDEX   253

TABLE OF CASES

References are to page numbers. **Bold** references indicate where material is set out in full.

Aiden Shipping Co Ltd v Interbulk Ltd [1986] AC 965, [1986] 2 All ER 409, HL	89
Bailey, Re [1977] 1 WLR 278, [1977] 2 All ER 26	114
Boydell v Gillespie (1970) 216 EG 1505	114
Citro, Re [1990] 3 All ER 952	114
Debtor (No 83 of 1988), Re A [1990] 1 WLR 708 sub nom	
Re Cove (A Debtor) [1990] 1 All ER 949	48, 56, 78
Debtor (No 2389 of 1989), Re A [1990] 3 All ER 984	5
Debtor (No 222 of 1990), Re A (1991) *The Times*, 27 June	10, 15, 23, 40, 53, 65, 70, 71, 73, 76
Debtor (No 259 of 1990), Re A [1992] 1 WLR 226	74, 75
Gorman, Re [1990] 1 All ER 717	116
Holliday, Re [1981] Ch 405, [1981] 2 WLR 996, [1980] 3 All ER 385, CA	114
Lowrie, Re [1981] 3 All ER 353	114
M, In Re (1991) *The Times*, 17 April	43
Naeem (A Bankrupt) (No 18 of 1988), Re [1990] 1 WLR 48	22, 30, 35, 44, 73, 83, 112
Pittortou, Re [1985] 1 All ER 285	116
Practice Direction (Bankruptcy: Voluntary Arrangements)	
[1992] 1 WLR 120	48, **51**, 57
Solomon, Re [1967] Ch 573, [1967] 2 WLR 172, [1966] 3 All ER 255	114
Turner, Re [1974] 1 WLR 1556, [1975] 1 All ER 5	114
Woodstock, Re (unreported) November 1979	116

TABLE OF STATUTES

References are to page numbers. **Bold** references indicate where material is set out in full.

Bankruptcy Act 1914	1, 2, 82, 181	(2)	43, 48
s 16	2	(3), (4)	48, 100, 169
s 21	2	(5)	48, 100
s 112(4)	2	(6)	50
Companies Act 1985	1	s 256	12, 15, 28, 53, 133, **212**
Company Directors Disqualification		(1)	51, 54, 59, 170, 171
Act 1986	13	(2)	55, 56
s 21(2)	14	(3)	57
County Courts Act 1984		(3)(a)	27
Part VI	181	(4)	50, 169
ss 112–114	2	(5), (6)	50, 56
Deeds of Arrangement Act 1914	1, 2, 71	s 257	72, 110, 173, 174, **213**
Drug Trafficking Offences Act 1986	43	s 258	15, 28, 110, **214**,
s 1	116		250
Finance Act 1988		(1)	61
s 21	118	(2)	36, 61, 136
Finance Act 1990	118, 119	(3)	27, 110
s 11	119, 251	(4)	18, 40, 43, 61, 75, 112, 134
Finance Act 1991	119	(5)	22, 61, 75, 134
Housing Act 1985		(7)	20
Part III	90	s 259	65, 70, 71, 101, 104, 110,
Housing and Planning Act 1986	90		175, 177, **214**
Insolvency Act 1985	1	s 260	5, 70, 110, 142, 177, **214**
Insolvency Act 1986		(2)	137
ss 1–7	9	(2)(a)	70
ss 252–263	243	(2)(b)	70, 83
s 252	7, 8, 43, 49, 165, 168,	(3)	71
	169, 210, **211**	(4)	71
(1)	8, 43	(5)	69, 72, 104, 177
(2)	207	s 261	110, 177, **215**
(2)(a)	43	(1)	69, 100
(2)(b)	43, 112	(1)(b)	101
s 253	3, 7, 49, 165, 173, **211**	(2)	101
(1)	44	s 262	5, 9, 26, 29, 40, 66,
(2)	4, 44		70, 71, 72, 73, 74, 76, 82,
(3)	43, 45, 47		93, 101, 110, 112, 142, 143,
(3)(a)	99		**215**, 251
(4)	45	(1)	74
s 254	5, 7, 49, 165, 168, **212**	(1)(a)	72
(1)	45	(1)(b)	71, 72
ss 255–263	3, 7	(2)	72
s 255	46, 49, **212**	(3)	77
(1)(a)	46	(4)	77
(1)(b)	46, 134	(4)(b)	77, 78
(1)(c)	9, 46	(5)	78
(1)(d)	46	(7)	78

Insolvency Act 1986 *continued*
s 263	11, 28, 79, 81, 110, 137, 153, 155, **216**
(1)	81
(2)	4, 27
(3)	15, 16, 23, 25, 37, 40, 81, 82, 83, 86, 97, 137, 141, 143, 159
(4)	15, 16, 23, 25, 27, 34, 35, 37, 40, 82, 83, 97, 142, 159
(5)	41, 83, 145
ss 264–271	1, 7
s 264	74, **217**
(1)	93
(1)(b)	109
(1)(c)	74, 93, 107, 137, 141, 252
(2)	94
s 271(3)	4
ss 272–385	7
s 272	102, **217**
(1), (2)	109
s 273	**217**, 244, 246
(1)(a), (b)	109
(1)(c)	93, 109
(1)(d)	109
(2)	110
s 274	109, 110, **218**
(1)	110, 196
(2), (3)	110
(5)	110
s 275	**218**
s 276	17, 19, 31, 74, 77, 81, 93, 94, 95, 97, 105, 107, 129, 141, 155, 156, **219**
(1)	179
(1)(a)	37, 39, 85, 94, 139
(b)	40, 71, 95
(c)	37, 39, 85, 95, 139
s 279	11
s 281(8)	116
s 282	**219**
(4)	101
s 283	**220**
(1)	19, 29
(2)	19, 29, 126, 150, 158
(2)(a)	33
(3)	29
(3)(a)	29, 107
s 284	35, 106, 107, **221**
(6)	106
s 285	**222**
s 288	102, 246
s 301	36

s 303	82
s 306	11, 103
ss 307–309	33, 158
s 310	11, 33, 159
(2)	33
s 312	11
ss 315–321	11, 30, 90
ss 322–325	38, 140
s 325(1)	143
s 326	11, 38, 140
s 328	140, 143
s 329	116, 140
s 330	140
s 333(3)	114
s 336	114
(1), (2)	114
(3)	115
(4)–(6)	114
s 337	114
(4)	115
(5)	114
ss 337–344	11
s 339	20, 22, 39, 127, 140, 141, 153, 245
s 340	20, 22, 39, 127, 140, 141, 154, 246
s 343	20, 127, 140, 141, 246
s 344	39
ss 353–362	39, 140, 141
s 366	11
s 373	7
s 374	7
s 375	7, 66, 72
(1)	107
s 383(2)	18
s 386	22, 102, 108, 197
s 387	108, 117
ss 388–398	4
s 388	
(2)(c)	4
(5)	4
s 389	
(1), (2)	4
s 390	
(1)	4
s 412	97
s 420	14
s 423	11, 83, 245
s 424	11
(1)(b)	83
s 425	11
s 435	22, 245
Sch 1	140, **222**
Sch 5	11, 140, **223**
Sch 6	21, 102, 108, 117, 197, **225**
Sch 9	97

Landlord and Tenant Act 1954   149
Law of Property Act 1925
  s 30   114, 115
Magistrates' Courts Act 1980   116
Matrimonial and Family Proceedings
  Act 1984   116
Matrimonial Homes Act 1983
  s 1   114

Social Security Pensions Act 1975   197
Trustee Act 1925
  s 41(2)   83
Value Added Tax Act 1983
  s 22(2)(a)   119

TABLE OF STATUTORY INSTRUMENTS

References are to page numbers. **Bold** references indicate where material is set out in full.

Administration of Insolvent Estates of		rr 5.7–5.11	53
Deceased Debtors Order 1986 (SI		r 5.7	50, **232**
1986/1999)	49	r 5.8	55, 192, **232**
Part III	56, 61, 68, 70, 72, 82, 100	(1)	55, 102
County Court Rules 1981		(2), (3)	55
Ord 39	2	r 5.9	**233**
Insolvency Proceedings (Monetary		(1)	55
Limits) Order 1986 (SI 1986/1996)	109	(c)	55
Insolvency Rules 1986 (SI 1986/1925)		(2)	55
rr 5.1–5.30	7, 243	(b)	102
r 5.1	13, **229**	(3)	55
(2)	99	r 5.10	12, 59, **233**
r 5.2	3, 5, **229**	(1)	56
r 5.3	3, 141, **229**	(2), (3)	51, 56
(1)	10, 16, 134	(4), (5)	56
(2)	134	r 5.11	57, **234**
(a)(i)	16	r 5.12	59, 171, **234**
(a)(ii)	17, 29	r 5.13	171, 172, **234**
(a)(iii)	18, 91, 134	(1)	59
(b)	19, 140	(2), (3)	60
(c)	20, 134	r 5.14	59, 137, **234**
(d)	22, 134	(2)	171
(e)	23, 134, 137	r 5.15	63, 137, **234**
(f), (g)	24, 134	(2)	174
(h)	24, 41, 134	r 5.16	64, **235**
(j)	25, 134, 140	r 5.17	65, 66, 73, 75, 137, **235**,
(k)–(l)	25, 134		250
(m)	25, 135	(1)–(3)	66
(n)	26, 91, 135, 140	(4), (5)	66, 75
(o)	27, 135	(6), (7)	66
(p)	28	(8), (9)	66, 75
(3)	15, 28, 36	r 5.18	48, **235**, 250
r 5.4	10, 166, 167, **231**	(1)	60, 64, 67, 137, 146, 173, 174
(1)–(5)	44	(2)	67
r 5.5	5, 46, 47, 166, 167, **231**	(3)	60, 67, 173
(1)	166	(b), (c)	67
(c)	100	(4)	60, 67, 76, 173
(2)	10, 15	(5)	67
(3)	5, 47, 100	(6)	64
(4)	5, 9, 47, 50, 102, 165	r 5.19	64, **236**
(b)	104	rr 5.20–5.28	79
r 5.5A	**231**	r 5.20	**237**
r 5.6	**231**	r 5.21	86, 103, **237**
(2)	48	(1)–(4)	27
(3)	56	r 5.22	**237**

Insolvency Rules 1986 *continued*
  r 5.22 *continued*
    (1)   51, 174
    (2), (3)   69, 174
    (4)   69, 174, 175
  r 5.23   69, 176, **238**
  r 5.24   176, **238**
    (1), (2)   69
  r 5.25   72, 78, **238**
  r 5.26   37, **239**, 252
    (1)–(5)   28, 81
  r 5.27   **239**
  r 5.28   103, **240**
  r 5.29   28, 41, 97, 137, 138, **240**
  r 5.30   97, **240**
  rr 6.6–6.36   96
  r 6.6   178
  r 6.9   178
  r 6.10(6)   108
  r 6.12   96
  r 6.23   109
  r 6.37   180
  r 6.41   182
  r 6.44   196
  r 6.59   192
  r 6.81   137
  r 6.96   197, 199
  r 6.99   199
  rr 6.150–6.166   36

rr 6.206–6.212   101
r 6.212A   101
r 6.224   25
r 7.2   72, 200, 201
rr 7.47–7.50   66
rr 8.1–8.7   251
r 8.1   202
r 12.3   143
  (2)   40
r 12.15   116
r 12.16   71
Sch 5   97, **241**
Insolvency (Amendment) Rules 1987
  (SI 1987/1919)
  r 83   22, 141
  r 84   44, 47
  r 85   7, 45
  r 93   179
Insolvent Partnership Order 1986
  (SI 1986/2142)   13
  art 1(2)(a)   14
  arts 7, 8   14
  art 10   14
  art 11   8, 14
  art 13   14
  art 15(3)   14
  Sch 2, Pt III   14
Value Added Tax (Bad Debt Relief)
  Regulations 1986 (SI 1986/335)   175

Chapter 1

AN INTRODUCTION

1.1 The Innovation

The Insolvency Act 1986 ('the Act') came into force on 29 December 1986 and brought with it major changes regarding both individuals and companies. The Act consolidated the Insolvency Act 1985 (most of which was never brought into force) and those parts of the Companies Act 1985 which dealt with receivership and winding up. Consequently, a new body of rules relating to insolvency has been made.[1]

The Act introduced wide-ranging and significant changes in the area of personal insolvency. It abolished the old two-stage bankruptcy procedure and replaced the receiving order followed by adjudication with a single bankruptcy order and acts of bankruptcy with a simplified procedure by way of creditor's petition.[2]

However, the single most fundamental innovation under the Act as regards individuals is the concept of the individual voluntary arrangement. The purpose of this innovation is to provide as an alternative to bankruptcy the means by which a debtor may settle with his creditors on such conditions and terms as may be agreed.

The former law continues to apply in the case of insolvencies which commenced prior to 29 December 1986. Consequently, it is not possible to convert a 1914 Act bankruptcy into a voluntary arrangement under the 1986 Act.

---

1 Insolvency Rules 1986, SI 1986/1925; Insolvency (Amendment) Rules 1987, SI 1987/1919.
2 See generally Insolvency Act 1986, ss 264–271.

1.2 The Position prior to 1986

Prior to the introduction of the Act, individual debtors had limited and restricted alternatives to formal bankruptcy.

1.2.1 Deeds of arrangement

Under the Deeds of Arrangement Act 1914, which is still in force, it was possible for a debtor to execute a deed of arrangement in favour of a named trustee in order to establish a mode of distribution of assets. There were, however, a number of grave disadvantages. First, a deed of arrangement is dependent on the assent of the creditors and, secondly, its very existence constitutes an act of bankruptcy. Deeds of arrangement have therefore been open to attack by non-assenting creditors and, if any such creditor was successful with a bankruptcy petition, he destroyed the effectiveness of the deed. These problems meant that, certainly in the 20 years prior to 1986, comparatively few deeds of arrangement were executed.

At one stage, it was recommended that the Deeds of Arrangement Act should be repealed, but this has not been implemented. The 1986 Act amends the 1914 Act in certain respects, principally by abolishing references to acts of bankruptcy. It is arguable, therefore, that it is now safer to adopt a deed of arrangement but, since 1986, there has in practice been no sign of them coming back into favour.

1.2.2 Compositions and arrangements under the Bankruptcy Act 1914

Under the old law, it was not possible for a debtor to enter into a binding agreement outside bankruptcy legislation. Section 16 of the Bankruptcy Act 1914 provided for a composition or scheme of arrangement with creditors, but this procedure could only be implemented if a receiving order was made. Under s 21, there were similar provisions if an order of adjudication had been made. The statutory requirements in general and, in particular, the requirement to provide for payment of not less than 25 pence in the pound on all provable unsecured claims, meant that these provisions were seldom invoked.

1.2.3 Informal moratoria

Because of the absence of a viable alternative to formal bankruptcy, debtors would frequently try to enter into an informal moratorium or agreement with creditors. Such arrangements were rarely successful. They did not have the effect of binding each and every creditor, and so any creditor minded to issue bankruptcy proceedings could destroy such an arrangement. Likewise, such arrangements could be rendered ineffective by creditors taking other legal proceedings, proceeding to and then enforcing judgment by the usual means of execution. Furthermore, any third party who adopted informally the role of trustee or supervisor of the arrangement had no legal standing or status and, consequently, no powers. Nor was there any formal control over the conduct of the debtor, and so such informal arrangements were frequently used by debtors to buy time, evade their responsibilities and postpone the inevitable. Consequently, proposals for an informal moratorium were often treated by creditors not only with suspicion but also with contempt. Arguably, any such informal moratorium or, indeed, proposal to implement one constituted an act of bankruptcy under the 1914 Act.

1.2.4 Administration orders[1]

Administration orders, while greatly under-used, remain an important option for debtors. Application may be made by the debtor, a creditor who has obtained judgment or the court of its own motion. Once an order is made, no creditor included may, without leave, present or join in a bankruptcy petition against the debtor, subject to the provisos to s 112(4).

---

1 See generally County Courts Act 1984, ss 112–114 and County Court Rules 1981, Ord 39.

1.3 The New Provision

The purpose of the introduction of the individual voluntary arrangement is to provide the machinery whereby a debtor can enter into an agreement with his creditors which is binding on all creditors, affords a degree of court protection, retains a degree of protection for those creditors who object to it and endeavours to maintain a proper regard and balance between the interests of the debtor, the creditors and the public.

The relevant provisions are to be found in Part VIII of the Act, which must always be read in conjunction with the Rules.

1.4 The Basic Procedure

The procedure by which a debtor enters into an individual voluntary arrangement is discussed in greater detail below, but a voluntary arrangement essentially comprises the following specific stages:

(1) preparation of the proposal,[1] ie the written document which sets out the precise terms of the arrangement between the debtor and cre' ors, a copy being sent to all creditors and which is voted on at the creditors' meeting;

(2) application for an interim order[2] made by the court having bankruptcy jurisdiction in respect of the debtor which, for a limited period of time, brings into effect a moratorium so as to permit the due consideration by the creditors of the proposal;

(3) nominee's report[3] on the debtor's proposal which indicates whether or not, in the nominee's opinion, a creditors' meeting should be summoned;

(4) creditors' meeting[4] which decides whether or not to accept the proposal; there must be a 75 per cent majority in favour by those creditors voting either in person or in proxy; if there is such a majority, then any dissenting minority are bound; and

(5) implementation of the scheme whereby the debtor, under the supervision of the supervisor, implements what is proposed, thereby leading to the payment to the creditors of the dividend or distribution envisaged by the proposal.

The nominee is the person who acts in connection with the proposal, and normally assists the debtor in its preparation and is obliged to deliver a report to the court on the proposal and which states whether or not a creditors' meeting is, in his opinion, to be convened. He will summon the creditors' meeting and act as chairman at it. If the creditors' meeting approves the proposal, the insolvency practitioner who supervises the implementation of the proposal is known as the supervisor.

A procedural table is set out at para 1.7 below.

---

1 Insolvency Rules 1986, rr 5.2, 5.3.
2 Insolvency Act 1986, ss 253, 255.
3 Ibid, s 256.
4 Ibid, s 257.
5 Ibid, ss 258–263.

1.5 The Nominee and Supervisor

An individual voluntary arrangement requires the involvement of a nominee and a supervisor, who may be the same person.[1] The nominee and supervisor must be licensed insolvency practitioners,[2] unless the offices are exercised by the official receiver.[3] Any person who acts as a nominee or supervisor while not a licensed insolvency practitioner is liable to imprisonment or a fine or both.[4]

A company may not be a licensed insolvency practitioner.[5]

The proposal must provide for a person, known as the nominee, to act in relation to the voluntary arrangement and, if the proposal is accepted by the creditors, that nominee may, but is not required to, become the supervisor of the arrangement.[6]

The role, duties and responsibilities of a nominee and supervisor are discussed elsewhere.[7]

---

1 See generally Insolvency Act 1986, ss 388–398.
2 Ibid, s 388 (2) (c).
3 Ibid, ss 388 (5), 389 (2).
4 Ibid, s 389 (1).
5 Ibid, s 390 (1).
6 Ibid; ss 253 (2), 263 (2).
7 See Chapter 5 (nominee) and para 3.3.4 et seq and Chapter 7 (supervisor).

1.6 The Nature of an Individual Voluntary Arrangement

In many respects, a voluntary arrangement can be regarded as a contract. Its essence is a legally binding agreement between debtor and creditors enforceable at law.[1] The classic definition of a contract is a promise by one party to another to do, or forbear from doing, certain specified acts. For a contract to be valid and legally enforceable, there must be:

(1) capacity to contract;
(2) intention to contract;
(3) consensus ad idem;
(4) valuable consideration;
(5) legality of purpose; and
(6) sufficient certainty of terms.

A voluntary arrangement by its nature will satisfy these tests and will invariably be in writing.

Of the classic types of contract, a voluntary arrangement can be seen as being 'of record', ie entered into through the machinery of a court of justice,[2] and at the same time 'quasi', ie founded by law on the circumstances.

The essential features of a voluntary arrangement in addition to those of a basic contract between debtor and creditor are the involvement of a third party, namely the nominee and supervisor, and the intervention of the court.[3]

---

1 The debtor's proposal is not, however, an offer to each creditor for the purposes of the
Insolvency Act 1986, s 271 (3), under which the court may dismiss a petition if it is satisfied
that an offer made by the debtor has been unreasonably refused. It is an offer made to a

class of creditors for the purposes of Part VIII of the Act: see *Re A Debtor (No 2389 of 1989)* [1990] 3 All ER 984 per Vinelott J.

2 Although the court does not as such approve the proposal; see paras 6.3.1–6.3.11 below and 1986 Act, s 262.

3 The court provides the machinery which permits the arrangement to come into force.

1.7 Flow Chart: Individual Voluntary Arrangement

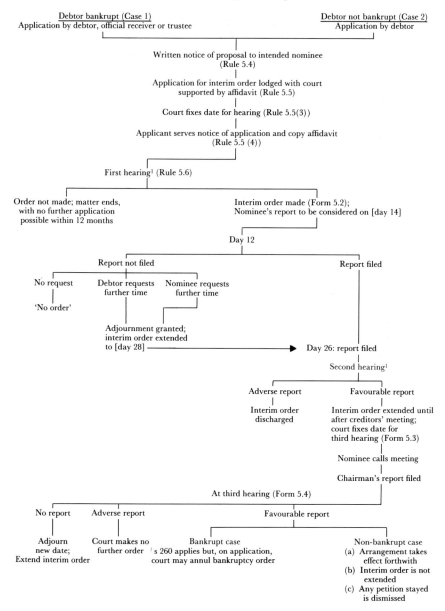

Debtor bankrupt (Case 1)
Application by debtor, official receiver or trustee

Debtor not bankrupt (Case 2)
Application by debtor

Written notice of proposal to intended nominee
(Rule 5.4)

Application for interim order lodged with court
supported by affidavit (Rule 5.5)

Court fixes date for hearing (Rule 5.5(3))

Applicant serves notice of application and copy affidavit
(Rule 5.5 (4))

First hearing[1] (Rule 5.6)

Order not made; matter ends,
with no further application
possible within 12 months

Interim order made (Form 5.2);
Nominee's report to be considered on [day 14]

Day 12

Report not filed

Report filed

No request

Debtor requests
further time

Nominee requests
further time

'No order'

Adjournment granted;
interim order extended
to [day 28] ──────────▶ Day 26: report filed

Second hearing[1]

Adverse report

Favourable report

Interim order
discharged

Interim order extended until
after creditors' meeting;
court fixes date for
third hearing (Form 5.3)

Nominee calls meeting

Chairman's report filed

At third hearing (Form 5.4)

No report

Adverse report

Favourable report

Adjourn
new date;
Extend interim order

Court makes no
further order

Bankrupt case
s 260 applies but, on application,
court may annul bankruptcy order

Non-bankrupt case
(a) Arrangement takes
effect forthwith
(b) Interim order is not
extended
(c) Any petition stayed
is dismissed

1 These hearings may be combined (see para 5.9 below).

Chapter 2

FORMATION OF THE INDIVIDUAL VOLUNTARY ARRANGEMENT

2.1 Sources of Law

The whole of the legislation relating to individual voluntary arrangements is to be found in Part VIII of the Insolvency Act 1986 comprising ss 252–263. Other provisions of the second group of Parts to the Act (ss 252–385) are relevant and will be considered in context. The principal rules are the Insolvency Rules 1986, as amended by the Insolvency (Amendment) Rules 1987. The rules of particular relevance to individual voluntary arrangements are found in Part 5 of the 1986 Rules (rr 5.1–5.30). Equally, other rules relating to individual insolvency may be relevant, including Part 7 on Court Procedure and Practice.

2.2 Jurisdiction

The High Court and the county courts have jurisdiction throughout England and Wales for the purposes of those parts of the Act which relate to voluntary arrangements.[1] Jurisdiction is exercised:

(a) by the High Court in relation to the proceedings which, in accordance with the rules, are allocated to the London insolvency districts; and
(b) by each county court in relation to the proceedings which are so allocated to the insolvency district of that court.[2]

The effect of this is that an application for an interim order should be made to the court having jurisdiction for the time being to entertain a bankruptcy petition (brought by either a creditor or debtor) in respect of the individual concerned.[3]

Section 375, dealing with appeals from courts exercising insolvency jurisdiction, relates to proceedings concerning voluntary arrangements.

---

1 Insolvency Act 1986, s 373.
2 The designation of insolvency districts is covered by ibid, s 374; not every county court has insolvency jurisdiction.
3 See Insolvency (Amendment) Rules 1987, r 85.

2.3 Capacity

Section 252 (1) of the Act specifies:

> In the circumstances specified below, the court may in the case of a debtor (being an individual) make an interim order under this section.

The interim order is the first step in the legal procedure leading to an individual voluntary arrangement, and no such arrangement can come into force and effect until an interim order has been made. A court may not make an interim order unless it is satisfied, inter alia, that no previous application has been made by the debtor for an interim order during the preceding 12 months.[1]

The wording of s 252 (1) makes it clear that the power of the court is discretionary, but nonetheless the overriding consideration is that an application may be made only by an individual. Since an individual has to be considered as being a single person, this precludes an application as such by a firm or partnership. The Act makes provision elsewhere for company voluntary arrangements.[2] Generally, firms and partnerships fall to be dealt with under the provisions of the Insolvent Partnership Order 1986.[3] Article 11 of the Order extends the application of Part VIII to individual partners of insolvent partnership as follows:

> Part I of the Act (Company Voluntary Arrangements) shall apply to corporate members and Part VIII (Individual Voluntary Arrangements) shall apply to individual members where insolvency orders are made against the partnership and an insolvent member with the modification that any reference to the creditors of the company or of the debtor, as the case may be, includes a reference to the creditors of the partnership.

It follows, therefore, that the operation of the Insolvent Partnership Order in this respect cannot come into play until such time as insolvency orders within the meaning of the Order have been made.

This gives rise to a serious practical difficulty. Many partnerships will find themselves insolvent and will wish to invoke the individual voluntary arrangement procedure before such time as insolvency orders are made under the Insolvent Partnership Order. It is clear that the partnership as such cannot apply under s 252.[4] Voluntary arrangements can, however, be brought into effect by the individual partners each making a separate application under s 252. Accordingly, if a firm has three partners, there would have to be three separate and distinct applications and proposals leading to three distinct individual voluntary arrangements. It is perfectly possible within the context of such a procedure to make each voluntary arrangement interdependent on the approval by the creditors of the others, thereby ensuring, so far as is possible, that all creditors are properly dealt with, all assets properly realised and no partner left vulnerable to further proceedings. This may in certain respects be seen as a device aimed at circumventing the plain provision of s 252. In the first four years of the operation of individual voluntary arrangements, numerous such applications have been made without any reported decision as to an effective challenge. In certain instances, applications have been made to the court by partners jointly, but this would appear to be a dangerous procedure because of the requirement of the section that the applicant must be an individual. Unless and until the matter is judicially decided, it can only be regarded as safe for partners seeking to enter into a voluntary arrangement to proceed by way of separate applications. The same considerations apply to other 'joint applications', such as husband and wife, co-habiting partners and quasi-partnerships.[5]

---

1 Insolvency Act 1986, s 255 (1) (c).
2 See generally ibid, ss 1–7.
3 SI 1986/2142. See para 2.8 below. The 'new' provisions relating to partnerships must be considered one of the least satisfactory aspects of the new legislation. These provisions only apply where the partnership is being wound up.
4 Ie 'J. Smith and Co. (a firm)' would not be a competent applicant.
5 In practice, a point by way of procedural defect is unlikely to be taken at the interim order stage unless by the court itself or possibly a trustee or official receiver who has to be served under Insolvency Rules 1986, r 5.5 (4). A challenge under the 1986 Act, s 262 (see paras 6.3.1–6.3.11 below) might be possible if a creditor could show that his position is worse under the arrangement than it would have been otherwise. In 'partnership' arrangements, care must be taken to ensure that partnership assets are applied first in respect of partnership liabilities and non-partnership assets applied in respect of non-partnership liabilities. Surpluses can be 'carried across'.

2.4 First Approach to the Nominee

The theory behind the legislation was that a debtor would prepare a proposal and take it to a licensed insolvency practitioner with a request that that practitioner act as nominee.[1] In practice, this rarely happens. The Act and, in particular, the Rules lay down very many technical matters that must be dealt with in the proposal and, as will be seen, very great care and attention needs to be applied to the preparation of the proposal so that it is in a form which can properly be considered by the creditors (who must be supplied with all information they need to arrive at a proper conclusion); in addition, there are a great many matters to be included in the proposal for which no provision is made in the Act or Rules.

The common practice is for the intended nominee[2] to assist the debtor in the preparation of the proposal, with the result that most proposals are professionally prepared. Since the official function of the nominee does not commence until he has been served with the proposal and has formally indicated his willingness to act in relation to that proposal, the intended nominee does not at this stage have any formal or legal standing; indeed, this provisional role is not recognised as such anywhere in the Act or Rules.

In the vast majority of cases, the preparation of the proposal is a time-consuming exercise. It is common for the intended nominee to require an advance payment of costs, though this is by no means the invariable practice of all licensed insolvency practitioners. It follows that a practitioner who acts as an intended nominee, and takes a fee for such role, will enter into a professional relationship with the debtor, thereby giving rise to the usual considerations of contract and duty of care. This potential liability will almost certainly arise even if the nominee accepts no fee at this stage or if his fee is dependent on the making of an interim order or the acceptance of the proposal by the creditors.

It follows that an intended nominee must exercise the greatest possible care and attention in assisting the debtor and in ensuring that the proposal is properly put together and complies with the requirements of the Act and Rules.[3]

---

1 See Insolvency Rules 1986, r 5.4.
2 This term applies to the nominee prior to the making of the interim order. See ibid, rr 5.4, 5.5 (2).
3 *Re A Debtor (No 222 of 1990)* (1991) *The Times*, 27 June.

2.5 Desirability of an Individual Voluntary Arrangement

2.5.1 The Rules

In his proposal, the debtor must provide a short explanation as to why, in his opinion, a voluntary arrangement is desirable and why his creditors may be expected to concur with such an arrangement.[1]

---

1 Insolvency Rules 1986, r 5.3 (1).

2.5.2 General considerations

For the debtor, the desirability of an individual voluntary arrangement will normally be the avoidance of bankruptcy, since most debtors are anxious to avoid the consequences of a bankruptcy order. It may also be the possibility of continuing in his existing trade or business. However, the debtor must show that a voluntary arrangement is desirable not only from his own point of view but also from that of the creditors. The attitude of creditors will of course vary from debtor to debtor. It is not always easy to anticipate human reaction to circumstances in which an individual creditor is likely to lose a considerable sum of money or feels aggrieved by the conduct of the debtor. Nevertheless, most creditors proceed on the basis of sound economic considerations. Put at its simplest, it is normally essential to establish that, by concurring in a voluntary arrangement, the creditors will or are likely to receive some enhanced benefit as against that resulting from a bankruptcy. The fundamental question for the creditor is "Am I likely to get a better dividend from a voluntary arrangement than from a bankruptcy?".

There are a number of factors which might make a voluntary arrangement a better commercial prospect than bankruptcy, including:

(1) the possibility of third party funds being injected;
(2) the waiver by parties of claims or rights;
(3) cheaper administrative costs, charges and expenses;
(4) quicker realisation of assets;
(5) the prospect of available funds by ongoing trading;
(6) the extension of the subsistence of a voluntary arrangement for a period longer than that for which a bankruptcy is likely to last[1], thereby increasing the time in which 'after-acquired assets'[2] may become available.

1 Normally two or three years: see Insolvency Act 1986, s 279.
2 See para 3.2.12 below.

2.5.3 Advantages and disadvantages

The debtor and the creditors need to assess the advantages and disadvantages of bankruptcy on the one hand and of an individual voluntary arrangement on the other. The most obvious advantages have been set out above. The principal disadvantage of a voluntary arrangement as opposed to bankruptcy is the virtual absence from the Act and Rules of any powers of the supervisor which are in any sense comparable to those of a trustee in bankruptcy. A trustee's powers are set out in Sch 5 to the Act[1] and, whilst these powers can be conferred by express provision in the proposal[2] on a supervisor, they will not have the same statutory force or effect. Furthermore, a supervisor is not able to protect the debtor's estate for the benefit of creditors in the same way as a trustee, nor do the debtor's assets vest in a supervisor as they do in a trustee.[3] Other relevant powers applicable to a trustee which are not applicable to a supervisor are:

(1) the ability to apply to the court for an income payments order;[4]
(2) the obligation on the debtor to surrender control to a trustee;[5]
(3) disclaimer;[6]
(4) distribution of property in specie;[7]
(5) the ability to take proceedings in his own name to realise assets;[8]
(6) the ability to attack transactions at an undervalue, preferences or extortionate credit transactions;[9]
(7) the power to make application for the examination on oath of the debtor or other parties.[10]

This list is by no means exhaustive. The official receiver has no role to play, save in Case 1 matters (as to which see Chapter 9), and the arrangement will not benefit from the general control by the court.[11]

For many debtors, the relief from bankruptcy is a material consideration, and an intended nominee must put to the debtor the alternatives of bankruptcy and individual voluntary arrangement, with all their respective implications.

1 See page 225.
2 They are not implied.
3 Insolvency Act 1986, s 306.
4 Ibid, s 310.
5 Ibid, s 312.
6 Ibid, ss 315–321.
7 Ibid, s 326.
8 Ibid, Sch 5, para 2.
9 Ibid, ss 337–344 and 423–425.
10 Ibid, s 366.
11 But see ibid, s 263 (application to court) and paras 7.1.1–7.1.8 below.

2.5.4 Co-operation

A material consideration for both the intended nominee and the creditors will be the likelihood of the co-operation and good faith of the debtor. The proposed arrangement is, after all, voluntary. If the nominee considers that the debtor will give anything less than his completely unqualified co-operation he is clearly under an obligation to indicate this to the court at the time of making his report.[1] Likewise, this is a matter on which the creditors will form their own view. Many creditors will have dealt with the debtor over a long period of time and they are normally in a good position to express an objective opinion as to the likelihood of co-operation.

Co-operation is particularly vital because of the very nature of a voluntary arrangement. The absence of a comprehensive statutory framework under which a voluntary arrangement is implemented and supervised lays a very considerable burden on the debtor to make it work. The fact that no assets vest in the supervisor means that, if assets have to be sold, it is the debtor who must effect the sale. If proceedings have to be taken to recover assets, it is the debtor who will have to take such proceedings. A debtor cannot enter into a voluntary arrangement and expect to walk away from a high degree of day-to-day responsibility for ensuring that the arrangement works and that its terms are complied with.

---

1 The report is made pursuant to Insolvency Act 1986, s 256; see also Insolvency Rules 1986, r 5.10 and Chapter 5.

2.6 Costs and Legal Aid

The administrative costs of a voluntary arrangement are likely to be considerably less than those of a bankruptcy involving similar assets. Whilst many supervisors are perfectly content to deduct their fees from realisations of assets, and indeed are unlikely to take on a voluntary arrangement without the realistic prospect of such realisations, nevertheless the setting-up costs are not inconsiderable. A great deal of time is likely to be spent on this matter by the nominee, both in his capacity as nominee and, prior to his formal appointment, as intended nominee. Legal costs may be incurred by virtue of the application to the court for the interim order. A debtor must, therefore, be in a position in most cases to make a substantial down-payment.

Where the debtor is an undischarged bankrupt or subject to an outstanding bankruptcy petition, there may well be practical difficulties. Sometimes it is possible to arrange for a third party or relative to make an advance.

Legal aid may be available to the debtor for the purpose of applying for an interim order. However, in practice, the Legal Aid Board is reluctant to grant legal aid in such circumstances. The debtor must establish financial eligibility but, even if he does so, the Legal Aid Board may conclude that the debtor does not fulfil the requirement that he will secure some financial benefit as a result of the proceedings; the mere avoidance of bankruptcy is unlikely to be enough. Subject to financial eligibility, if the debtor can demonstrate that as a result of the voluntary arrangement he will retain some asset which otherwise would be lost in bankruptcy, the attitude of the Legal Aid Board may well be different.

In such circumstances, however, the effect of the legal aid statutory charge must be borne in mind and brought to the attention of the debtor. In any event, if the debtor is legally aided, the proposal must provide for the operation of the statutory charge. The Legal Aid Board may also take the view that it is not for the taxpayer to fund the implementation of a voluntary arrangement, but rather for the creditors on whom, presumably, the proposal is supposed to confer a benefit.

2.7 Case 1 and Case 2

A debtor may apply for an interim order and seek to enter into a voluntary arrangement in two separate sets of circumstances: if the debtor is an undischarged bankrupt, the rules refer to the matter as being Case 1; where he is not an undischarged bankrupt, the rules refer to the matter as being Case 2.[1]

---

1 See Insolvency Rules 1986, r 5.1.

2.8 Partnership as Debtor

Under the new legislation, the treatment of partnerships probably represents one of the most unsatisfactory changes which has been brought about. Generally as regards a proposed petitioning creditor, four courses of action are provided by the Insolvent Partnership Order 1986.[1] The principal change brought by the subordinate legislation is that the partnership itself is no longer treated as in bankruptcy, but as a case for winding up and the partnership is treated as an unregistered company.[2] Where individual insolvency proceedings in bankruptcy are brought against two or more members of an insolvent partnership at the same time as proceedings against the insolvent partnership itself, all the petitions must be presented to the Companies Court having jurisdiction. Only when insolvency proceedings are brought against an individual member, or where all the members of an insolvent partnership are individual members and they present a petition against themselves, are the petitions brought in the bankruptcy court.

Nevertheless, some principles of the old law remain. Accordingly, the separate assets of the partners go first to pay separate debts whilst the assets of the partnership go first to pay joint debts, and separate accounts must be kept. Only in the event of a surplus in either estate does such surplus go to meet the shortfall, if any, in the other estate.[3]

One consequence of a partnership being treated as a company for winding-up purposes is that the partners are treated as directors for the purpose of the Company Directors Disqualification Act 1986 and any winding-up order made thereon and, accordingly, may be liable to proceedings against them for disqualification.

The four courses of action open to a petitioning creditor are:

(1) to wind up the insolvent partnership alone;[4]
(2) to wind up the insolvent partnership, there being petitions against two or more insolvent members;[5]

(3) proceedings against the members of the partnership not involving winding up of the partnership as an unregistered company;[6] and
(4) proceedings against one or more members of the partnership without
involving the others and without presenting a petition for the winding up
of the partnership as an unregistered company.[7]

The relevant provisions of Insolvency Act 1986 relating to corporate and
individual members are extended to the situation where an insolvency order is
made against the partnership;[8] however, the provisions relating to the conversion of a debtor's petition into a voluntary arrangement do not apply in
relation to partnerships.[9]

1 SI 1986/2142, made pursuant to Insolvency Act 1986, s 420 and Company Directors
Disqualification Act 1986, s 21 (2).
2 Insolvent Partnership Order 1986, art 1 (2) (a).
3 See generally ibid, art 10.
4 Ibid, art 7.
5 Ibid, art 8.
6 Ibid, art 13.
7 Ibid, art 15 (3).
8 See ibid, art 11 and para 2.3 above.
9 See ibid, Sch 2, Part III, para 9.

Chapter 3

THE PROPOSAL

3.1 Requirements of the Act and Rules

3.1.1 Introduction

The most important aspect of a voluntary arrangement is the preparation of the proposal which must be in writing[1] and should be in a single document, although this is not necessary. The proposal must conform to the requirements of the Insolvency Act and Rules[2] and must deal with a great variety of other matters.[3] The proposal must be in place before an application is made to the court for an interim order.[4]

The author of the proposal is the debtor himself but, in almost every proposal, the debtor will rely on the professional assistance of the nominee for actual drafting and preparation.[5]

---

1 However, this is not stated in the Act or Rules.
2 The vital importance of strict compliance with the Rules is demonstrated in *Re A Debtor (No 222 of 1990)* (1991) *The Times*, 27 June, where Harman J was extremely critical of a proposal that did not deal adequately with the Rules.
3 See paras 3.2.1–3.3.26 below.
4 See Insolvency Rules 1986, r 5.5 (2) as amended and generally Chapter 4.
5 A number of specific provisions which may be included in a proposal are set out in Appendix 1; in this section, these specimen clauses are referred to in square brackets.

3.1.2 Amendment of the proposal

The proposal may, with the agreement in writing of the nominee, be amended at any time up to the delivery of a nominee's report to the court under Insolvency Act 1986, s 256.[1] Furthermore, the proposal may be modified and amended at the creditors' meeting called under s 258 of the Act for the consideration of the debtor's proposal, provided that the debtor agrees to such modifications and amendments. There is no provision for amendment of a proposal after it has been approved by the creditors and so, if it is sought to make provision for such amendments to be permitted, specific provision must be made in the proposal itself.[2] It is considered that, after the creditors have approved the proposal, the court does not have power to allow or order an amendment under s 263 (3) or (4).[3]

---

1 Insolvency Rules 1986, r 5.3 (3); see generally Chapter 5.
2 If such a provision is included, it must be drafted with care and certainty as to the reasons

---

why, and the circumstances in which, such amendment might be necessary. An example
might be provision for the extension of the arrangement's duration.
3 Applications to the court by the debtor, creditors or other persons (s 263 (3)) and the
supervisor (s 263 (4)).

3.1.3 Contents of the proposal

Numerous matters must be dealt with in the proposal and, for ease of
reference, these are dealt with in the order in which they appear in Rule 5.3
and in accordance with the numbering of the Rule.

> (1) The debtor's proposal shall provide a short explanation why, in his opinion,
> a voluntary arrangement under Part VIII is desirable, and give reasons why
> his creditors may be expected to concur with such an arrangement.

It is clearly desirable to include in this explanation some relevant history of the
debtor's background, including an explanation as to why he is now insolvent.
It may sometimes be appropriate to include brief extracts from trading
accounts for previous years to show and explain a deterioration in trading or
other fortunes. The debtor should be frank and honest so as to demonstrate
that he is a person whom the creditors can trust, notwithstanding past
difficulties, and in whom the creditors can have confidence to see a voluntary
arrangement succeed.

> (2) The following matters shall be stated or otherwise dealt with in the
> proposal—
>   (a) The following matters so far as within the debtor's immediate[1]
>   knowledge—
>   (i) his assets with an estimate of their respective values;

The debtor must set out the full extent of his assets, both within and outside the
jurisdiction of the court.[2] This section of the proposal should include prospective or contingent assets with a statement as to the likelihood of realisation. It
is not for the debtor to speculate on matters of possible inheritance, though
clearly he must declare any actual vested or contingent interest in a trust. The
debtor must declare any asset in which he has a beneficial interest. If he holds
an asset purely in a trustee capacity without enjoying any beneficial interest,
there is no obligation upon him to disclose it, although he would be well
advised to disclose the position, explaining that he has no beneficial interest.
Any omission later discovered by the creditors is bound to undermine their
confidence in the debtor. [See, for example, Appendix 1, p 148, Clauses 1–4.]

The debtor must give an estimate of the value of each asset. Since many
voluntary arrangements are constructed urgently, often because of a steadily
deteriorating financial position, outstanding litigation or pending bankruptcy
proceedings, it is frequently not practicable to obtain and provide a proper
professional valuation of assets. In any event, funds may not permit such an
exercise. Nevertheless, the debtor must value the assets realistically and make
clear the basis of valuation so that there is no danger of the creditors being
misled. At this stage, a clear obligation falls on the intended nominee. A
professional person knows the importance of providing accurate information
to creditors.

If the debtor is seeking to sell his private dwellinghouse, the proposal should specify the realistic selling price and not the asking price, as to which appropriate enquiries should be made. [See for example Appendix 1, p 149, Clauses 5–9.] With many assets there will be grave difficulties in arriving at a realistic valuation. Work in progress and book debts are notoriously difficult to value. [See Appendix 1, pp 156, 7, Clauses 36, 37.] The approach should be one of prudent caution and conservatism. Where it is possible to obtain proper professional valuations of assets, this should be done. This might include the surrender value of life policies, the valuation of motor vehicles, fixed plant and equipment.

If, in a particular case, the debtor has made a proper attempt to arrive at proper and realistic valuations, having regard to the constraints of time and funds, the creditors will not be able to complain if the valuations turn out to be optimistic; however, they will have a right to complain, with potentially serious consequences,[3] if it can subsequently be demonstrated that no real thought was given to the figures to be included in the proposal.

It is desirable to include in the proposal an express provision that the failure by the debtor or supervisor to realise an asset for the estimated value shown in the proposal shall not give rise to failure or default.[4]

The debtor must also consider, in assessing the value of assets, any particular difficulties with realisation: an asset may have a limited market; freehold dwellinghouses, for example, will be subject to the vagaries of the property market; the sale of leaseholds invariably gives rise to special difficulties, not least the necessity of obtaining the consent of the landlord where there are considerable arrears of rent or other breaches of covenant. [See Appendix 1, p 149, Clause 9.] A valuation of a lease is not an easy matter and, if it is not possible to obtain a professional valuation, this should be expressly pointed out in the proposal.

The likely costs of realisation should be shown, so that when calculating funds available for distribution the proposal proceeds on the basis of net figures, that is to say, the estimated gross realisation less the costs of sale and, where applicable, the extent of liabilities charged or otherwise secured against that particular asset.

---

1 This seems to imply that detailed enquiry or investigation is not necessary, but care must be taken to ensure reasonable accuracy. A debtor cannot take 'a stab in the dark'.
2 Clearly assets abroad must be disclosed.
3 See Insolvency Act 1986, s 276 (Default Petitions) and generally Chapter 8.
4 This is designed to protect 'innocent', as opposed to 'culpable', misvaluation or under-realisation.

    (ii)   the extent (if any) to which the assets are charged in favour of creditors [See Appendix 1, p 151, Clauses 17, 18]

Secured creditors must be shown and fully disclosed. This affects the equity in any particular asset. A secured creditor is someone whose debt is secured to the extent that the person to whom the debt is owed holds any security for the debt (whether a mortgage, charge, lien or other security) over any property of the person by whom the debt is owed.[1]

The most obvious examples[2] are:

(a) the holder of a mortgage or legal charge, including an equitable charge;
(b) a creditor with the benefit of a reservation of title clause;
(c) finance companies holding hire purchase agreements, credit sale agreements, lease hire agreements or the like;
(d) the holders of liens.

The creditors' meeting must not approve any proposal or modification which affects the right of a secured creditor of the debtor to enforce his security except with the concurrence of the creditor concerned.[3] Accordingly, the rights of secured creditors are fully protected.

If there is the slightest doubt as to the extent of security or, indeed, the validity of any security, the proposal must clearly state this.

---

1 Insolvency Act 1986, s 383 (2).
2 This list is not exhaustive. Careful enquiry must be made of the debtor. Frequently debtors will not be fully aware of the existence or significance of reservation of title clauses. There may be insufficient time to investigate the basis upon which stock was acquired. The proposal should contain a general saving provision to cover this situation.
3 Ibid, s 258 (4).

(iii) the extent (if any) to which particular assets are to be excluded from the voluntary arrangement [See Appendix 1, p 150, Clauses 11–14]

Unlike in bankruptcy, the debtor can choose to exclude any particular asset. In theory there is no limit, although practical considerations will dictate otherwise.

In bankruptcy, a bankrupt's estate is defined as comprising:

(a) all property belonging to or vested in the bankrupt at the commencement of the bankruptcy; and
(b) any property which by virtue of any of the following provisions of this Part is comprised in that estate or is treated as falling within the preceding paragraph.[1]

The statutory exceptions are:

(a) such tools, books, vehicles and other items of equipment as are necessary to the bankrupt for use personally by him in his employment, business or vacation;
(b) such clothing, bedding, furniture, household equipment and provisions as are necessary for satisfying the basic domestic needs of the bankrupt and his family.[2]

It is perfectly proper for a debtor to exclude from a voluntary arrangement such assets as would be excluded from his estate in the event of him being made bankrupt. If, however, the debtor chooses to include in his voluntary arrangement any such asset and it is of any particular value, then that is clearly a material consideration in suggesting that the voluntary arrangement is preferable and likely to be accepted by creditors.

If the debtor seeks to exclude any other asset, he must give good reasons as creditors are likely to question such exclusions at the creditors' meeting. A mere whim or considerations of sentimentality are unlikely ever to be sufficient. If, however, the debtor can convince the creditors that he seeks to exclude particular assets because they are required by him for ongoing business purposes,[3] and it is part of the proposal that the ongoing business is to generate funds to be made available for the creditors, then provided that the continuation of the business is viable, it would be proper to seek to exclude such assets.

There should be provision that, if the ongoing business fails or is terminated, the excluded assets are sold and the proceeds of sale brought in to the funds available for distribution. For example, if the debtor's business is haulage and the business is to continue, then clearly the vehicles will be excluded. The proposal will include a provision that, if the business is terminated, then the vehicles will be sold and the proceeds of sale, after discharge of any hire purchase or the like, made available. Again, if an asset is to be excluded in consideration of an injection of cash, this may well be acceptable to the creditors provided that the cash sum equals or exceeds the value of the asset. It may also be perfectly reasonable to exclude an asset which it is thought is likely to be difficult or expensive to realise. The proposal must, however, set out all the relevant facts so the creditors can reach a proper decision.

---

1 Insolvency Act 1986, s 283 (1).
2 Ibid, s 283 (2).
3 Such as stock in trade or work in progress.

(*b*) particulars of any property other than assets of the debtor himself which is proposed to be included in arrangement, the source of such property and the terms on which it is to be made available for inclusion [Appendix 1, p 151, Clauses 15, 16]

Third parties may agree to make assets available for a variety of reasons, although the most common reason is to prevent the bankruptcy of a debtor. Such an offer must be spelt out in detail, and the third party must be identified, as must the terms on which any such asset is to be made available.[1] A mere statement in the proposal that an undisclosed third party is willing to contribute an asset or sum of money in the event of the proposal being accepted will not be sufficient. It is desirable for there to be annexed to the proposal a letter or document signed by the third party confirming the arrangement and its terms. By doing so, the third party is not made a party as such to the proposal, but the proposal may provide that the failure by the third party to perform constitutes default on the part of the debtor within the meaning of Insolvency Act 1986, s 276.

There is no limit to the categories of third parties who may be willing to contribute an asset. A common example is the debtor's spouse who may be willing to make concessions regarding, for example, the matrimonial home or her rights. Benevolent relatives or even employers may be prepared to put up funds.

It is desirable for any third party to be properly advised as to the implications of their involvement. This is particularly the case if they are forgoing a legal right or remedy. The intended nominee should satisfy himself that such advice has been given. He should make clear to the third party that he has an absolute right to take independent advice and, in certain circumstances, should insist that such independent advice be taken.[2]

---

1 This is particularly the case if conditions are attached.
2 If, for example, a spouse agrees to waive a good 'exoneration' claim (see Chapter 11). See also Appendix 2, p 205.

(c) the nature and amount of the debtor's liabilities (so far as within his immediate[1] knowledge), the manner in which they are proposed to be met, postponed or otherwise dealt with by means of the arrangement and (in particular)—

   (i)   how it is proposed to deal with preferential creditors (defined in section[2] 258 (7)) and creditors who are, or claim to be, secured,

   (ii) how associates[3] of the debtor (being creditors of his) are proposed to be treated under the agreement, and

   (iii) In Case 1, whether, to the debtor's knowledge, claims have been made under Section 339 (Transactions at an Undervalue), Section 340 (Preferences) or Section 343 (Extortionate Credit Transactions) or there are circumstances giving rise to the possibility of such claims and, in Case 2, whether there are circumstances which would give rise to the possibility of such claims in the event that he should be adjudged bankrupt[4] [See Appendix 1, pp 153, 4, Clauses 24–28]

and where any such circumstances are present, whether, and if so how, it is proposed under the voluntary arrangement to make provision for wholly or partly indemnifying the insolvent estate in respect of such claims

The voluntary arrangement must set out with as much accuracy as is possible the debtor's liabilities. The debtor and the intended nominee must make every reasonable and proper enquiry as to the full extent of liabilities and the identity of each and every creditor.

This is by no means an easy task and there is always the risk that a liability will either be understated or missed completely. These are matters which can be catered for in the proposal itself.

As with assets, time will often not permit detailed enquiry. Whilst the nominee should request from each and every known creditor an up-to-date statement of liability, this is a costly exercise and potentially time-consuming. Furthermore, it may in certain cases be tactically unwise lest such an enquiry encourages a creditor to bring on a bankruptcy petition or expedite outstanding legal process.

Secured liabilities need particular consideration; if a secured liability is likely to increase during the period from the date that the proposal is prepared until such time as the asset in question is realised, this must be expressly stated in the proposal with a realistic estimate of the amount by which the liability will increase. If, for example, the proposal provides for the sale of a freehold property which, at the date of the proposal, is valued at £60,000 with an

outstanding liability by way of mortgage of £50,000, and if it is unlikely that
the debtor will be in a position to make any payments to keep down the secured
liability, it is clear that the ostensible equity which may be vital to the
voluntary arrangement will be eroded. It follows that, in such circumstances,
the proposal must set out the true facts and whether or not the debtor is to keep
up any such payments and, if not, why not.

The categories of preferential creditors are shown in Sch 6 to the Insolvency
Act 1986. The creditors' meeting may not approve any proposal or modification under which any preferential debt of the debtor is to be paid otherwise
than in priority to such of his debts as are not preferential debts.[5] This
represents the situation in bankruptcy. Accordingly, preferential claims must
be paid in full before any dividend is paid to unsecured creditors. It is most
unlikely that any preferential creditor will agree to waive its right, although
this may occur in certain very limited circumstances. For example, if a debtor
has no assets at all and, in order to save bankruptcy, a third party is willing to
inject £10,000 into a voluntary arrangement, the third party may specify that
this is on the basis that all creditors, both preferential and unsecured, are
treated equally and *pari passu*. In such circumstances, the preferential creditor
may take a commercial view that it is sensible to accept such a proposition on
the basis that one penny in the pound is better than nothing at all. However,
such a situation will rarely arise. [See Appendix 1, p 151, Clause 19.]

The position of secured creditors has been dealt with above.[6] The proposal
must provide how secured creditors are to be dealt with.[7] This will largely
depend on negotiation between the debtor, or more likely the nominee, and the
secured creditor. The secured creditor's rights remain intact. It may
be possible to negotiate an arrangement with a secured creditor that it
will not enforce its security for a specified period in order to secure a more
orderly and, hopefully, more beneficial realisation of the asset. If any such
agreement has been reached or is proposed, then this should be set out in the
proposal.[8]

Whilst a landlord does not constitute a secured creditor as such, it is
arguably even more important to endeavour to agree terms with a landlord
who has a right of forfeiture than with a secured creditor.[9]

Associates, if creditors, must be identified. Difficulty may arise with alleged
associates such as reputed spouses or illegitimate children.

The reason for including the third provision is clear: if, in a Case 1 or Case 2
voluntary arrangement, it can be demonstrated that any such claim could be
made with a reasonable degree of success, this will be material to the creditors'
decision. A supervisor, unlike a trustee, has no power to bring an action in
respect of any such matter. Therefore, by proceeding with a voluntary
arrangement, the creditors may deprive themselves of a potentially valuable
asset. On the other hand, the creditors will give due consideration as to the
strength of any such claim and the cost involved in prosecuting it to a
satisfactory conclusion.[10]

A simple example of a transaction at an undervalue would be where the
debtor makes a gift of a particular asset to his spouse. In bankruptcy, the value
of such an asset could be recovered for the estate. More complicated situations
arise where there is the suggestion that an asset has been disposed of for less

than its true consideration, and this will always be a matter of degree. If the debtor has disposed of an asset to a spouse in accordance with a professionally prepared valuation, such a valuation is unlikely to be impeachable, even though a second or further valuation may raise doubts as to whether the valuation relied on was wholly accurate. The essential point is that the transaction in question must be brought fully to the creditors' attention, and they must decide, in effect, whether to accept it or reject the arrangement and see the matter dealt with in bankruptcy.

Where there is the possibility of such a claim, it is always possible for the third party involved to make some offer to compromise the claim and thereby generate further funds for the arrangement. In such a case, the proposal must contain the fullest possible particulars, including the basis of the compromise and any terms on which the payment is to be made.

It will always be difficult to satisfy the indemnity provision because, if prima facie a case is made out that there has been a transaction at an undervalue, a preference or an extortionate credit transaction, the creditors will probably be reluctant to approve a voluntary arrangement. Indemnity may arise by the potential respondent to any such claim agreeing to compromise it and making some payment available to the arrangement in return for the arrangement being approved and thereby no claim being brought against him.[11]

---

1 See note 1 to (2) above.
2 The subsection in turn refers to Insolvency Act 1986, s 386.
3 Defined in ibid, s 435. Associates have particular significance when considering the relevance of the avoidance provisions relating to bankruptcy; see ibid, ss 339, 340.
4 See Insolvency (Amendment) Rules 1987, r 83.
5 Insolvency Act 1986, s 258 (5).
6 See (ii) at page 17 above.
7 If there is doubt as to the validity or extent of any security, this must be specified and a full explanation given. It may be that a secured creditor will in fact only be partly secured and will wish to claim for the unsecured balance. Again this must be allowed for.
8 The proposal must specify whether or not and, if so, how interest payments are to be made. If no interest payments are to be made, the secured indebtedness will increase, thereby reducing the 'equity' and possibly putting the arrangement in jeopardy.
9 For the position with landlords, see generally *Re Naeem (A Bankrupt) (No 18 of 1988)* [1990] 1 WLR 48 per Hoffman J.
10 For a detailed examination of the subject matter of such claims, see, for example, *Muir Hunter on Personal Insolvency* (Stevens, 1987), paras 3-292 to 3-301/2. Such an examination is outside the scope of this work. In essence, the purpose of these sections is to restore for the benefit of creditors assets which have wrongly been disposed of prior to the commencement of the bankruptcy.
11 If such is proposed, the proposal should include written confirmation of the same by the proposed respondent. As will be seen later (Chapter 9), in a Case 1 it might be possible, notwithstanding the approval of the arrangement, for the bankruptcy to continue so as to allow the prosecution of such a claim or its continuation. This would greatly complicate an arrangement and would necessitate very careful drafting. The trustee in bankruptcy would have to retain control over sufficient funds to enable the action to be pursued and to cover the possibility of an order for adverse costs.

(*d*) whether any, and if so what, guarantees have been given of the debtor's debts by other persons specifying which (if any) of the guarantors are associates[1] of his [Appendix 1, p 155, Clause 29]

The creditors are clearly entitled to know if some person other than a debtor is liable for any of the debtor's liabilities.[2] The debtor may have been in a partnership which is ostensibly solvent with other partners remaining liable for partnership debts. It may be the case that any such liabilities are excluded from the voluntary arrangement leaving the particular creditor to proceed against the other liable parties, but if this course of action is adopted there is a substantial risk that the creditor in question who will not be bound by the voluntary arrangement will then proceed against the debtor by way of bankruptcy proceedings or otherwise and thereby jeopardise the whole arrangement.[3]

1 See note 3 to (*c*) above.
2 Any such guarantor who discharges the liability may by subrogation be entitled to claim in the arrangement in the shoes of the creditor. Guarantors should be given notice of the arrangement.
3 In any event, notice should be given to all creditors.

(*e*) the proposed duration of the voluntary arrangement [Appendix 1, p 155, Clause 30]

'Duration' here means the period of time from the date of the creditors' meeting until such time as it is expected that the terms of the voluntary arrangement will have been complied with, ie all relevant assets realised and a final dividend paid. The voluntary arrangement can last for as long as the debtor proposes,[1] although the creditors will be anxious to see a return of funds within the quickest possible time. Accordingly, the debtor, in conjunction with the nominee, must take a realistic view. Consideration must be given to the length of time that will be required to realise assets, having regard to market conditions, any peculiar difficulties and the need to agree creditors' claims. If it is intended that the proposed duration should be extended, or be capable of being extended, the proposal must make express provision as to how this is to be done. There is no provision in the Act or Rules for extending a voluntary arrangement and it is only arguable that the court would have power to extend under s 263 (3), (4). It will only be in exceptional circumstances that a voluntary arrangement will last for longer than two years. This may be relevant in a case where there is to be ongoing trading for which wholly special considerations apply or possibly litigation to be concluded. Experience shows that sufficient thought is seldom given to the proposed duration of the scheme, with particular reference to the length of time allowed for the process of realisation of assets. This is particularly important in a depressed property market where the realisation of the asset is difficult. Consideration must also be given as to whether or not any litigation will be necessary to realise assets such as book debts and work in progress. In anything other than the simplest of proposals, it is always wise to make provision for extension of the proposed duration.

1 In *Re A Debtor (No 222 of 1990)* (1991) *The Times*, 27 June, the judge was extremely critical of the fact that in the proposal in that case the duration of the arrangement was not spelt out. It seems that the duration must be expressed in terms of a period of time certain.

(*f*) the proposed dates of distributions to creditors, with estimates of their amounts

Great care must be taken in putting forward dates on which the creditors will receive interim and final dividends. Dates must be realistically arrived at, having regard to the considerations mentioned above. The proposal may provide for only a final dividend to be paid on the conclusion of the arrangement. The nominee must also bear in mind any peculiar difficulties that may exist in quantifying creditors' claims. Strictly speaking, he will not be in a position to pay any dividend until all claims are known and agreed. This may, for example, be difficult where one unsecured claim represents either contingent claims or the possible residual unsecured liability on an otherwise secured claim which cannot be quantified until the asset in question is realised.

(*g*) the amount proposed to be paid to the nominee (as such) by way of remuneration and expenses

The remuneration referred to here is that of the nominee for acting as nominee and does not include his remuneration as supervisor. The position of a nominee is dealt with below.[1] In order that the creditors know where they stand, it is desirable for the amount to be expressed in a specific sum of money and, if payment has already been made to the nominee, this should be indicated. Again, it should be expressly stated whether or not the nominee's remuneration includes or excludes sums to be paid to the debtor's solicitor, if any, for undertaking the necessary legal work.[2] Expenses should be quantified and defined.

---

1 See Chapter 5.
2 This is likely to be limited to the application for the interim order.

(*h*) the manner in which it is proposed that the supervisor of the arrangement should be remunerated and his expenses defrayed

The same considerations apply as stated above relating to the nominee's remuneration, although the remuneration of the supervisor is far more difficult to anticipate than that of the nominee. Whilst a supervisor from his experience may well be able to give a reasonably accurate estimate as to his likely remuneration, experience shows that during the course of the administration of the arrangement many factors may arise which could not have been anticipated. It is therefore preferable for the supervisor to provide for his remuneration to be paid on an hourly basis, taking into account work actually and reasonably undertaken and the appropriate level of skill and responsibility employed and involved. However, creditors may not always be happy with a provision in such general terms, and a reasonable balance must be struck between the supervisor and the creditors. Specific provision may be made in the proposal for the means of calculating and agreeing the supervisor's remuneration, either by resolution of a creditors' committee, if any, or of the general body of creditors, or by the court.[1] If the supervisor is likely to incur expenses as a result of employing solicitors, estate agents or other professional advisers, the proposal should make provision for this and for all such fees and expenses to be paid in priority to preferential creditors. Creditors cannot reasonably object to the preparation of an order of priority of payment similar to that in bankruptcy.[2]

---

1 This would involve an application under Insolvency Act 1986, s 263 (3), (4).
2 See, for example, Insolvency Rules 1986, r 6.224; however, if this were adopted, obvious amendments would need to be made to exclude those items which would have no application to a voluntary arrangement.

(*j*) whether, for the purposes of the arrangement, any guarantees are to be offered by any persons other than a debtor, and whether (if so) any security is to be given or sought [Appendix 1, p 155, Clause 29]

A third party may on occasions offer to contribute to the available funds and assets, whether by way of a formal guarantee or by providing security in some manner. The terms of the contribution must be spelt out and full particulars given to the creditors. It is important for any such guarantor to be given proper independent advice on his potential liability.

(*k*) the manner in which funds held for the purposes of the arrangement are to be banked, invested or otherwise dealt with pending distribution to creditors

The proposal should provide for all funds realised to be paid to the supervisor. The supervisor should be empowered to open such bank accounts as are necessary and, furthermore, to invest in a personal capacity in such investments as may be appropriate. It is unlikely that there will ever be the need to embark on long-term investments. In essence, the supervisor should always proceed on the basis of paying money out to creditors as quickly as is reasonably possible, although there will inevitably be cases where the supervisor is prevented from making an early distribution, for example because of difficulties in agreeing the full extent of creditors' claims for the purpose of dividend. It is undesirable for funds to be retained under the control of the debtor.[1]

---

1 See para 3.3.3 below for discussion of the possibility of constituting the debtor as holding assets on trust.

(*l*) the manner in which funds held for the purpose of payment to creditors, and not so paid on the termination of the arrangement, are to be dealt with

The supervisor will generally be responsible for the payment of dividends and distributions. If any dividend or distribution for any reason remains uncollected, for example where a creditor disappears and cannot be contacted, provision must be made in the proposal concerning the funds due [see Appendix 1, p 143, SC 20.2]. Otherwise, an application may be made to the court under Insolvency Act 1986, s 263(4) for directions and/or an order that the money be paid into court.

(*m*) if the debtor has any business, the manner in which it is proposed to be conducted during the course of the arrangement

Consideration is given below[1] to the particular considerations that arise with an ongoing business. It is clear that, if the debtor intends to continue his business, this must be set out in the fullest possible terms. However, creditors are bound to approach any such proposal with a high degree of suspicion and scepticism because, although the proposal may state that the business is to be continued for the purpose of generating funds for the arrangement, they may well take the view that, if the particular business has failed, it is unlikely to succeed if essentially the same business is being run by the same person and, in addition to meeting all its current ongoing liabilities, is also expected to generate a super profit over and above that required by the debtor for living purposes so as to provide surplus cash for the benefit of the creditors. Experience shows that a reasonably high percentage of voluntary arrangements which involve an ongoing business arrangement fail[2] or become subject to the default provisions. The creditors will need to know who is to conduct the business and, in particular, will need to know the role that the supervisor is to play in overseeing the business. If, for example, a proposal provides that a business is to continue for a period of two years so as to generate funds, it is inevitable that, if the supervisor is to play an active role in supervising the business, this will greatly increase the remuneration payable to the supervisor.

---

1 See para 3.3.13 below.
2 As to failure of an arrangement, see Chapter 8.

(*n*)   details of any further credit facilities which it is intended to arrange for the debtor, and how the debts so arising are to be paid [Appendix 1, p 156, Clause 35]

The creditors should treat with suspicion any proposal that there should be further credit facilities, especially if it is suggested that they should provide such facilities. No provision in the proposal can force them to do so against their wishes,[1] and it is clear that they could only be expected to provide further credit facilities if they agreed to the proposal, they were totally satisfied that they would be repaid and that their debt would not increase. The credit facilities may be required for the business to continue or, in another situation, for the completion of outstanding work-in-progress. If the voluntary arrangement concerns a builder, it may be proposed that the builder has credit facilities to enable him to finish particular building projects. Any such proposal needs to be examined with the greatest of care and realistic figures forecasts and cashflow projections produced. The identity of a provider of credit, and the terms on which the further credit is to be repaid, including provision as to interest, should be made known. Creditors will generally be reluctant to accept a voluntary arrangement if the arrangement itself is likely to give rise to further liabilities which may not be satisfied and which may result in the bankruptcy of the debtor. The supervisor would be most unwise to incur any personal liability for further credit facilities or for their repayment. Any credit facilities will have to remain the sole liability of the debtor.

---

1 Any such provision would open the way for a challenge under Insolvency Act 1986, s 262.

(*o*) the functions which are to be undertaken by the supervisor of the
arrangement

Arrangements, by their very nature, will have individual features which make
each one unique. The Act and Rules are virtually silent on the functions of the
supervisor, his powers, duties and responsibilities. This topic is considered in
further detail below.[1] The Act provides:

> The person who is for the time being carrying out, in relation to the voluntary
> arrangement, the functions conferred by virtue of the approval on the nominee
> (or his replacement under section 256 (3) (a) or 258 (3)) shall be known as the
> supervisor of the voluntary arrangement.[2]

The Act confers on the supervisor the right to apply to the court 'for
directions in relation to any particular matter arising under the voluntary
arrangement'.[3] The Rules place on the debtor an obligation to put the
supervisor into possession of the assets included in the arrangement,[4] subject
to special provisions for a Case 1 arrangement.[5] The supervisor is also under
an obligation to keep certain specified accounts and records of his acts and
dealings in connection with the arrangement, including in particular records
and receipts of payments of money.[6] He is also under an obligation to prepare
an abstract of such receipts and payments and send those to a specified class of
person.[7] Apart from these provisions and those relating to the completion of
the arrangement,[8] the Act and Rules are silent on the functions of the
supervisor. Accordingly, these must be spelt out in the voluntary arrangement.

The creditors are entitled to know exactly what role the supervisor will play.
If it is proposed in any way to constitute the supervisor as a trustee, this should
be expressly stated. The functions to be performed by a supervisor will vary
greatly. In a voluntary arrangement where, for instance, the entire scheme is
based solely on the payment in of a sum of money by a third party, the
supervisor's function will be to collect in the third party funds, agree creditors'
claims and then pay out. On the other hand, the arrangement may be far more
complicated, lasting for a much longer period of time, involving ongoing
trading or perhaps the completion of work in progress or a building project or a
situation where difficulties may arise in realising assets such as book debts.
This demonstrates the importance of a flexible approach to each individual
arrangement, and shows that one cannot merely adopt a standard form of
proposal and set of conditions which may be wholly unnecessary in certain
cases and wholly deficient in others. The nominee will either have been
involved in the preparation of the proposal or will have had an opportunity to
comment on it prior to its approval by the creditors so, in every instance, it is
open to the nominee to comment on the functions that will be expected of him
and to indicate whether or not he considers the proposal to be adequate in this
respect.

---

1 See Chapter 7.
2 Insolvency Act 1986, s 263 (2).
3 Ibid, s 263 (4).
4 Insolvency Rules 1986, r 5.21 (1).
5 Ibid, r 5.21 (2)–(4).

6 Ibid, r 5.26 (1).
7 Ibid, r 5.26 (2)–(5).
8 Ibid, r 5.29.

(*p*) the name, address and qualification of the person proposed as supervisor of the voluntary arrangement and confirmation that he is (so far as the debtor is aware) qualified to act as an insolvency practitioner in relation to him

The person who is nominee for the purpose of the proposal becomes the supervisor of the voluntary arrangement when the proposal is approved, unless he is replaced under s 256 or 258.[1] The debtor must set out the information in relation to the nominee although he will generally have to rely on the nominee's assurance that he, the nominee, is qualified to act. Arguably, the creditors are entitled to proof of the nominee's due qualification.

1 Insolvency Act 1986, s 263.

(3) With the agreement in writing of the nominee, the debtor's proposal may be amended at any time up to the delivery of the former's report to the court under section 256.

Delivery of the nominee's report is dealt with below.[1] In certain circumstances, it may be necessary to amend the proposal, as originally prepared, in the light of intervening circumstances, for example where additional assets or, more usually, liabilities are ascertained, or the nominee discovers a material fact not previously made known to him by the debtor.

1 See Chapter 5.

3.2 Particular Assets and Liabilities

3.2.1 Introduction

The proposal must satisfy the requirements of the Act and Rules as to assets and liabilities; in addition, it is generally desirable for the proposal to give more information than is required by the Act and Rules. This is necessary for two reasons: first, so that the creditors can have the fullest possible information to enable them to form a reasoned judgment as to whether or not to support the proposal; and, secondly, the creditors must be satisfied that their position is no worse than it would be in bankruptcy. Furthermore, if the proposal considers particular assets and liabilities in detail, not only will it show that care has been taken in preparing the proposal, but it also highlights the fact that certain assets, where applicable, are to be made available under the voluntary arrangement which would not otherwise be available in bankruptcy.

3.2.2 Exclusion of assets and liabilities

Since the debtor is the originator of the proposal, he may propose that particular assets or liabilities are excluded from the proposal. In relation to assets, the exclusion of an asset which would otherwise be available in bankruptcy[1] may only be made with good reason, but there can be no objection to the exclusion of an asset which would not form part of a bankrupt's estate.[2] If an asset is excluded and no reason is given, this is likely to lead to the rejection of the proposal. If business assets are to be excluded because the proposal envisages the continuation of trading, this must be made clear and the creditors are entitled to be reassured that ongoing trading will be both realistic and beneficial. Where the debtor holds property on trust and has no beneficial interest therein the situation must be made clear.[3] If there is doubt as to entitlement to an asset, this must also be specified and the reasons for doubt should be made clear. If it is envisaged that steps are to be taken to establish title or entitlement, the proposal should indicate the steps to be taken and by whom, the likely time scale and expense.

The omission of categories of liabilities from the proposal may at first sight be beneficial to the creditors who are to be bound. However, the situation needs to be considered carefully. If, for whatever reason, a liability is excluded and cannot otherwise be dealt with, there is the danger that a creditor who is not bound by the arrangement may pursue independent proceedings against the debtor, possibly involving bankruptcy proceedings, which could jeopardise the proposal as a whole. If a particular liability is to be excluded, therefore, it is essential not only that it should be identified but also that satisfactory reasons are put forward and a viable indication as to how the liability will be satisfied is shown. It seems that, if it is proposed that a creditor be omitted from the scheme, that creditor would have a right of challenge.[4]

---

1 See Insolvency Rules 1986, r 5.3 (2) (a) (ii) at para 3.1.3 above.
2 See ibid, r 5.3 (2) (a) (ii) at para 3.1.3 above and Insolvency Act 1986, s 283 (1)–(3).
3 For the position in bankruptcy, see ibid, s 283 (3) (a) which implies that the debtor has no beneficial interest in the property.
4 See ibid, s 262 and Chapter 8.

3.2.3 *Freeholds*

In most instances of personal insolvency, the principal asset of the debtor will be his private dwelling or his share in the private dwelling. This gives rise to a number of considerations:

(a) *Valuation.* Some realistic attempt must be made to arrive at a proper valuation of the property, having regard to current market conditions, together with an equally realistic valuation of outgoings and how such outgoings, including mortgage payments, are to be met until sale. If a mortgagee is in the process of taking enforcement proceedings or is likely so to do, this needs to be indicated. The creditors will be interested in the equity available and this must be clearly stated and all qualifications made clear.

(b) *Title.* If the property is jointly owned, this must be shown in the proposal and the position and attitude of the joint owner made clear. The question of the matrimonial home is considered later.[1] Special considerations will arise as to property owned jointly in a partnership. Where the matrimonial home is to be sold, the debtor should be specifically advised as to the possible effect of rendering himself and his family homeless on a voluntary basis. If property is to be sold, the proposal should indicate who is to have the conduct and who is to have the right to instruct agents and solicitors and to agree the asking price and method of sale.

---

1 See Chapter 11.

3.2.4 Leaseholds

These are likely to be more problematic than freeholds. At the time of preparation of the proposal, the intended nominee should endeavour to see a copy of the lease and should come to some conclusion as to whether or not the entry into a voluntary arrangement gives rise to a right to forfeiture. Other breaches of covenant on the part of the tenant debtor may exist, and these will have a material effect on the marketability of the lease and valuation. Most leases will require the consent of the landlord to assignment and, wherever possible, the attitude of the landlord should be ascertained before the proposal is presented to the creditors. There is little point in including a leasehold as having a realisable value if, having regard to the attitude of the landlord and his potential claims, a sale is likely to be frustrated. The nominee will almost always need to approach the landlord at an early stage to explain his involvement in the matter, outline the proposed course of action and ascertain the attitude of the landlord and the likelihood of his co-operation. The proposal should then be framed accordingly, or else the result of such enquiries set out in the nominee's report.

If a leasehold interest is to be kept for any period of time, either pending sale or for the purpose of the debtor's business, the proposal must set out how the rent and other outgoings are to be paid. To prevent forfeiture, it will also be necessary to make provision for the payment of any arrears of rent or other sums due to the landlord.

A voluntary arrangement binds the debtor's creditors only as creditors and does not affect any proprietary rights, such as the right of a landlord to forfeit the lease, subject to the court's discretion to grant relief.[1] If forfeiture is likely, the proposal must deal with the possibility of an application for relief against forfeiture and ways in which this is to be funded.

No right of disclaimer arises in favour of a supervisor.[2]

---

1 See *Re Naeem (A Bankrupt) (No 18 of 1988)* [1990] 1 WLR 48 per Hoffman J.
2 For the position in bankruptcy see Insolvency Act 1986, ss 315–321. In appropriate cases, the landlord may accept a surrender.

3.2.5 Book debts

Creditors will often be suspicious as to figures provided in relation to the likely realisable value of book debts, and the debtor and his intended nominee must always have regard to the default provisions that exist in the Act.[1] In view of the amount of time that is normally available for the preparation of a proposal, it is clearly unrealistic for the proposal to contain a wholly accurate estimate as to the realisable value of such debts. Nevertheless, an attempt must be made. If the debtor is aware that book debts are likely to be contested, this must be explained. If steps will have to be taken to collect in book debts, the proposal must indicate who is to be responsible for this and how the collection process will be financed; in such circumstances, legal aid may be available. However, it will be of little comfort to the creditors to see that all available funds have been spent on litigating uncollectable book debts, and it is far better for the proposal to take a pessimistic view as to realisable values.

---

1 See Insolvency Act 1986, s 276 and Chapter 8.

3.2.6 *Work in progress and unfinished work*

Where the debtor has been in business, there will often be work in progress and unfinished contracts or engagements. Like book debts, such assets are notoriously difficult to value, and the sums actually realised often fall far short of projected realisable values. A conservative approach should be adopted. The nominee may feel that he cannot rely on the debtor's assessment of work in progress and unfinished work, and that he is not professionally qualified to reach an independent conclusion as to an accurate valuation and anticipated realisation. In such a case, the proposal should provide for the supervisor to engage a suitably qualified surveyor or other professional to assess the situation at once and reach an agreement with the other contracting parties. It will always be dangerous to include in a proposal any definite amount for realisation of such assets, since there will always be some degree of doubt as to the level of realisation.

The precise position in relation to each and every item should be set out. If it is envisaged that funds are to be expended on completing work, this must be explained, together with the necessary funding arrangements. If set-offs and counterclaims are likely to exist, this also must be made clear. If the voluntary arrangement itself gives rise to the termination of a contract or engagement, this must be ascertained and explained.

3.2.7 *'Securities' (stocks and shares)*

A true valuation of quoted securities held by the debtor may be obtained relatively easily; however, problems will arise in relation to unquoted securities and, in particular, shares held by the debtor in private companies. The memorandum and articles of association of such companies will normally contain restrictions on the realisation of such shares. If such securities exist, they must be included in the proposal, together with all relevant considerations and factors as to their realisation and valuation. A detailed examination of the valuation of such shares is outside the scope of this work.

3.2.8 *Joint assets*

In bankruptcy, the debtor's beneficial interest in joint assets forms part of his estate, and the same considerations should apply in an arrangement. Not only does the extent of the debtor's interest need to be identified, but the proposal must make clear what steps need to be taken to achieve realisation. If the other joint owner is willing to co-operate, that fact can be indicated and a letter of consent to realisation signed by the joint owner can be attached as an exhibit to the proposal. If the joint owner is unlikely to co-operate or if, at the time the proposal is prepared, it is clear that there is a dispute between the joint owners, the proposal must indicate what steps will be taken. It must be remembered that the supervisor as such will have no power to realise assets in his own name, since none of the statutory powers available to a trustee are available to a supervisor. It will fall to the debtor to take the appropriate steps under the supervision and direction of the supervisor. The proposal must set out what is envisaged and what the likely expense of realisation will be. Any particular difficulties should be highlighted, especially if they are likely to have a material effect on the duration of the arrangement. If the joint owner indicates concurrence, it is prudent to ensure that he is aware of the implications and is advised as to his rights.

3.2.9 Life assurance policies

Surrender values should be obtained, together with confirmation as to the identity of the debtor as beneficiary and whether or not the policies are charged. Pension policies may also give rise to specific considerations. The nominee should satisfy himself as to the precise terms of any pension policy to which the debtor is entitled and, in particular, whether or not it has any surrender value, which is unlikely. No obligation should need to be included in the arrangement to continue the payment of premiums unless it is clear that there will be a resulting benefit to the creditors. In certain cases, the debtor may be entitled to a pension as a result of policies to which he has contributed; this will constitute income arising during the arrangement and should be accounted for.

3.2.10 Liens and charges generally

All encumbrances should be identified and quantified. The proposal should indicate whether or not any steps are to be taken, and if so by whom, to challenge the validity of encumbrances and the likely effect on the arrangement as to duration and cost. The intended nominee would be well advised, if time and circumstances permit, to investigate the extent and nature of any encumbrances. If they purport to grant some sort of option in favour of the chargee to re-possess or re-acquire on beneficial terms, this will clearly affect the realisable value and should be identified accordingly. As regards freehold and leasehold property, the intended nominee would be well advised to make land charge and Land Registry searches to verify the extent of encumbrances on land. This is a relatively simple exercise, and an intended nominee may well be criticised for not taking this basic step if, after acceptance of the proposal, it is ascertained that property is subject to more charges than anticipated or is subject to some other encumbrance, such as an option or possibly, in the case of land, a covenant prohibiting development.

3.2.11 Motor vehicles

Some motor vehicles may be excluded from the proposal if they are necessary to the debtor for use personally by him in his employment, business or vocation.[1] Otherwise, vehicles should be included at a proper valuation and the extent of encumbrances shown. Most insolvency practitioners will have established lines of communication with experts specialising in the valuation of motor vehicles, so valuation should not prove difficult. Particular care needs to be taken as regards any motor vehicle which may have any historic, antique or collector's interest or if a vehicle has the benefit of a personalised number plate. If a motor vehicle has a minimal equity, after the likely costs of sale have been taken into account, the creditors may agree for it to be excluded.

---

1 Cf Insolvency Act 1986, s 283 (2) (a).

3.2.12 After-acquired property

In bankruptcy, after-acquired assets that devolve on the bankrupt prior to discharge may be claimed by the trustee.[1] It is therefore logical for such a provision to be made in the proposal for a voluntary arrangement. The debtor should make available, from the after-acquired assets that devolve on him during the arrangement, sufficient after-acquired assets to pay all the creditors in full with interest applicable. The proposal should specifically require the debtor to notify the supervisor of after-acquired assets and of the obligation to make them available. After-acquired assets which would be excluded in bankruptcy may properly be excluded from a voluntary arrangement.[2]

---

1 See Insolvency Act 1986, ss 307–309.
2 See (iii) at page 18 above.

3.2.13 Income arising during the arrangement

In bankruptcy, a trustee may apply to the court for an income payments order.[1] The court, if minded to make an order, is obliged not to reduce the income of the bankrupt below what appears to the court to be necessary for meeting the reasonable domestic needs of the bankrupt and his family.[2] Similar provision may be made in a voluntary arrangement, but the obligation on the debtor should be no more onerous than would be the case in bankruptcy. Due account should be taken in quantifying the contribution as regards the incidence of taxation, national insurance contributions, reasonable expenses for earning the income and such other deductions as are reasonable in all the circumstances. The debtor should be required to notify the supervisor of all material changes in his income and to provide the supervisor with all relevant and necessary information. A supervisor will have no power to apply to the court for an income payments order as such. Accordingly, the proposal should specify the amount and frequency of contributions from income and should, where appropriate, contain provision as to how the contribution is to be reviewed.

---

1 Insolvency Act 1986, s 310.
2 Ibid, s 310 (2).

3.3 Specific Considerations

3.3.1 General

In this section, a number of matters which may need inclusion in a proposal are considered. It is certainly not suggested that every matter which follows needs to be included in each and every proposal. Each proposal is an individual document and must be prepared with the characteristics of a particular case in mind.

3.3.2 *Incorporation of standard conditions*

Many insolvency practitioners use their own standard conditions.[1] In this section, these standard conditions are referred to by use of the abbreviation 'SC' followed by the relevant number. However, these need to be treated with care: the person responsible for preparing a proposal should give due consideration not only to the necessity of incorporating standard conditions but also to any standard conditions which are not to apply and any necessary variations. A simple proposal does not need to be encumbered with rigid time-consuming and potentially expensive procedures. Creditors' interests need to be borne in mind, as they will certainly not want to read lengthy legalistic conditions. On the other hand, the proposal must make it clear that standard conditions are incorporated. The standard conditions to be used should be annexed to the proposal, and there should be a clear indication that the standard conditions form an integral part of the proposal. If any conflict or ambiguity arises between the proposal itself and the standard conditions, provision should be made as to which prevails. The supervisor may be given power to determine such conflict or ambiguity or, accordingly, may be entitled to apply to the court for a determination.[2] The proposal may provide that approval by the creditors of the proposal should be deemed to include approval and acceptance of the standard conditions.

---

1 See Appendix 1, p 136 for a specimen set.
2 Insolvency Act 1986, s 263 (4).

3.3.3 *Beneficial entitlement to assets*

After the proposal has been accepted by the creditors and the supervisor has been appointed, beneficial ownership of the assets which form part of the arrangement remain vested in the debtor and do not vest in the supervisor.[1] A potential difficulty may arise if the debtor is subsequently adjudged bankrupt, either as a result of default in the arrangement or as a result of a petition brought by a creditor who was not bound or whose debt came into existence after the approval of the arrangement.[2] One particular problem is the restriction placed on a debtor as regards the disposal of his property after a bankruptcy petition has been presented. The Act provides that such a disposition within the relevant period is void except to the extent that it is made with the consent of the court or is subsequently ratified by the court.[3] The relevant period is from the day of presentation to the day of vesting of the bankrupt's estate in a trustee. Whilst there are saving provisions for dispositions made in good faith and without notice, nevertheless it seems that, since the assets forming part of the arrangement remain in the beneficial ownership of the debtor, the presentation of a petition will effectively frustrate the operation of the arrangement. The proposal may, therefore, provide for the assets in question to be held by the debtor on trust for the supervisor and/or the creditors bound generally so as to bring the assets outside the debtor's estate for the purpose of bankruptcy.[4] Furthermore, the Act provides that the restrictions on the disposition of property following presentation of a petition do not affect any disposition made by a person of property held by him on trust for any other person. Clearly the supervisor needs to consider the implications of being constituted trustee.

1 See para 2.5.2 above and *Re Naeem* [1990] 1 WLR 48 at 51A.
2 As to the effect on an arrangement of the subsequent bankruptcy of the debtor, see paras 10.1–10.7 below.
3 Insolvency Act 1986, s 284.
4 See Appendix 1, p 138, SC 7.2

3.3.4 Supervisor's role, position and powers [SC 11.1] [1]

The Act and Rules are virtually silent on such matters. The Act provides that the supervisor is to carry out the functions conferred by virtue of the approval of the arrangement by the creditors. The supervisor is given power to apply to the court for directions in relation to any particular matter arising under the voluntary arrangement.[2] Otherwise, the role, position, powers, duties and responsibilities of the supervisor are as set out in the proposal and, accordingly, the proposal must be quite clear as to such matters.

1 Page 140.
2 Insolvency Act 1986, s 263 (4).

3.3.5 Failure and default [SC 15] [1]

If it is envisaged that default should embrace events or happenings wider than those provided for in the Act, specific provision must be contained in the proposal.

1 See generally Chapter 8 and page 141.

3.3.6 Warranty [SC 4] [1]

Assurance should be given to the creditors that the debtor has made a full and complete disclosure to the nominee of all relevant matters, whether by express warranty included in the proposal or otherwise.

1 Page 136.

3.3.7 Extension of time [SC 5.2] [1]

The Rules provide that the proposal must specify the duration of the arrangement, but circumstances may arise whereby it is desired to extend the duration, for example because the realisation of a particular asset has taken longer than was anticipated. Furthermore, the proposal may provide that the debtor is to contribute, within a specified period of time, a certain sum of money by way of voluntary contribution. The proposal may contain provision for extension of the specified duration, which may be done in a number of ways: first, the proposal itself may confer on the supervisor the right to extend the duration; alternatively, the proposal may provide for the matter to be dealt with by way of a resolution of the creditors' committee, or by convening a meeting of all the creditors bound and passing an appropriate resolution. It would appear that the court does not have power to extend the duration.

---

1 Page 137.

3.3.8 Amendment of the proposal generally [SC 26] [1]

Whilst there is specific provision for the amendment of the proposal up to and including the creditors' meeting,[2] there is no provision in either the Act or Rules for the amendment of the terms of the proposal after it has been accepted by the creditors. The proposal constitutes the whole agreement between debtor and creditors. Nevertheless, circumstances may arise whereby it is desirable for the proposal to be amended in some material particular; for example, the question of duration has been dealt with above. Arguably, the supervisor could apply to the court for directions but, even if the court accepted jurisdiction, it might well conclude that it would be wrong to make material alterations to the terms of an agreement without notice to all the creditors and without giving the creditors a right to make representations. It follows that, if it is considered likely that amendments will be needed after approval, the proposal itself should contain specific provision setting out the procedure and formula. There is probably no objection to conferring on the supervisor the right to effect minor or insignificant amendments. Major or material amendments should, it is submitted, only be made with the approval of either the creditors' committee or all the creditors.

---

1 Page 146.
2 Insolvency Act 1986, s 258 (2); Insolvency Rules 1986, r 5.3 (3).

3.3.9 Creditors' committee

No provision is made in the Act or Rules for the establishment of a creditors' committee, in contrast to the situation in bankruptcy.[1] In appropriate cases, a creditors' committee may be desirable, in which case the proposal must make specific provision for this and must lay down the responsibilities, duties and powers of the creditors' committee.[2]

---

1 See Insolvency Act 1986, s 301; Insolvency Rules 1986, rr 6.150–6.166.
2 See, for example, SC 5.4, 16, 21.4.

3.3.10 Creditors' meeting

It is desirable for the proposal to contain a provision empowering the supervisor to convene a meeting of creditors in certain circumstances. In the normal course of events, the supervisor keeps creditors informed as to the progress in the voluntary arrangement.[1] A creditors' meeting may be desirable from time to time, for example, to pass a resolution to seek the bankruptcy of the debtor or to deal with some other unforeseen situation. Circumstances may also arise where the supervisor feels that it is in the interests of the creditors generally to take their view on a situation instead of, or as a prerequisite to, an application to the court for directions[2] or, alternatively, in a situation of doubt to avoid the risk of either the debtor or a creditor applying to the court to reverse or modify an act or decision of the supervisor.[3]

1 See the requirements of Insolvency Rules 1986, r 5.26.
2 Under Insolvency Act 1986, s 263 (4); see also SC 5.2, 5.4, 6.1, 13, 15.2, 16, 18.4, 21.4, 24.1, 26.
3 Such applications are under ibid, s 263 (3).

3.3.11 *Powers of attorney [SC 7.1]*

Since the debtor's property remains vested in him, any legal documents required to be signed for the disposition of property or otherwise must be signed by the debtor himself. The proposal may provide for the debtor to give to the supervisor a power of attorney to deal with such matters on the debtor's behalf.

3.3.12 *Requirements on the debtor [SC 7]*

The proposal generally specifies the continuing obligations on the debtor. In any event, the debtor is liable to carry out all the terms of the proposal which may contain specific provision as to the debtor's obligations in relation to:

(a) doing all things that the supervisor shall require
(b) instituting or defending legal proceedings which affect or concern the proposal
(c) applying for legal aid for such proceedings
(d) attending upon the supervisor when required
(e) delivering to the supervisor upon receipt any communication which may affect or concern the arrangement.

Failure to comply with such requirements would constitute default within the meaning of the Act.[1]

1 See Insolvency Act 1986, s 276 (1) (a), (c) and Chapter 8.

3.3.13 *Continuation of debtor's business [SC 8]*

This is a matter which requires specific consideration. From what is contained in the proposal and supporting documents, the creditors must be satisfied that the continuation of the business is viable. Past trading accounts should be made available and realistic forecasts, cashflow statements and projections prepared. Arrangements as to suppliers, employees and all other aspects of the business need to be made quite clear. The co-operation of HM Customs and Excise as regards continued VAT registration may be problematic. The proposal should make clear the duration of continued trading, the circumstances, if any, in which such trading is to cease, the fact that the debtor will continue trading on his own account and in his own name, together with restrictions as may be appropriate. These are generally matters which can satisfactorily be dealt with by the inclusion of standard conditions. Nevertheless, it must be stressed that every business is different, so that the particular circumstances of the business in question and the implications of ongoing trading need to be thought out with care and precision. The supervisor should be afforded full access to the business and its records, and there should be an obligation on the debtor to provide the supervisor with regular information and maintain all proper accounts, records and banking arrangements. Generally speaking, it would be unwise for a proposal to permit a debtor to continue trading on a credit basis, especially where there is the likelihood of a new body of creditors coming into existence.

3.3.14 Tax and VAT [SC 9] [1]

In all instances and, in particular, where there is to be ongoing trading, it should be made clear in the proposal that the debtor alone remains responsible for all taxation liabilities, including liability for VAT. Where the proposal provides for contributions to be made by the debtor to the arrangement out of the profits of continued trading, it is desirable for the term 'profits' to be defined and to make clear the basis upon which contributions are to be calculated. The Inland Revenue and HM Customs and Excise will almost certainly support a proposal only if it contains provision for all outstanding accounts and returns to be completed and made within a specified period of time, normally three months. The nominee should ascertain exactly what accounts or returns are outstanding and should anticipate this point and include a specific provision in the proposal. If he does not, the revenue authorities will almost certainly seek to effect amendments at the creditors' meeting itself.

---

1 See generally Chapter 12.

3.3.15 Application of bankruptcy principles [SC 12]

Generally speaking, creditors should never be in a worse position than they would have been if the debtor had been adjudged bankrupt. Accordingly, specific provisions which bear comparison to provisions in bankruptcy may be included in the proposal. These may include incorporation of Insolvency Act 1986, ss 322 (Proof of Debts), 323 (Mutual Credit and Set-Off), 324 (Distribution by Means of Dividend), 325 (Claims by Unsatisfied Creditors) and 326 (Distribution of Property in Specie).

3.3.16 Wrongdoing by the debtor [SC 13] [1]

The part of the Act dealing with bankruptcy refers to a number of instances of potential wrongdoing: these include the adjustment of prior transactions by reference to transactions at an undervalue,[2] preferences,[3] avoidance of general assignment of book debts[4] and numerous offences collectively described as wrongdoing by the bankrupt before and after bankruptcy.[5] As regards a number of these matters, if there is the suggestion that at the time of the creditors' meeting facts exist which may give rise to such claims, they are to be referred to in the proposal so that the creditors can make a decision as to whether or not to allow the debtor's affairs to proceed to bankruptcy when the statutory powers arise. If such facts exist at the material time and the creditors accept the proposal, they have done so in full knowledge of the facts and cannot complain. If, however, it comes to light after the acceptance of the proposal that such wrongdoing existed and was not disclosed or alternatively there has been wrongdoing within the meaning of the sections, then the proposal may provide for the termination of the scheme, whether or not such acts constitute default within the meaning of the Act. The proposal must be very clear and specific on such matters. There cannot be room for any ambiguity. It would be wrong to leave dealing with such matters to the sole discretion of the supervisor. It would be right to empower and, indeed, direct him to refer such matters to either the creditors' committee or the creditors' meeting for a determination as to the appropriate course of action in accordance with the proposal.

1 As to failure of the scheme and default, see generally Chapter 8.
2 Insolvency Act 1986, s 339.
3 Ibid, s 340.
4 Ibid, s 344.
5 Ibid, ss 353–362.

3.3.17 Failure to realise [SC 15.1 (d)]

There will be instances where the supervisor or debtor is unable to realise an asset for the sum specified or estimated in the proposal. This may prima facie give rise to default,[1] which may in certain circumstances be unfair to the debtor. In bankruptcy, creditors are given no guarantee as to what a particular asset will realise. If, therefore, it is to be provided that failure to realise an asset for a particular sum or, indeed, any sum at all is not to constitute either default or failure of the scheme (presupposing that such a concept is incorporated into the proposal), the proposal must contain specific provision to this effect.

1 Insolvency Act 1986, s 276 (1) (a) or (c).

3.3.18 Inclusion of creditors not bound [SC 18.3]

It will not be unusual to discover after approval of the scheme that there exist creditors who were not given notice of the arrangements and therefore are not bound. It may be desired to include such creditors into the scheme and, indeed, such creditors may desire to be included. Such a provision may be incorporated in the proposal. If no such provision exists, it appears that such creditors cannot be included. A creditor who is not bound cannot subsequently be bound against his will.

3.3.19 Advertisement of claims [SC 18]

The proposal may provide for the supervisor to be empowered to advertise for claims in an appropriate local newspaper.[1]

1 The debtor must be made aware of such a proposal. Voluntary arrangements, unlike bankruptcy, are not advertised. The debtor may wish, for good reasons, to avoid publicity other than is inevitable as a result of the circulation of his creditors.

3.3.20 Agreement of claims [SC 18]

Creditors must lodge a proof of debt with the nominee prior to the creditors' meeting.[1] This proof of debt will be used initially for voting purposes. The extent of the creditor's claim may or may not be agreed at the time of the creditors' meeting. If a particular creditor's claim is not agreed at this time, the meeting should be advised accordingly and the proposal should contain provision as to how disputed claims are to be resolved; this obligation may be conferred on the supervisor. It is desirable for all claims to be agreed so far as possible before the holding of a creditors' meeting so that all creditors at the meeting know the extent of ranking liabilities,[2] although this is not always possible. A creditors' meeting is not the correct forum to agree actual amounts or to deal with disputed debts. Judicial guidance has been given.[3] Disputed and contingent debts should be shown at their 'worst' so that the creditors can see the 'bottom line position'. Where a claim is disputed or contingent, the nominee should take care to explain to the creditor that his claim is being admitted for voting purposes only and that agreement and quantification of the claim will follow.

---

1 Chapter 5.

2 Otherwise, the arrangement may be put in jeopardy by claims being more than was thought likely. This may give rise to allegations that creditors were misled: see Insolvency Act 1986, s 276 (1) (b). The court would be able to adjudicate on the extent of a creditor's claim on an application under ibid, s 263 (3) or (4).

3 *Re A Debtor (No 222 of 1990)* (1991) *The Times*, 27 June.

3.3.21 Interest

The right of a secured creditor entitled to interest to continue charging interest until paid in full can be interfered with only if the creditor concurs.[1] Other categories of creditors may be entitled to interest by contract or statute. Otherwise, creditors are not entitled to claim interest. The proposal should be clear as to how interest is to be dealt with and quantified. Other than secured creditors, the proposal may provide for all interest to cease running as from the date of the approval at the creditors' meeting, although this may give rise to a challenge.[2]

---

1 See Insolvency Act 1986, s 258 (4).

2 Under ibid, s 262.

3.3.22 Non-provable claims

In bankruptcy, certain claims are not provable.[1] There seems no reason why such claims cannot be included in a voluntary arrangement, but natural justice would seem to indicate that, if a claim is not provable in bankruptcy, it should not be provable in a voluntary arrangement.

---

1 See Insolvency Rules 1986, r 12.3 (2).

3.3.23 Payment to supervisor on account of fees [SC 21]

The proposal may provide for the supervisor to draw sums on account of his fees and disbursements from time to time as he thinks fit.

3.3.24 Agreement of fees [SC 21.4]

The proposal must contain details as to the basis on which the supervisor is to be remunerated.[1] If the proposal does not provide for a fixed sum, it should provide for the basis on which the remuneration is to be calculated and agreed.

---

1 See Insolvency Rules 1986, r 5.3 (2) (h).

3.3.25 Certificate of compliance [SC 23]

The proposal may provide that, on due completion of the arrangement, the supervisor is to send to each creditor bound a certificate of due completion. There is no prescribed form.[1]

---

1 But see Insolvency Rules 1986, r 5.29.

3.3.26 Vacancy in office of supervisor [SC 24]

The Act provides[1] that the court is to have power whenever it is expedient to appoint a person to carry out the functions of the supervisor and it is inexpedient, difficult or impracticable for an appointment to be made without the assistance of the court, for the court to make an order appointing a qualified person to act either in substitution for the existing supervisor or to fill a vacancy arising, for example, on death. The supervisor may purport to have resigned.[2] To avoid the expense of an application to the court, the proposal may make provision for the method by which the office of supervisor may be filled if a vacancy arises.

---

1 Insolvency Act 1986, s 263 (5).
2 The Act and Rules do not make provision for resignation. If a resignation is effected, the debtor or a creditor would have to apply under ibid, s 263 (5).

Chapter 4

PROCEEDINGS FOR THE INTERIM ORDER

4.1 Introduction

Once the proposal has been prepared, application can be made to the court for an interim order. The power of the court to make an interim order is discretionary.[1] The application will in most instances be made by the debtor himself.[2]

---

1 Insolvency Act 1986, s 252 (1); the word 'may' is used.
2 See ibid, s 253 (3).

4.2 Purpose of the Interim Order

As is specified in the heading to s 252 of the Act, the purpose of the interim order is to effect a moratorium. Section 255 (2) provides that 'the court may make an order if it thinks that it would be appropriate to do so for the purpose of facilitating the consideration and implementation of the debtor's proposal'. Whilst the interim order is in force:

(a) no bankruptcy petition relating to the debtor may be presented or proceeded with,[1] and
(b) no other proceedings, and no execution or other legal process, may be commenced or continued against the debtor or his property except with the leave of the court.[2]

If a bankruptcy petition has been presented prior to the application for the interim order and it comes on for hearing, it will almost certainly be adjourned. The term 'no other proceedings and no execution or other legal process' is wide-ranging and would include proceedings for forfeiture by a landlord under a lease.[3] In the context of this subsection, the reference to 'the court' is a reference to the court hearing the application for the interim order.

---

1 Insolvency Act 1986, s 252 (2) (a).
2 Ibid, s 252 (2) (b). This appears to be an all-embracing provision, but the effect of this prohibition is likely to be eroded by the courts in proper cases. See *In Re M* (1991) *The Times*, 17 April: an interim order does not affect the right of the prosecution under the Drug Trafficking Offences Act 1986 to make an order appointing a receiver for the realisable property of a debtor against whom criminal proceedings have been instituted. The section will not generally prevent secured creditors from enforcing their security in the long term, in view of the provisions of Insolvency Act 1986, s 258 (4).

3 But only for as long as the interim order is in place. See *Re Naeem* [1990] 1 WLR 48 at
  50E.

4.3 Involvement of the Nominee

The debtor must give written notice of the proposal to the intended nominee.[1]
The notice must be accompanied by a copy of the proposal[2] and must be
delivered either to the nominee himself or to a person authorised to take
delivery of documents on his behalf.[3] If the intended nominee agrees to act, he
must endorse a copy of the notice accordingly.[4] A copy of the notice duly
endorsed is to be returned by the nominee to the debtor at the address specified
by the debtor in the notice.[5] In a Case 1 matter, the debtor must also give
notice of his proposal to the official receiver and to any trustee who has been
appointed, and the notice must contain the name and address of the insolvency
practitioner who has agreed to act as nominee, who may or may not be the
same person as the trustee.[6]

1 Insolvency Rules 1986, r 5.4 (1).
2 Insolvency (Amendment) Rules 1987, r 84.
3 Insolvency Rules 1986, r 5.4 (2).
4 Ibid, r 5.4 (3).
5 Ibid, r 5.4 (4).
6 Ibid, r 5.4 (5).

4.4 The Application

The application for an interim order may be made where a debtor intends to
make a proposal for a composition to satisfy his debts or a scheme of
arrangement.[1] Either is referred to as a voluntary arrangement. In reality, the
difference between a composition in satisfaction of a debtor's debts and a
scheme of arrangement of a debtor's affairs is seldom apparent from a
proposal. The real difference appears to be that, in a scheme of arrangement,
the debtor makes over his assets to be administered by a trustee,[2] and, in a
composition, the debtor keeps his assets and undertakes to pay over to his
creditors a certain sum of money. This distinction is ancient and, in practice,
most voluntary arrangements are likely to be a combination of both, although
such an arrangement is essentially a composition. Most proposals will involve
elements of a scheme of arrangement and will have the effect of being a
composition in satisfaction of debts. As has already been seen, the proposal
must provide for a person to act in relation to the voluntary arrangement,
either as trustee or otherwise, for the purpose of supervising its implementation. Rarely will a supervisor be willing to become a trustee in the full sense of
the word. Nevertheless, this distinction between 'as trustee' and 'otherwise
. . . supervising' is consistent with the theoretical difference between a composition and a scheme of arrangement.

1 See Insolvency Act 1986, s 253 (1) and Appendix 2, p 169.
2 Hence the reason for ibid, s 253 (2) specifying the alternatives of 'trustee' or 'otherwise . . .
  supervising'.

4.5 Who May Apply?

The Act[1] provides that, if the debtor is an undischarged bankrupt, an application for an interim order may be made by either the debtor, the trustee or the official receiver and, in any other case, it must be made by the debtor. An application by the debtor calls for no particular comment at this stage. It is probably unlikely that the official receiver will make an application, but application by a trustee in bankruptcy is more likely. A bankruptcy order will frequently be made against a debtor who has either not heard of voluntary arrangements or otherwise has not had an opportunity to consider one.[2] There will also certainly be cases where the debtor has been dilatory in giving proper consideration to his own affairs. Therefore, even if a bankruptcy order is made, a view may be taken by the debtor, the trustee or the official receiver that it is in the interests of the creditors as well as the debtor for the bankruptcy to be 'converted' into a voluntary arrangement. Where the debtor is an undischarged bankrupt, he is not permitted to make an application himself unless he has given notice of his proposal to the official receiver and, if one has been appointed, the trustee.[3] Special provisions apply where a bankruptcy petition presented by the debtor himself is pending.[4]

---

1 Insolvency Act 1986, s 253 (3).
2 But see paras 10.8.1–10.8.5 below.
3 Ibid, s 253 (4).
4 See paras 10.8.1–10.8.5 below.

4.6 Effect of Application

As soon as the application has been filed with the court, the court to which the application has been made[1] may stay any action, execution or other legal process against the property or person of the debtor.[2] Such applications, save in extreme cases, should be on notice. Having regard to the comparatively short time which is normally involved in proceedings for an interim order, the court will normally make an order for stay so as to protect the interests of the creditors generally. Furthermore, any court[3] in which proceedings are pending against an individual may, on proof that an application has been made,[4] stay the proceedings or allow them to continue on such terms as it thinks fit. The court is likely to stay proceedings if it considers that there would be prejudice to the arrangement by allowing the particular proceedings to continue.

---

1 See Insolvency (Amendment) Rules 1987, r 85.
2 Insolvency Act 1986, s 254 (1). The power is discretionary; there is no automatic stay as on the making of the interim order.
3 This need not be the court to which the application for the interim order is made.
4 Normally in the form of a sealed copy of the application, supported by an affidavit.

4.7 Cases in which an Interim Order can be Made[1]

Both the Act and Rules lay down certain basic requirements which must be satisfied in each case. The Act contains four mandatory conditions. The court must be satisfied that:

(a) the debtor intends to make a proposal;[2]
(b) on the day of making the application, the debtor is either an undischarged bankrupt or in a position to petition for his own bankruptcy;[3]
(c) no previous application has been made by the debtor for an interim order in the preceding 12 months;[4] and
(d) the nominee is properly qualified and willing to act.[5]

The application[6] must be accompanied by an affidavit,[7] normally sworn by the debtor,[8] which must deal with certain specified matters:

(a) the reasons for making the application;
(b) particulars of any execution or other legal process which, to the debtor's knowledge, has been commenced against him;
(c) statement that he is an undischarged bankrupt or, as the case may be, able to petition for his own bankruptcy;
(d) that no such previous application has been made 'by or in respect of'[9] the debtor in the period of 12 months ending with the date of the affidavit and
(e) that the nominee is duly qualified and willing to act.

A copy of the notice to the intended nominee[10] must be exhibited, together with a copy of the proposal.[11]

Whilst, in essence, the Act and Rules lay down the same requirements, there are differences. Under the Rules, the debtor must specify particulars of all outstanding legal proceedings against him, and of particular importance will be disclosure of the existence of any outstanding bankruptcy petitions. Whilst the Act precludes an application where there has been a previous application made by the debtor in the preceding 12-month period, the Rules go further and suggest that no application can be made if there has been a previous application 'by or in respect of' the debtor. This appears to suggest that, even if the debtor has not made a previous application within the 12-month period, an application by a trustee or the official receiver precludes the court from entertaining a further application until the 12-month period has expired.

The debtor must rely on the nominee for confirmation of his due qualification. There have been instances of courts rejecting applications for interim orders where there was no corroborating proof of due qualification. This can be overcome by a copy of the nominee's certification being exhibited or, alternatively, by the nominee depositing a copy of his licence with the court from which he normally takes appointments.

---

1 See generally Insolvency Act 1986, s 255 and Insolvency Rules 1986, r 5.5.
2 Insolvency Act 1986, s 255 (1) (a).
3 Ibid, s 255 (1) (b).
4 Ibid, s 255 (1) (c).
5 Ibid, s 255 (1) (d).
6 See Appendix 2, p 165.

7 See Insolvency Rules 1986, r 5.5 and Appendix 2, p 166.
8 Or by whoever makes the application.
9 See Insolvency Act 1986, s 253 (3) for a summary of those who might have applied 'in respect of' the debtor.
10 See Appendix 2, p 167.
11 Insolvency (Amendment) Rules 1987, r 84.

4.8 Service

On filing the application, a hearing date is fixed.[1] At least two days' notice must be given in a Case 1 arrangement to the bankrupt, the official receiver and the trustee, depending on which of those three is not the applicant and, in a Case 2, to any creditor who has presented a petition; in either case, notice must be given to the nominee.[2]

1 Insolvency Rules 1986, r 5.5 (3).
2 Ibid, r 5.5 (4).

4.9 Hearing of the Application

The hearing will be in chambers before a district judge. Anyone who has to be given notice of the application may appear or be represented. The court is not bound to make an interim order, nor does it exist to 'rubber-stamp' applications.[1] The matter must be dealt with judicially.[2] The Act provides that the court may make an order if it thinks it would be appropriate to do so for the purpose of facilitating the consideration and implementation of the debtor's proposal.[3] The Rules provide that the court, in deciding whether to make an interim order, must take into account any representations made by a person entitled to attend.[4]

The court is therefore entitled to look at the whole proposal and, amongst other things, reach a view as to whether or not it is a proposal that ought to go to the creditors.[5] It has sometimes been argued that, at this stage, the court should not, in effect, exercise a veto, but should work on the principle that it is ultimately for the creditors to decide. The logic of this approach is patently obvious. Nevertheless, not only must the court be satisfied that the requirements of the Act and Rules to date have been satisfied, but must also act judicially. In a Case 1, the official receiver or trustee may appear and raise matters unknown to the nominee and possibly to the detriment of the debtor. There may be instances where the official receiver or trustee has experienced the non-co-operation of the debtor or the deliberate concealment of assets. These are clearly matters most pertinent to a voluntary arrangement. The court must take all matters into consideration and then, on the totality of the evidence, decide whether or not the application should be granted. It is the practice of some courts to deal with applications for an interim order without any hearing at all. This was previously thought to be a questionable practice,[6] but it is now provided for by a High Court Practice Direction[7] which may equally be applied in a county court. The making of an interim order may materially affect the rights of creditors; individual creditors may be prejudiced by an interim order being made to the extent that it prevents them from pursuing outstanding litigation. The court must be seen to be doing the right thing and dealing with the matter properly.

1 Although this is frequently the case.
2 See generally *In Re A Debtor (No 83 of 1988)* [1990] 1 WLR 708 per Scott J. Whilst not concerned directly with the actual granting of an interim order, this case, which on its facts is unusual, indicates that in proper cases the courts may dismiss applications. This case concerned the failure to hold a creditors' meeting. The judge held, on the evidence available, that a 75 per cent majority (see Rule 5.18) could not be obtained. Arguably a similar situation could arise on the hearing of the application for the interim order.
3 Insolvency Act 1986, s 255 (2).
4 Insolvency Rules 1986, r 5.6 (2).
5 See *In Re A Debtor (No 83 of 1988)*, note 2 above.
6 See the wording of the 1986 Act, s 255 (2) in relation to the obligation imposed on the court.
7 *Practice Direction (Bankruptcy: Voluntary Arrangements)* [1992] 1 WLR 120, reproduced at para 4.16 below.

4.10 Where Debtor is an Undischarged Bankrupt

The interim order may contain provision as to the conduct of the bankruptcy and the administration of the bankrupt's estate during the period for which it is in force.[1] Such provision may stay proceedings in the bankruptcy or modify any provision in the Act or Rules relating to the debtor's bankruptcy.[2] The interim order must not, however, make any provision relaxing or removing any of the requirements of the Act and Rules relating to bankruptcy unless the court is satisfied that such provision is unlikely to result in any significant diminution in, or in the value of, the debtor's estate for the purposes of the bankruptcy.[3] It is not immediately clear as to the extent of an order capable of being made under these provisions. The qualification is that any order so made must not diminish the quantum or value of the bankrupt's estate. If, for example, the trustee in bankruptcy has already entered into a binding contract for the sale of an asset, then in the normal course of events such contract should be permitted to proceed to completion. This would be the case even though the trustee completing such a transaction may incur greater costs and expenses than would be the case if the asset was realised in the context of the voluntary arrangement. Similarly, if the trustee had embarked on litigation, an order might be made as to the conduct of such litigation. The fact is that the further the bankruptcy has proceeded, the more difficult it will be to convert it into a voluntary arrangement. Consequently, if an application for an interim order is made in the very early stages of the bankruptcy, then it is unlikely that any substantive relief need be sought under these particular provisions. Possibly a stay of advertisement might be appropriate. Conversely, the further the administration of the estate in bankruptcy has proceeded, the less likely it will be for a voluntary arrangement to be appropriate and the more difficult and complicated it will be for the court to make any sensible or meaningful orders under these subsections.[4]

1 Insolvency Act 1986, s 255 (3).
2 Ibid, s 255 (4).
3 Ibid, s 255 (5).
4 See generally Chapter 9.

4.11 Where Debtor dies before the Court has made an Interim Order

Where a debtor dies after a voluntary arrangement has been approved, there appears to be no reason why the arrangement cannot be concluded, although the death of the debtor may, depending on the terms of the arrangement, in effect frustrate or otherwise destroy the viability and practical working out of the arrangement. Much will depend on the position in each individual case.

It does not seem possible for a voluntary arrangement to be proposed by the personal representatives or administrators of a deceased who, if insolvent, must administer the estate, subject to the provisions of the Administration of Insolvent Estates of Deceased Debtors Order 1986.[1]

---

1 SI 1986/1999.

4.12 Where Debtor dies after the Court has made an Interim Order

Pursuant to the Administration of Insolvent Estates of Deceased Debtors Order 1986, which came into force on 29 December 1986, most of the sections of Part VIII of the Insolvency Act 1986 apply, but generally with modifications. In general terms, an insolvency administration order means an order for the administration in bankruptcy of the insolvent estate of a deceased debtor, being an individual at the date of his death, and an insolvency administration petition means a petition for an insolvency administration order.

It is expressly provided that provisions of the Act apply where the court has made an interim order under s 252 in respect of an individual who subsequently dies. This being the case, it is clear that the provisions of the Act relating to applications for an interim order[1] are not relevant, since the interim order must already have been made.

---

1 Insolvency Act 1986, ss 252–255.

4.13 Official Receiver/Trustee

It has already been seen that, in a Case 1, the official receiver and, if appointed, the trustee must be served with the application for an interim order and they are entitled to attend and be represented at the hearing. It will always be wise for the nominee, where he is not the trustee, to liaise as closely as possible with the official receiver and trustee, since both are likely to have useful information. The attitude of both may well be crucial to the success of the application and the subsequent success of the voluntary arrangement. If the nominee and proposed supervisor is someone different from the trustee, then professional rivalry should not in any instance be allowed to interfere with a proper and professional flow of information between trustee and nominee. As many applications for voluntary arrangements in Case 1 situations will be brought in the very early days of a bankruptcy, an immediate approach by the intending nominee to the official receiver is desirable and should certainly be made well before the application for an interim order is made. Official receivers are bound to co-operate and should not be unnecessarily obstructive; they are entitled to make their views known. Matters of relevance, detriment and concern must be brought to the attention of the court.[1]

---

1 Eg lack of co-operation on the part of the debtor, concealment of assets or other offences, failure to surrender to the proceedings or possible voidable transactions.

4.14 Duration of Interim Order

If an interim order is made, it ceases to have effect at the end of the period of 14 days from the day after the order is made.[1] Application in appropriate circumstances may be made for the interim order to be extended.[2] Such an application can arise in a number of circumstances:

(a) if the nominee defaults in submitting his report;
(b) if the nominee seeks more time for the purpose of dealing with his report;
(c) if more time is necessary for considering the debtor's proposal;
(d) if there is a challenge; or
(e) if the creditors' meeting needs to be adjourned.

Prima facie, a 14-day period is short. This is for good reason: once the interim order is made, a moratorium comes into existence and, without leave, creditors may not commence or continue proceedings. In Case 1, where a bankruptcy order has already been made, the creditors are fully protected because of the intervention of the official receiver or trustee, and the bankrupt's assets will remain under their control. This is not the case, however, where no bankruptcy order has been made. The bankrupt's assets are vulnerable in the instance of a dishonest debtor who seeks an interim order for the purpose of enabling him to evade his responsibilities and escape from his creditors with the benefit of his assets. As has been seen, the powers of a nominee are very limited. To an extent, the creditors are at risk during the period of the interim order. If the nominee believes that the debtor is misbehaving, it seems that he has the right to go back to the court to ask for the interim order to be discharged.[3] A creditor could also seek relief by way of injunction.

---

1 Insolvency Act 1986, s 255 (6).
2 Ibid, s 256 (4), (5).
3 Ibid, s 256 (6).

4.15 Form of Order and Service

The form of interim order is specified[1] although, in Case 1, it needs appropriate amendment.[2] The order should be served on those parties who were required to be served with the application.[3]

---

1 See Appendix 2, p 169.
2 See Appendix 2, p 169, note 1.
3 See Insolvency Rules 1986, rr 5.5 (4), 5.7.

4.16 Practice Direction (Bankruptcy: Voluntary Arrangements)[1]

1 In suitable cases the High Court registrars will normally be prepared to make orders under Part VIII of the Insolvency Act 1986 (individual voluntary arrangements) without the attendance of either party, provided there is no bankruptcy order in existence and (so far as is known) no pending petition. The cases are:

(1) A 14-day interim order with the application adjourned 14 days for consideration of the nominee's report, where the papers are in order and the nominee's signed consent to act includes a waiver of notice of the application or a consent by the nominee to the making of an interim order without attendance.

(2) A standard order on consideration of the nominee's report, extending the interim order to a date seven weeks after the date of the proposed meeting, directing the meeting to be summoned and adjourning to a date about three weeks after the meeting. Such an order may be made without attendance if the nominee's report has been delivered to the court and complies with section 256(1) of the Insolvency Act 1986 and rule 5.10(2) and (3) of the Insolvency Rules 1986 and proposes a date for the meeting not less than 14 nor more than 28 days after the date of the "hearing".

(3) A "concertina" order, combining orders as under sub-paragraphs (1) and (2) above. Such an order may be made without attendance if the initial application for an interim order is accompanied by a report of the nominee and the conditions set out in sub-paragraphs (1) and (2) above are satisfied.

(4) A final order on consideration of the chairman's report. Such an order may be made without attendance if the chairman's report has been filed and complies with rule 5.22(1) of the Rules of 1986. The order will record the effect of the chairman's report and discharge the interim order.

2 Provided that the conditions as under paragraph 1(2) and (4) above are satisfied and that the appropriate report has been lodged with the court in due time the parties need not attend or be represented on the adjourned hearing for consideration of the nominee's report or of the chairman's report (as the case may be) unless they are notified by the court that attendance is required. Sealed copies of the order made (in all four cases as above) will be posted by the court to the applicant or his solicitor and to the nominee.

3 The procedure outlined above is designed to save time and costs but is not intended to discourage attendance.

4 Practitioners are reminded that whenever a document is filed the correct case number, code and year (e.g. 123/IO/92) should appear at the top right-hand corner. A note should be attached stating the date and time of the next hearing (if any).

T. L. DEWHURST
Chief Bankruptcy Registrar

13 December 1991

---

1 [1992] 1 WLR 120.

Chapter 5

ROLE OF THE NOMINEE AND NOMINEE'S REPORT

5.1 Introduction

The theory behind the Act was that the debtor would prepare a proposal and then hand it to the nominee for consideration. This will rarely be the case, and the nominee in his capacity as intended nominee is likely to have been heavily involved in the matter since the very conception of the voluntary arrangement. Whilst the proposal always remains the debtor's proposal, it will also to a certain extent be the nominee's proposal.

5.2 Nominee's Report[1]

After the nominee has been given notice of the proposal and has signified his willingness to act, his first formal duty is to give consideration to the proposal. He must submit a report to the court, whether or not he is the person who has prepared the proposal. Where the nominee has not been involved in the preparation of the proposal, the extent of his consideration will clearly be much greater than would otherwise be the case.

In *Re A Debtor (No 222 of 1990)*,[2] Harman J was extremely critical of the nominee's report filed in that matter. From the comments made by the judge, which were not actually central to the decision in the case, it is clear that, even if the proposal has to a large extent been prepared by the nominee, the nominee must nevertheless bring a "considered opinion of the sort which one would expect of a professional accountant and a licensed insolvency practitioner to bear upon the nature of the proposals". The judge criticised the nominee for bringing "no critical eye whatever to bear upon the debtor's statements of assets and liabilities", and he added that no attempt had been made to assess whether the proposal was in accordance with the Rules. He concluded that "no competent insolvency practitioner could properly have said that the report was fit for consideration". It is clear that the nominee must express an objective judgment, and it seems desirable for the report to contain an express statement that the proposal does comply with all the provisions of the Act and Rules.

---

1 See generally Insolvency Act 1986, s 256 and Insolvency Rules 1986, rr 5.7–5.11.
2 (1991) *The Times*, 27 June.

5.3 Form and Purpose of the Report

The report does not have to be in specified form.[1] Its purpose is not to approve the proposal but to say whether, in the nominee's opinion, a meeting of the debtor's creditors should be summoned to consider the debtor's proposal.[2] The nominee must conclude that taking everything into account there is a proposal which is worthy of consideration by the creditors. If he so concludes, his report must indicate the date, time and place at which the creditors' meeting should be held.

---

1 However, see page 133.
2 Insolvency Act 1986, s 256 (1).

5.4 Nominee's Powers

These are limited but important. It must be remembered that the statutory powers conferred on a nominee were drafted on the assumption that the proposal would be prepared by a person other than the nominee. The debtor is obliged to submit to the nominee not only the proposal but also a statement of affairs containing such particulars of his creditors, debts, liabilities and assets as may be prescribed and such other information as may be prescribed;[1] the prescribed information is that set out in the Rules. In Case 1, if a debtor has already delivered a statement of affairs, he need not deliver a further one unless so required by the nominee with a view to supplementing or amplifying the original statement.[2] In Case 2, the debtor must within seven days after his proposal is delivered to the nominee, or within such longer time as the nominee may allow, deliver to the nominee a statement of his affairs.[3] The statement must be certified by the debtor that it is correct to the best of his knowledge and belief.[4]

   If the nominee concludes that he has insufficient information to enable him to prepare a report, he is empowered[5] to require the debtor to provide him with:

(a) further and better particulars as to the circumstances in which, and the reasons why, he is insolvent or (as the case may be) threatened with insolvency;

(b) particulars of any previous proposals which have been made by him under the Act; and

(c) any further information in respect of his affairs which the nominee thinks necessary for the purpose of the report.[6]

   Furthermore, the nominee is entitled[7] to require the debtor to inform him whether and in what circumstances he has at any time been concerned in the affairs of a company, whether or not incorporated in England and Wales, which has become insolvent, or whether he has been adjudged bankrupt or entered into an arrangement with his creditors. For the purpose of allowing the nominee to consider the proposal, the debtor must give the nominee access to his accounts and records.[8]

1 Insolvency Act 1986, s 256 (2); Insolvency Rules 1986, r 5.8.
2 Ibid, r 5.8 (1).
3 Ibid, r 5.8 (2).
4 Ibid, r 5.8 (3).
5 Ibid, r 5.9 (1).
6 This provision of r 5.9 (1) (c) is very wide and enables the nominee to obtain any information that might be relevant.
7 Ibid, r 5.9 (2).
8 Ibid, r 5.9 (3).

5.5 Consideration of the Report

The interim order will specify the date and time when the court will consider the report.[1] The report must be delivered by the nominee to the court not less than two days before the interim order ceases to have effect.[2] The nominee must also deliver with his report a copy of the proposal with amendments, if any, and a copy or summary of any statement of affairs provided by the debtor.[3] If the nominee concludes that a creditors' meeting should be held, his report must include his comments on the proposal.[4] If the nominee concludes otherwise, he must give his reasons.[5] The court must endorse on the nominee's report the date on which the report is filed in court.[6] Any creditor of the debtor is entitled at all reasonable times on any business day to inspect the file.[7] A copy of the report must be given to any party who is entitled to attend the hearing of the interim order.[8]

If the nominee himself, as will normally be the case, has been instrumental in the preparation of the proposal, it will be very unusual for him to make an adverse report. Nevertheless, there will be instances where, since the making of the interim order, matters have come to light which would lead the nominee to make an adverse report. He may, for example, have discovered matters detrimental to the debtor, such as the non-disclosure of assets, the withholding of information, the non-disclosure of liabilities and possibly the realisation by the debtor of assets in a manner which would be detrimental to the arrangement. It is also possible that, in Case 1, representations have been made by either the official receiver or the trustee which would lead the nominee to an adverse conclusion. If such circumstances arise, the nominee is duty bound to report these matters to the court.

At the hearing, the report is considered and the court must take into account all representations which are made. This is no rubber stamping exercise[9] and the court must act judicially. It is not bound to accept the nominee's recommendation, although the court rarely declines to permit the matter to proceed if faced with a favourable report. The court must be satisfied that a meeting of the debtor's creditors should be summoned to consider the proposal. This clearly indicates that the court must have careful regard to the proposal, the report and all representations made by parties entitled to attend. If the court concludes that no useful purpose would be served by directing a creditors' meeting to be held, the court would be quite entitled to decline to allow the matter to proceed any further and to order the discharge of the interim order.[10] For instance, the court might have information before it which made it clear that the proposal was bound to fail at a creditors' meeting because of the attitude of creditors holding more than 25 per cent of votes in value.[11] Nevertheless, the court should be careful in depriving creditors of the opportunity to vote.

If the court is satisfied that the matter should go to a creditors' meeting, the court will direct that the interim order be extended for such further period as may be specified for the purpose of allowing the meeting to be held.[12]

There is express power for the court to discharge an interim order if it is satisfied, on application by the nominee, that the debtor has failed to comply with his obligations under s 256 (2) of the Act or that for any other reason it would be inappropriate for a meeting of the debtor's creditors to be summoned to consider the debtor's proposal.[13] The test as to whether or not it would be inappropriate will largely involve consideration of the same matters as the court must take into account for it to be satisfied that a meeting of debtor's creditors should be summoned.

---

1 Insolvency Rules 1986, r 5.6 (3).
2 Ibid, r 5.10 (1).
3 Ibid, r 5.10 (2).
4 Ibid, r 5.10 (3).
5 Ibid, r 5.10 (3).
6 Ibid, r 5.10 (4).
7 Ibid, r 5.10 (4).
8 Ibid, r 5.10 (5).
9–11 See generally *In Re A Debtor (No 83 of 1988)* [1990] 1 WLR 708.
12 Insolvency Act 1986, s 256 (5).
13 Ibid, s 256 (6).

5.6 Effect of Death of Debtor

If the individual has died before he has submitted his proposal and statement of affairs, the nominee must, as soon as the death is known, give notice to the court, which will discharge the interim order.[1] However, it is highly unlikely that an interim order will have come into existence without the proposal having been prepared, even though modifications may be in the process of consideration.

---

1 Administration of Insolvent Estates of Deceased Debtors Order 1986, Part III, para 1.

5.7 Replacement of Nominee[1]

Where a nominee has failed to submit a report in accordance with the requirements of the Act and Rules, the court has a discretionary power, on application by the debtor, either to direct that the nominee be replaced by another person qualified to act as an insolvency practitioner and to direct that the interim order shall continue or, if the order has ceased to have effect, be renewed for such further period as the court may specify. If the debtor intends to apply to the court for such an order, the nominee must be given at least seven days' notice of the application. No specific procedure is laid down for the replacement of the nominee on what is in effect the ground of default.

1 See Insolvency Act 1986, s 256 (3) and Insolvency Rules 1986, r 5.11.

5.8 Form of Order

The order is in specified form[1] and will specify a date and place on which the matter will come back before the court for consideration of the report of the chairman of the creditors' meeting.

1 See Appendix 2, p 169.

5.9 One-stage Procedure ('Concertina Order')

The Act and Rules envisage a two-stage procedure: first, an application is made for an interim order and that application is heard; then, if the interim order is made, the matter comes back before the court for consideration of the nominee's report. In many instances, especially Case 2 matters, this is an unnecessarily complex procedure involving unnecessary delay and expense. Accordingly, the practice has arisen for the court to be invited to consider the nominee's report at the same time as the application for the interim order.[1] Most courts are willing to adopt such a procedure and frequently will do so, even in Case 1 applications. In Case 1 applications, the debtor and nominee should seek to secure the co-operation of the official receiver and trustee, if any. It will be largely a matter of judgment in each individual case as to whether or not it is appropriate to proceed in this way. In certain instances, where the proposal may have been put together extremely quickly and the interim order sought within a very short period of time, the nominee may conclude that it would not be right to proceed in this way and that the period of time between the making of the interim order and the consideration of his report is vital to allow him to give further consideration to the matter, possibly with a view to suggesting to the debtor that amendments be made to the proposal. If, however, the one-stage procedure is adopted, the form of order will need to be amended[2] and all the parties entitled to be served at either stage must be notified.

1 This is now recognised by *Practice Direction (Bankruptcy: Voluntary Arrangements)* [1991] 1 WLR 120, reproduced at para 4.16 above.
2 See Appendix 2, p 170.

Chapter 6

CREDITORS' MEETING

6.1 General

6.1.1 Order for meeting

On the occasion of the hearing of the application for consideration of the nominee's report, the court may direct that the interim order be extended for the purpose of enabling the debtor's proposal to be considered by his creditors. If the nominee has recommended that a meeting of creditors should be summoned, he must in his report indicate the date on which and time and place at which he proposes the meeting should be held.[1]

---

1 Insolvency Act 1986, s 256 (1).

6.1.2 Timing and venue of meeting

The date on which the meeting is to be held must be not less than 14 nor more than 28 days from the date on which the nominee's report is filed in court[1] nor more than 28 days from that on which the report is considered by the court under r 5.12.[2] The meeting must be summoned to start between 10am and 4pm on a business day, and the nominee must have regard to the convenience of creditors.[2] Normally the nominee will summon the creditors' meeting to be held at his office or some other appropriate venue such as a local hotel. The question of convenience will depend on the circumstances of each individual case. If the majority of creditors reside in the same area as that of the debtor and the place of the nominee's office, the nominee's office would normally be regarded as being convenient. What would clearly be inconvenient is a case where, for example, the nominee practised in London and the debtor and most of the creditors were located in Cornwall or Northumberland. In such instance, it would be inappropriate and greatly inconvenient for the creditors if the meeting were held in London.[4]

---

1 Ie under Insolvency Rules 1986, r 5.10.
2 Ibid, r 5.13(1).
3 Ibid, r 5.14.
4 In any event, in such a situation it would rarely be desirable for such a nominee to act. The nominee, especially if he is to be supervisor, should be reasonably local to the debtor.

6.1.3 *Notification of meeting* [1]

The nominee calls the meeting and must give notice to each of the debtor's creditors of whose claim and address he is aware. The term 'debtor's creditors' includes, as regards a debtor who is an undischarged bankrupt, every person who is a creditor of his in respect of a bankruptcy debt and every other person who would be such a creditor if the bankruptcy had commenced on the day on which notice of the meeting is given. Generally, the debtor's creditors are those listed in the statement of affairs, together with all other creditors of whom the nominee is otherwise aware. Even if the nominee is satisfied that a secured creditor is wholly secured, notice should still be given to such creditor. The term 'creditor' clearly includes a contingent creditor and also a creditor whose claim is disputed in whole or in part.

---

1 Insolvency Rules 1986, r 5.13 (2), (3).

6.1.4 *Form of notice*

There is no prescribed form,[1] but the notice must state the purpose of the meeting and the effect of the Rule relating to requisite majorities,[2] and each creditor notified must be supplied with a copy of the proposal, a copy of the statement of affairs or, if the nominee thinks fit, a summary of it (the summary to include a list of the creditors and the amounts of their debts) and a copy of the nominee's comments on the proposal.[3] Where the proposal incorporates standard conditions, copies of those conditions should be sent. The strict requirements of the Rules are not exhaustive as to the advance documentation to be sent to creditors, and proof of debt forms and proxy forms should be supplied.[4] If the circumstances so dictate, it may be appropriate to send to the creditors copies of valuations, reports on ongoing litigation and such other material as may assist the creditors in making a proper decision.

---

1 However, see Appendix 2, p 172.
2 Insolvency Rules 1986, r 5.18 (1), (3), (4).
3 Ibid, r 5.13 (3).
4 See Appendix 2, pp 197, 202.

6.1.5 *Preliminaries to the meeting*

The nominee, in conjunction with the debtor, must give due consideration as to what other steps need to be taken prior to the holding of the creditors' meeting. In many cases, personal contact between the nominee and specific creditors may well be desirable. This is particularly the case if any individual creditor is likely to have sufficient voting strength to defeat the proposal. Both the nominee and debtor may well receive general enquiries from creditors prior to the meeting, and these should be dealt with in a courteous and helpful manner and the nominee should agree with the debtor on the way in which such enquiries are to be dealt with. These should be a consistency of approach between the nominee and the debtor. Where litigation against the debtor is ongoing, the creditor or his solicitors should as a matter of courtesy be supplied with a copy of the interim order and of the order directing the holding of a creditors' meeting.

6.1.6 *Debtor's presence at meeting*

Whilst neither the Act nor the rules specifically require the debtor to attend the creditors' meeting, it will always be essential for him to do so. Creditors are likely to be unimpressed if the debtor fails to attend. It is more than a matter of courtesy. The debtor owes it to his creditors to attend, so that he can offer an explanation as to his predicament and answer questions that may properly be put to him. Furthermore, the creditors' meeting may be asked to consider modifications, which cannot be approved without the consent of the debtor.[1] Where a creditors' meeting is convened to consider two or more linked proposals, each debtor should attend. Creditors may well vote against a proposal as a matter of principle if the debtor fails to attend without good reason.

---

1 See para 6.1.8 below.

6.1.7 *Purpose of meeting*

The Act[1] specifically provides that the purpose of the creditors' meeting is to decide whether to approve the proposed voluntary arrangement; the creditors may approve modifications to the proposal, but only with the debtor's consent.

---

1 Insolvency Act 1986, s 258 (1), (2). This whole section applies without modification in the event of the death of the debtor: Administration of Insolvent Estates of Deceased Debtors Order 1986, Part III, para 3.

6.1.8 *Modifications to the proposal*

Any modification may be proposed, and each one must be specifically consented to by the debtor.[1] In many instances, creditors will have given notice of proposed modifications to either the nominee or debtor prior to the meeting. There is no obligation on them to do so but, if this is done, it gives the nominee an opportunity to consider the effect of such modifications, discuss them with the debtor and advise him thereon. If substantial modifications are raised at the meeting itself, it may in certain circumstances be desirable to seek an adjournment[2] of the meeting so as to permit proper consideration of the modifications and their effect on the proposal as a whole. It will also permit re-drafting of the proposal document, which is difficult to achieve during the course of a meeting. A possible modification may be to appoint another duly qualified insolvency practitioner to act as supervisor in the place of the nominee. Any modification which affects the rights of secured creditors or preferential creditors may not be agreed without the consent of such credi-tors.[3] The circumstances in which secured creditors may agree such a modification are rare. Preferential creditors may be persuaded to rank *pari passu* with unsecured creditors if it can be demonstrated to their satisfaction that, in the event of the debtor's bankruptcy, they would receive nothing or less in their preferential capacity.[4]

---

1 Insolvency Act 1986, s 258 (2).
2 See para 6.1.14 below.
3 Ibid, s 258 (4), (5).

4 This would normally only be the case where the proposal provides for the injection of third
   party assets.

6.1.9 'Hijacking'

This term is used to describe the situation where a creditor proposes the
appointment of another insolvency practitioner as supervisor in place of the
nominee. Competition between insolvency practitioners for appointments is
sometimes fierce. The appointment of another supervisor may well be for good
reasons. The creditors may in certain instances feel that the nominee or his
firm is too closely associated with the debtor. Often it may simply be the fact
that a particular creditor or group of creditors prefers an insolvency practitioner that it knows better; equally, the creditors may have been persuaded to
support the appointment of another supervisor who has directly or indirectly
sought support. The nominee should throughout adopt a thoroughly professional and objective view. Unseemly 'infighting' between rival insolvency
practitioners at a creditors' meeting is to be avoided.

6.1.10 Joint supervisors

There may be a modification proposed to the effect that another insolvency
practitioner acts jointly with the nominee, or, indeed, that joint supervisors are
appointed, neither of whom is the nominee. Joint appointments are permitted
but, except in very large arrangements, it is undesirable for joint supervisors to
be from different firms as this will normally lead to increased costs. Joint
supervisors from the same firm can be advantageous, by providing protection
in the event of the death, illness, retirement or other non-availability of a single
supervisor. Frequently, joint supervisors are appointed purely to accom-
modate the wishes of different camps of creditors who each traditionally
support a particular insolvency practice. If this is the only way to reach
agreement between otherwise competing creditors, joint supervisors may have
to be agreed on; otherwise, there are few advantages in having joint supervisors and, in any event, if they are proposed, the reasons and the financial
implications should be spelt out, either in the proposal or at the creditors'
meeting.

6.1.11 Conduct of meeting

There is no specified formula. The creditors will have been sent in advance all
the relevant paperwork and, accordingly, will be considerably better informed
than creditors attending, for example, a meeting summoned for a creditors'
voluntary liquidation. In many cases, creditors will have had the opportunity,
prior to the meeting, to raise with the nominee their particular concerns and
anxieties, and the nominee will have had an opportunity to consider these and
deal with them, possibly leading to amendments to the proposal. This process
will also have enabled the nominee to ascertain and, insofar as is possible, deal
with the particular requirements of specific creditors such as landlords, the
Inland Revenue or HM Customs and Excise. It is normally desirable for the
nominee, who acts as chairman,[1] to open the meeting with appropriate
introductions and a statement as to the extent to which he and his firm have
been involved with the affairs of the debtor other than in connection with the
arrangement. The nominee should then explain to the creditors the effect of

the proposal and its essential ingredients; there is no need for the nominee to read the proposal verbatim. All appropriate explanations on the figures and, in particular, valuations of assets should be given, together with a realistic indication of the possible outcome of the arrangement compared to that of bankruptcy. ·

The nominee should then invite questions, comments and observations from the creditors which may be addressed either to the nominee or the debtor himself. Full, frank and honest answers should be given to every question and no attempt made to evade areas of actual or potential difficulty. Many creditors will attend meetings with a sense of grievance, and it is incumbent on the nominee to ensure that the meeting is conducted in a businesslike and orderly fashion. If the meeting gets out of hand, the nominee should not hesitate in ordering a brief adjournment. If points arise that need detailed consideration, the nominee may adjourn either to another day or, if appropriate, for a short period of time to enable consultations to take place.[2] In his dealings with the creditors, the nominee should seek to achieve a fair and proper balance between the interests of the creditors on the one hand and of the debtor on the other. The nominee should ensure that creditors are met on arrival and a full record is taken of their name, address and amount of their claim.

---

1 See para 6.1.12 below.
2 See para 6.1.14 below.

6.1.12 Chairman [1]

The nominee should be the chairman of the meeting but, if for any reason he is unable to attend personally, he may nominate another person to act as chairman in his place. Any person so nominated must be either a duly qualified insolvency practitioner or an employee of the nominee or his firm who is experienced in insolvency matters. It is normally desirable for the nominee to be present personally, although this will often be impossible in the case of large insolvency practices which are at any given time involved on a large number of cases. Nevertheless, many creditors like to see the nominee himself, and to be assured that he is taking a personal interest and concern in the case. If the nominee himself cannot be present, he must ensure that his replacement has sufficient knowledge of the particular case, and experience generally of handling creditors' meetings, to ensure that the meeting is conducted properly.

---

1 Insolvency Rules 1986, r 5.15.

6.1.13 Proxies [1]

The Rules provide for voting by proxy, which may be in favour of the chairman of the meeting or any other person. The chairman is not by virtue of any proxy held by him able to vote to increase or reduce the amount of the remuneration or expenses of the nominee or the supervisor of the arrangement, unless the proxy specifically directs him to vote in that way. If the chairman uses a proxy contrary to such provision, his vote with that proxy does not count towards any required majority.

---

1 See Insolvency Rules 1986, rr 5.16, 5.18 (1), (6); for the form of proxy see Appendix 2, p 202.

6.1.14 Adjournments [1]

The creditors' meeting may from time to time be adjourned. If, at the first creditors' meeting, the requisite majority for approval of the arrangement with or without modifications has not been obtained, the chairman may or, if it is so resolved, must adjourn the meeting for not more than 14 days. If there are further adjournments, the final adjournment must not be to a day later than 14 days after that on which the meeting was originally held. If the meeting is adjourned, the chairman must give notice of that fact to the court, and it may be necessary to apply to the court for an extension of the interim order. If, after any final adjournment of the meeting, the proposal with or without modifications is not agreed to, it is deemed to be rejected. In certain circumstances, an adjournment may be necessary so as to afford the chairman and the debtor a proper opportunity either to consider proposed modifications and their effect on the arrangement generally, or to deal with unforeseen matters arising at the creditors' meeting.

---

1 Insolvency Rules 1986, r 5.19.

6.1.15 Voting rights [1]

The following rules apply:

(1) Subject to the limitations set out below, every creditor who was given notice of the creditors' meeting is entitled to vote at the meeting or any adjournment of it.[2] It is therefore important that notice is given to all known creditors. If a person purporting to be a creditor attends the meeting but has not been given notice, the nominee should make due enquiry as to that person's status and, if satisfied that he is a creditor, should permit him to attend and vote. If satisfied that the person is not a creditor, the nominee should not permit him to attend the meeting.

(2) In Case 1 (ie where the debtor is an undischarged bankrupt), votes are calculated according to the amount of the creditor's debt as at the date of the bankruptcy order and, in Case 2, votes are calculated according to the amount of the debt as at the date of the meeting.[3]

It follows that, in Case 1, the bankruptcy creditors prove and vote in accordance with their debts in the bankruptcy. In Case 1 arrangements, there may be other creditors who have arisen since the making of the bankruptcy order. The votes of those creditors will be calculated according to the amount of the debt as at the date of the meeting, and care must be taken to ensure that, so far as possible, the quantification of creditors' claims has been agreed at the commencement of the meeting.

(3) A creditor may not vote in respect of a debt for an unliquidated amount or any debt whose value is not ascertained, except where the chairman

agrees to give the debt an estimated minimum value for the purpose of entitlement to vote.[4] This is clearly a matter which the nominee should seek to agree before the creditors' meeting. Unliquidated and unascertained debts can cause considerable problems, not least of which is preparing any realistic forecast as to total liabilities and therefore likely dividend outcome. Where it is anticipated that there may be unliquidated claims, this must be specifically dealt with in the proposal and a procedure outlined for ascertaining or agreeing such claims.

(4) The chairman has power to admit or reject a creditor's claim for the purpose of his entitlement to vote, and this power is exercisable in respect of the whole or any part of the claim.[5]

The power to reject should only be exercised after the fullest possible enquiry and after permitting the creditor the opportunity to submit all relevant documentation and other evidence to substantiate his claim and to make the fullest possible representation. If a debt is disputed, the creditor may be entitled to vote, but it should be made clear that this does not constitute acceptance of the claim.

(5) The chairman's decision on entitlement to vote is subject to appeal to the court by any creditor or by the debtor.[6] It follows that, if a creditor is aggrieved by the chairman's decision, the matter may be appealed to the court by either creditor or debtor. This provision and those that follow show the court's powers on any such appeal are wide, since the court may in reversing or verifying the chairman's decision or holding a vote to be invalid, order another meeting to be summoned or refuse to act unless the matter gives rise to unfair prejudice or to a material irregularity.[7] Consequently, the court may refuse to make any order, even if it determines that a vote has been improperly included or rejected, provided it is satisfied that the inclusion or rejection of the vote would have made no material difference to the outcome of the creditors' meeting.

The appeal procedure is regulated by the Act and Rules,[8] and any appeal should be brought within 28 days from the date on which the chairman's report to the court is made under s 259 of the Act.[9]

(6) If the chairman is in doubt as to whether a claim should be admitted or rejected, he must mark it as objected to and allow the creditor to vote, subject to his vote being subsequently declared invalid if the objection to the claim is sustained.[10]

(7) As to appeals, see note 7 to (5) above.

(8) As to time-limits, see note 9 to (5) above.

(9) The chairman is not personally liable for any costs incurred by any person in respect of an appeal under r 5.17.[11]

Rule 5.17 was considered in detail in *Re A Debtor (No 222 of 1990)*[12] where applications came before Harman J by way of appeal[13] and by way of challenge.[14] The following conclusions can be drawn from that case, where the judge was most critical of the nominee.

(1) Since every creditor who is given notice of the creditors' meeting is entitled to vote at the meeting, one starts with the presumption that persons summoned to the meeting will be entitled to vote. In this particular case,

some five creditors were given notice of the meeting and therefore were prima facie entitled to vote. The nominee disallowed the creditors from voting on the basis that their claims were unliquidated and/or subject to dispute and counterclaim, thereby making it impossible to ascertain their value. However, it appears from the judgment that the matter really turned on the fact that the claims were contingent and disputed.

(2) Although persons who were not creditors of the debtor would not normally be given notice of the meeting, the chairman would be empowered to rule on the claimed position of any such creditor.

(3) The scheme of r 5.17 is a simple one, and the creditors' meeting is not the place to go into a lengthy debate as to the exact status of a debt, nor is it the time to consider such matters as the Companies Court may have to consider, for example in relation to whether a debt is bona fide disputed on substantial grounds.

(4) The chairman has clearly defined powers and, if he is in doubt as to whether a vote should be allowed, he should mark the vote as objected to and allow the creditor to vote.

On the facts of the case, the judge concluded, and this seemed to be accepted by the parties, that there was no point in ordering a further creditors' meeting since it was clear that the agreed creditors would have voted against the proposal and that would have been fatal.

The judge also described as bizarre the apparent view of the nominee/chairman that the creditors in question, who were not entitled to vote, were nevertheless bound by the arrangement.

---

1 See generally Insolvency Rules 1986, r 5.17.
2 Ibid, r 5.17 (1).
3 Ibid, r 5.17 (2).
4 Ibid, r 5.17 (3).
5 Ibid, r 5.17 (4).
6 Ibid, r 5.17 (5).
7 Ibid, r 5.17 (7).
8 Insolvency Act 1986, s 375; Insolvency Rules 1986, rr 7.47–7.50.
9 Ibid, r 5.17 (8).
10 Ibid, r 5.17 (6).
11 Ibid, r 5.17 (9).
12 (1991) *The Times*, 27 June.
13 Ie under Insolvency Rules 1986, r 5.17.
14 Ie under Insolvency Act 1986, s 262.

6.1.16 Requisite majorities

For a proposal to be approved, with or without modifications, there must be a majority in excess of three-quarters in value of creditors present in person or by proxy and voting;[1] by contrast, any other resolution requires only a majority in excess of one half in value.[2] However, certain obligations are imposed on the chairman of the meeting by virtue of subsequent provisions.[3]

The chairman must be satisfied as to the admissibility of claims. The creditor must, if he is to be entitled to vote, have given notice of his claim to the chairman, or the nominee[4] if different. Since these provisions draw no distinction between Case 1 and Case 2 arrangements, it is unclear whether a Case 1 creditor must give further written notice of his claim; to be safe, he should do so.

A wholly or partly secured creditor is excluded to the extent of his security which he will need to state, or estimate the value of, in his notice; likewise, a creditor secured on a bill of exchange must comply with the requirements as to the liabilities of prior parties and security.[6]

The provisions as to invalid resolutions are problematic:

Any resolution is invalid if those voting against it include more than half in value of the creditors, counting in these latter only those—

(a) to whom notice of the meeting was sent;
(b) whose votes are not to be left out of account under paragraph (3); and
(c) who are not, to the best of the chairman's belief, associates of the debtor.[2]

This could have been worded more clearly, and seems to mean that a resolution is defeated if an analysis of the creditors' voting results in the exclusion of:

(a) persons to whom notice of the meeting was not sent;
(b) persons excluded under r 5.18 (3); and
(c) associates;

so as to leave more than half the remaining creditors voting against the resolution.

It is for the chairman[7] to decide on the inadmissibility of a creditor's right to vote and as to whether any creditor is an associate of the debtor, in the light of the debtor's statement of affairs or any other information supplied. The debtor is under an obligation to disclose associates' claims. Again, there is provision for appeal against the decision of the chairman.

It would appear that, if a majority qualified under the rule is eliminated and the remaining votes are split equally, the resolution is not defeated.

Creditors who are associates must be dealt with specifically in the proposal and statement of affairs. So as to avoid difficulties at the meeting itself, the chairman should always be satisfied before the meeting as to those creditors who are or may be associates.

---

1 Insolvency Rules 1986, r 5.18 (1).
2 Ibid, r 5.18 (2).
3 Ibid, r 5.18 (3)–(5).
4 Ibid, r 5.18 (3).
5 Ibid, r 5.18 (3) (b).
6 Ibid, r 5.18 (3) (c).
7 Ibid, r 5.18 (5).

6.1.17 *Effect of death of debtor*

Where the individual dies before a creditors' meeting has been held, no such meeting will be held and, if the individual was at the date of his death an undischarged bankrupt, the personal representatives must give notice of the death to the trustee of his estate and the official receiver.[1] It seems that, if notice has been given for the meeting to be held but the meeting is not in fact held, the notice must be cancelled. In the event of there being no personal representative, it is arguably the nominee who must carry out this obligation.

---

1 Administration of Insolvent Estates of Deceased Debtors Order 1986, Part III, para 2.

6.1.18 Steps to be taken after the meeting

The chairman of the meeting, who may or may not be the nominee, must prepare a report. No form is specified,[1] although the report must contain certain information,[2] namely:

(a) whether the proposal for the arrangement was approved or rejected and, if approved, with what modifications, if any;

(b) the resolutions which were taken at the meeting and the decision on each one;

(c) a list of the creditors, with their respective values, who were present or represented at the meeting and an indication of how they voted on each resolution; and

(d) such further information, if any, as the chairman thinks appropriate to make known to the court.

A copy of the report must be filed with the court within four days of the meeting and the court must cause that copy to be endorsed with the date of filing.[3] The order of the court directing the creditors' meeting to be held will specify the date, place and time for the court to give consideration to the chairman's report.

In the event of the arrangement being approved, this hearing will normally be a formality and most courts will permit the matter to be dealt with without attendance. In such circumstances, no order is required and the court will merely be invited to note the report.[4]

If the report states that the meeting has rejected the proposal, the court has a discretionary power to discharge any interim order which is in force in relation to the debtor, and it will always do so unless there is a challenge.

All creditors to whom notice of the meeting is sent and, in Case 1 arrangements, the official receiver and the trustee, if any, must also be given notice of the result of the meeting, this being achieved most conveniently by sending them a copy of the report.[5]

No particular difficulties should arise in complying with paragraphs (a) to (c) above. The chairman, however, must give due consideration as to any matter which should be included under (d). In the event of the arrangement being approved, there will usually be no such matters to report but, if the chairman is aware of a possible challenge from a dissatisfied creditor, this is a matter which should be referred to.

In the event of the arrangement being rejected the chairman may, but is not required to, include brief reasons as to why, in his opinion, the creditors declined to accept the proposal.

1 But see Appendix 2, p 174.
2 Insolvency Rules 1986, r 5.22 (2).
3 Ibid, r 5.22 (3).
4 Unless, in a Case 1 matter, a bankruptcy order is to be annulled; see Insolvency Act 1986, s 261 (1) and para 9.7 below. Note also s 260 (5) which provides that the bankruptcy petition ceases to have effect unless the court orders otherwise.
5 Insolvency Rules 1986, r 5.22 (4).

6.1.19 *Registration of the voluntary arrangement*

A register of individual voluntary arrangements, which is open to public inspection, is maintained and must contain specified information.[1] Apart from this provision, and the public awareness which will arise as a result of the creditors' meeting and communications sent to creditors, there are no provisions in the Act and Rules to bring the existence of a voluntary arrangement to the attention of the general public.

1 Insolvency Rules 1986, r 5.23; see also Appendix 2, p 176.

6.1.20 *Reports to Secretary of State*

Immediately after the chairman of the creditors' meeting has filed in court a report that the meeting has approved the voluntary arrangement, he must report this to the Secretary of State[1] with certain specified information, namely:

(a) the name and address of the debtor;
(b) the date on which the arrangement was approved by the creditors;
(c) the name and address of the supervisor; and
(d) the court in which the chairman's report has been filed.[2]

A person who is appointed to act as supervisor, whether in the first instance or by way of replacement of another person previously appointed, must at once give written notice to the Secretary of State of his appointment. Similarly, if he vacates office as supervisor, he must at once give written notice of that fact.[3]

Although it would appear that these reporting requirements impose some supervision of voluntary arrangements by the Secretary of State, this is not, in practice, the case.

1 See Appendix 2, p 176.
2 Insolvency Rules 1986, r 5.24 (1).
3 Ibid, r 5.24 (2).

6.2 Effect of Approval

6.2.1 *General* [1]

The creditors' meeting alone approves the arrangement, either as originally proposed or subject to such modifications as may have been agreed. At no stage does the court formally approve the proposal, although it may have considered its merits at the hearing of the application for the interim order or at the hearing for consideration of the nominee's report. Furthermore, the merits of the proposal as regards specific creditors, and the conduct of the creditors' meeting or any adjournment thereof, may subsequently be considered by the court on any application by way of challenge.[2]

1 See Insolvency Act 1986, s 260. In the event of the death of the debtor, this section applies with the modification that it ceases to apply on or after the death of the individual: Administration of Insolvent Estates of Deceased Debtors Order 1986, Part III, para 4. The effect of this provision is unclear, but appears to suggest that the creditors are no longer bound by the proposal that they have approved.
2 Ie under Insolvency Act 1986, s 262; see further paras 6.3.1–6.3.11 below.

6.2.2 Essential effect of approval

The approved arrangement takes effect as if made by the debtor at the meeting.[1] This means that the actual agreement is made at the creditors' meeting and no further orders of the court are necessary. As soon as an affirmative vote is taken at the meeting the arrangement becomes binding; the chairman's report[2] in essence takes the matter no further and is merely a procedural requirement.

Furthermore, the approved arrangement binds every person who in accordance with the rules had notice of, and was entitled to vote at, the meeting (whether or not he was present or represented at it) as if he were a party to the arrangement.[3] This underlines the importance of notice being given to everyone who is or may be a creditor and who would be entitled to vote at the meeting.[4]

1 Insolvency Act 1986, s 260 (2) (a).
2 Ibid, s 259. This section applies without modification in the event of the death of the debtor: Administration of Insolvent Estates of Deceased Debtors Order 1986, Part III, para 4.
3 Insolvency Act 1986, s 260 (2) (b).
4 See also *Re A Debtor (No 222 of 1990)* (1991) *The Times*, 27 June: a creditor not entitled to vote cannot be bound.

6.2.3 Creditors who are not bound

A creditor who is not given notice of the arrangement will not be bound and will be entitled to pursue legal remedies against the debtor. Whilst in certain cases, on their own facts, it might be possible to argue constructive or implied notice, this is likely to be limited to very rare cases and should not be relied upon. There is no provision in the Act or Rules for advertisement of the creditors' meeting in either *The London Gazette* or a local newspaper. Such a notice could prima facie be given, but its effect is doubtful. Such a notice should only be given with the express consent of the debtor and in rare circumstances, since the debtor will generally wish to avoid the publicity which would arise as a result of such advertisement being given. The failure to bind a creditor might give rise to a challenge by a deprived creditor.[1] If a creditor who is not bound subsequently pursues bankruptcy proceedings against the debtor, it is not considered that any bankruptcy order subsequently made in any sense invalidates, terminates or otherwise sets aside the arrangement.[2] A dispute might arise as to whether or not a creditor has been given actual notice, in which case the debtor may be able to rely on the provisions relating to non-receipt of notice of meeting.[3]

The situation may arise where no notice is sent to a creditor whose existence is known. This might be a deliberate act because, for whatever reason, it was not desired to bind that particular creditor. This may well constitute a material irregularity as referred to in s 262 (1) (b) of the Act.[4] Each situation will turn on its own facts and will depend, first, on why the creditor was omitted and, secondly, whether or not his vote would have made any difference. In the latter case, the court may direct a further meeting to be held.

1 Insolvency Act 1986, s 262; see paras 6.3.1–6.3.11 below.
2 See generally paras 10.1–10.7 below.
3 Insolvency Rules 1986, r 12.16.
4 Arguably, the deliberate omission of a creditor is also a 'false or misleading' particular within s 276 (1) (b) of the Act. See also *Re A Debtor (No 222 of 1990)* (1991) *The Times*, 27 June.

6.2.4 *Creditors whose details must be given*
The short answer is all creditors, whether actual or contingent.[1]

1 See *Re A Debtor (No 222 of 1990)* (1991) *Times*, 27 June and generally para 6.1.15 above.

6.2.5 *Deeds of Arrangement Act 1914*
The 1914 Act does not apply to an approved voluntary arrangement.[1] Without this provision, it would apply.

1 Insolvency Act 1986, s 260 (3).

6.2.6 *Effect on interim order*
The interim order, which is still in force, as regards the debtor up to the end of the period of 28 days from the day on which the report concerning the creditors' meeting was made to the court,[1] ceases to have effect at the end of that period.[2] This is subject to any order made by the court under s 262 for its continuation. The order made on the hearing to consider the nominee's report will specify the period of time for which the interim order is continued.[3]

1 Ie under Insolvency Act 1986, s 259.
2 Ibid, s 260 (4).
3 See Appendix 2, p 177.

6.2.7 *Dismissal of bankruptcy petition*
Where proceedings on a bankruptcy petition have been stayed by an interim order which ceases to have effect as a result of the approval of the arrangement, that petition is deemed, unless the court otherwise orders, to have been dismissed.[1] This is a curious provision since it is based on the outcome of the creditors' meeting and no court order is necessary to give effect to it, since the deemed dismissal occurs not as a result of a court order but as a result of

the statutory provision. However, when a bankruptcy petition is dismissed, an order is generally made to vacate the land charge registration and it seems that, where an arrangement is approved, such an order is also required. In these circumstances, it seems desirable for a specific order to be made on the occasion of the consideration of the chairman's report[2] not only for the express dismissal of the petition but also for the vacation of the land charges entries and any other orders that may be appropriate.

1 Insolvency Act 1986, s 260 (5).
2 See para 6.1.18 above.

6.2.8 *Revival of petition*

It appears that it is not possible for a petition which has been subject to deemed dismissal to be reinstated by virtue of the review provisions contained in the Act.[1] The reason for this is that the power to review arises only in relation to an order made by the court in exercise of its jurisdiction under the Act, and no order is actually made until the hearing for consideration of the report of the chairman of the creditors' meeting. However, if a successful challenge to the meeting's decision is made,[2] it seems quite illogical to suggest that the petition would not thereby be revived.

1 Insolvency Act 1986, s 375.
2 Ie under ibid, s 262.

6.3 Challenge of the Meeting's Decision[1]

6.3.1 *General Considerations*

An application for challenge is brought under s 262 of the Act, and will be by way of ordinary application.[2] Only two grounds are specified, namely:

(a) where a voluntary arrangement approved by a creditors' meeting summoned under s 257 of the Act unfairly prejudices the interests of a creditor of the debtor;[3]
(b) where there has been some material irregularity at or in relation to such a meeting.[4]

Those who can make the application are limited.[5] The categories include the debtor, a person entitled in accordance with the Rules to vote at the creditors' meeting, the nominee or his replacement and, if the debtor is an undischarged bankrupt, the trustee of his estate or the official receiver.

In the event of the death of the debtor, s 262 of the Act ceases to apply on or after the death of the individual.[6]

1 See generally Insolvency Act 1986, s 262 and Insolvency Rules 1986, r 5.25.
2 Under ibid, r 7.2; see also Appendix 2, p 201.
3 Insolvency Act 1986, s 262 (1) (a).
4 Ibid, s 262 (1) (b).
5 Ibid, s 262 (2); see also para 6.3.5 below.
6 Administration of Insolvent Estates of Deceased Debtors Order 1986, Part III, para 4.

6.3.2 Approval and refusal

On the face of it, a challenge might be made both to the approval and also to the refusal to approve. A challenge as to refusal might be brought by the debtor or a disappointed creditor. It seems however that, on the express wording of the section, a disappointed creditor may not challenge a refusal to approve except on the basis of a material irregularity, and the same is probably true of other persons entitled to apply.

6.3.3 Unfair prejudice

It is difficult to draw any exhaustive conclusions as to what might constitute unfair prejudice.

In *Re Naeem (A Bankrupt) (No 18 of 1988)*,[1] the debtor, who was an undischarged bankrupt, sought approval for a voluntary arrangement. The arrangement as approved provided, inter alia, for the bankrupt's leasehold interest in a shop, under a lease which contained a forfeiture provision, to be placed on the market at once and sold as soon as possible. The landlord, a creditor for arrears of rent under the lease, obtained from the registrar an order revoking the creditor's approval of the arrangements on the grounds that it was unfairly prejudicial to his interests. The respondents to the application, the bankrupt, his nominee and two creditors, were ordered to pay the costs of the landlord's application.

In allowing the appeal, the court held that the voluntary arrangement was intended to bind the bankrupt's creditors only as creditors and did not affect any proprietary rights such as that of the landlord to forfeit the lease (subject to the court's discretion to grant relief). Since the effect of the arrangement was to modify the claims of all the creditors, there would be no unfairness to the landlord as a creditor in the modification of his claim for rent affairs, accordingly, the registrar was wrong to revoke the creditors' approval of arrangement.[2]

The court also expressed the view that it was wrong for the nominee and creditors to be respondents to the application and equally wrong that they should be ordered to pay the costs.[3] This was subject to the proviso that, if there had been some personal conduct on the part of the nominee which would justify an order for costs against him, the result might have been otherwise. The costs of a successful application under s 262 should ordinarily be paid out of the bankrupt's estate.[4]

In *Re A Debtor (No 222 of 1990)*,[5] where there had been a clear irregularity at the creditors' meeting and some five creditors had not been entitled to vote, the judge upheld their challenge under s 262. The judge ordered the nominee to pay one half of the agreed costs of the aggrieved creditors. The judge was prevented from making an order against the nominee for all the costs of the successful applicants since the appeals were brought under r 5.17 *and* s 262.[6]

It is clear that an arrangement that purports to treat secured or preferential creditors in a manner contrary to that prescribed[7] would be a ground for a successful challenge. Other possible grounds for a successful challenge might be:

(a) refusing a creditor entitled to vote the right to vote or be present at the meeting;

(b) approving an arrangement which treated unsecured creditors ostensibly ranking pari passu differently, ie conferring a preference on particular categories of unsecured creditors;

(c) failure to treat partnership assets and liabilities correctly;[8]

(d) provision in the arrangement whereby post-bankruptcy creditors are entitled to participate in assets in the bankruptcy which, if the bankrupt's estate were distributed, would not be the case.[9]

In *Re A Debtor (No 259 of 1990)*,[10] consideration was given to what is meant by unfair prejudice and material irregularity within the meaning of s 262 (1) of the Act. The case concerned a relatively small arrangement where there were virtually no assets, the aggrieved creditor being a former business associate of the debtor and a creditor of the debtor pursuant to a right to indemnity. The creditor, through his solicitor, attended the meeting but had no proxy and did not vote. The representative apparently asked questions relating to the debts said to be owing to four other creditors. It seems from the judgment that the representative did not suggest that the chairman ought to investigate the matter further or that there ought to be an adjournment. The arrangement proposed the payment of a dividend of 10 pence in the pound, the funds to be made available by a creditor since the debtor had no assets. The creditors approved the arrangement unanimously.

Before the appeal, there had been two applications, the first of which was brought solely on the ground of unfair prejudice but, on review, it was alleged that there had been material irregularity. The substance of the allegation was that the debts owed to the creditors who voted for the arrangement were suspect. Mr Registrar Scott took the view that the matters raised, which were, in any event, incapable of being resolved on affidavit, did not relate to anything which could be called unfair prejudice within the meaning of the section. The Registrar took the view that unfair prejudice within the section referred to prejudice caused by the terms of the scheme itself. It meant that the scheme had to be framed in a manner which prejudiced a creditor in a way which was unfair, as compared with the position if the scheme had been framed in a different way. Hoffman J agreed "that, as a matter of construction, s 262 is talking about unfairness brought about by the terms of the voluntary arrangement". He accepted the contention that this view was supported by the scheme of the Act and "in particular, by the provisions of s 264 (1) (c) and s 276". The judge observed that a creditor who is bound by an arrangement can nevertheless present a petition under s 264 provided he can satisfy the requirements of s 276. In the particular case, the judge held that, if the debtor's statement of affairs was in fact a fabrication, the aggrieved creditor was not without a remedy, and he could present a petition for bankruptcy, notwithstanding the voluntary arrangement.

The judge also stated that such a conclusion was supported by the provisions of the Rules dealing with the question of the admission of creditors to vote at the meeting. He referred in particular to the power of the chairman to admit or reject a creditor's claim for the purpose of entitlement to vote,[11] the fact that the chairman's decision on entitlement to vote is subject to appeal[12] and the fact that such an appeal must be brought within 28 days of the day on which the chairman's report is made to the court.[13] Accordingly, if the aggrieved creditor wanted to challenge the validity of claims made by creditors who voted in favour of the scheme, then he could do so under r 5.17, but had not done so.

The judge looked at the terms of the scheme and observed that all the creditors were to receive 10 pence in the pound and all the money was to come from a third party. He said, "It seems to me quite impossible to say that the terms of the scheme operate in a manner which is unfairly prejudicial. He was put in exactly the same position as all other creditors".

Whilst there is a substantial body of precedent on the term "unfair prejudice" under the old law by reference to the use of the term "person aggrieved",[14] the term "unfair prejudice" suggests some basic inequality in the treatment of creditors which a professionally prepared proposal should not contain.

---

1 [1990] 1 WLR 48.
2 Clearly therefore proprietary rights cannot be affected.
3 Only the debtor should be a respondent (or the party who made the application for the interim order, if not the debtor).
4 *Re Naeem*, note 1 above, at 51A, B.
5 (1991) *The Times* 27 June, per Harman J; see further para 6.1.15 above.
6 Insolvency Rules 1986, r 5.17 (9).
7 Insolvency Act 1986, s 258 (4), (5).
8 See note 5 to para 2.3 above.
9 See generally paras 10.1–10.7 below.
10 [1992]1 WLR 226, per Hoffman J.
11 Insolvency Rules 1986, r 5.17 (4).
12 Ibid, r 5.17 (5).
13 Ibid, r 5.17 (8).
14 See, for example, *Muir Hunter on Personal Insolvency* (Stevens, 1987) at para 3-049 and *Williams and Muir Hunter on Bankruptcy* (Stevens, 19th Edition) at pp 462–3.

6.3.4 Material irregularities

A material irregularity would seem to include any failure to comply with the requirements of the Act and Rules, as previously discussed, which is not de minimis. If there has been a defect in procedure which, if followed correctly, would have made no difference to the outcome, such an irregularity is not material. Obvious instances of material irregularity would be changing the venue of the creditors' meeting without proper notice to all creditors, the failure to supply required information, arguably the failure of the debtor to be present at the creditors' meeting, breaches of the rules relating to the admissibility of claims, the incorrect application of rules relating to voting rights[1] and majorities, and the failure of the chairman to adjourn if bound to do so.

In *Re A Debtor (No 259 of 1990)*,[2] the complaint of material irregularity was based on the fact that a creditor was not given notice of the meeting. It seems that the creditor in question was entitled to payments under a maintenance order, and the debtor was intending to apply for the maintenance order to be varied and for the arrears to be remitted. The debtor did not consider this creditor to be a creditor but, for the purposes of the appeal, the creditor was regarded as a creditor and it was held that she should have been given notice of the meeting. The judge agreed with the finding of the Registrar that the irregularity was not material because the creditor's presence at the meeting could not have affected the outcome. Her claim was for about £3,000 but, in the judge's words, "It does not really matter what the amount of her claim was, because under Rule 5.18 (4) the resolution would have been invalid if those voting against it, including more than half in value of the creditors, counting in these latter, that is to say, the creditors, only those – and then there are various categories including (c) – who are not to the best of the chairman's belief associates of the debtor". No-one voted against the resolution and, even if the aggrieved creditor had voted, her vote would not have been counted because she was an associate. Accordingly, the judge did not consider the omission of notice to this creditor to be a material irregularity.

The judge commented that the appellant felt that the debtor had "got away with a voluntary arrangement which had the effect of protecting him from a closer investigation of his business dealings". The judge made it clear that there was a remedy under s 262. In any event, he found it difficult to see what the creditor would have gained from 'scrapping the voluntary arrangement". On the basis of the evidence before him, there was nothing to suggest that further assets available to creditors remained to be uncovered. If a bankruptcy order were to have been made, the third party "would no doubt disappear from the scene, and there is nothing to suggest that the trustee would have any funds with which to pursue the elaborate investigation which . . . the creditor . . . wanted to have made".

In dismissing the appeal with costs, the judge concluded, "There are limits to the amount of money which can efficiently be spent on investigations of this kind, and I rather doubt whether it is in anyone's interests for this matter to be taken any further".

---

1 See, for example, *Re A Debtor (No 222 of 1990)* (1991) *The Times*, 27 June.
2 [1992] 1 WLR 226.

6.3.5 *Categories of applicant*

The four classes of individuals who are entitled to challenge will clearly do so for quite different reasons:

(a) A debtor would only seek to challenge if the arrangement was refused or was modified otherwise than with his consent.

(b) A creditor would seek to challenge on any of the bases discussed in the preceding paragraphs.

(c) A nominee might challenge a refusal, if it was open to him to do so, for depriving him of the opportunity of administering the proposed arrangement or for a modification thereto which was not consented to by the debtor. The mere fact, however, that a supervisor who is not the nominee is appointed would not in itself seem to be grounds for a challenge unless, for example, improper allegations were made about the conduct of the nominee which were ill-founded.

(d) A trustee and an official receiver are to be regarded as separate applicants. A trustee might consider a challenge if he considered it prejudicial to the interests of the bankrupt and the creditors in the bankruptcy and/or the administration of the estate generally. The official receiver might consider a challenge on the basis of "public interest", but nevertheless is bound to show either unfair prejudice or material irregularity. There is nothing in the Act or Rules which indicates that either the trustee or the official receiver is to be given notice of the creditors' meeting or, indeed, is entitled to attend and make representations at the meeting.

It is quite clear that there must be a good reason for challenging the decision. The fact that minority creditors were disappointed in the outcome could not in itself be sufficient since the Rules specifically provide for a majority decision. Likewise, the fact that the outcome would be less beneficial than that in bankruptcy would not of itself be sufficient; in any event, such a proposition is unlikely. Misconduct by the debtor as such would also be insufficient.

6.3.6 Time-limits

An application cannot be made after the end of the period of 28 days beginning with the day on which the report of the creditors' meeting was made to the court.[1] The court might extend the time-limit under its interest jurisdiction but is unlikely to do so, except in wholly exceptional circumstances, since this would frustrate the whole purpose of the arrangement and its implementation. An aggrieved creditor seeking to challenge the arrangement out of time would be better advised to consider whether or not grounds are open to him to bring a petition for default.[2]

---

1 Insolvency Act 1986, s 262 (3).
2 Ibid, s 276; see further Chapter 8.

6.3.7 Powers of the court

On hearing an application by way of challenge, the court may, but is not bound to, do one or both of the following:

(a) revoke or suspend any approval given by the meeting;
(b) give a direction to any person for the summoning of a further meeting of the debtor's creditors to consider any revised proposal he may make or, where there has been some material irregularity, reconsider his original proposal.[1]

The mere suspension of the arrangement in itself will achieve nothing. Suspension, it seems, must go hand in hand with an order summoning a further meeting of creditors. The fact that the debtor may be given an opportunity to reconsider his proposal would seem to be relevant to a challenge on the basis of material irregularity.

---

1 Insolvency Act 1986, s 262 (4).

6.3.8 Further proposal

If the court gives a direction under s 262 (4) (b) of the Act for the summoning of a meeting to consider a revised proposal and it is satisfied that the debtor does not intend to submit such a proposal, it must revoke the direction and revoke or suspend any approval given at the previous meeting.[1] The reasons for the debtor refusing to reconsider may be financial or otherwise: he may not be able to afford the process, or he may simply be unwilling. It seems clear that, if this situation arises, the court is likely to revoke the approval because suspension alone would leave a situation of perpetual uncertainty.

1 Insolvency Act 1986, s 262 (5).

6.3.9 *Extension of interim order*
Where the court gives a direction under s 262 (4) (b), it may also give a direction continuing, or, as the case may be, renewing for such period as may be specified, the effect of any interim order. This will be essential if there is to be a further meeting of creditors. The court is, however, quite entitled to consider all the circumstances and conclude, in the light of its knowledge of the attitude of creditors or otherwise, that the holding of a further meeting is pointless.[1] There may, for instance, be clear evidence before the court that a majority could not in any circumstances be obtained for the approval of the proposal. In such circumstances, the court would almost inevitably refuse any further extension of time for the holding of the meeting and would make orders to bring the proceedings for a voluntary arrangement to an end.

1 *Re A Debtor (No 83 of 1988)* [1990] 1 WLR 708, sub nom *Re Cove (A Debtor)* [1990] 1 All ER 949.

6.3.10 *Saving provisions*
Where the court gives a direction or revokes or suspends any approval of an arrangement by the creditors' meeting, it may give directions as it thinks fit, with particular regard to things done since the first creditors' meeting and things done since the meeting as could not have been done if an interim order had been in force in relation to the debtor when they were done.[1]

1 Insolvency Act 1986, s 262 (7), which allows the court to validate acts which take place on the assumption that the approval was valid.

6.3.11 *Procedure* [1]
In a Case 1 matter, the applicant must serve the order on the debtor, the official receiver and the trustee; in Case 2 he must serve it on the debtor and, in either case, on the supervisor. If the order includes a direction by the court for the summoning of a further creditors' meeting, notice must also be given to the person directed by the court to summon the meeting. The debtor or, as the case may be, trustee or, if there is no trustee, the official receiver must, immediately on receiving the order, give notice to all persons who were sent notice of the creditors' meeting which approved the voluntary arrangement or who, not having been sent that notice, appear to be affected by the order; he must also, within seven days of those persons receiving a copy of the order, or within such longer period as the court may allow, give notice to the court whether it is intended to make a revised proposal to creditors or to invite reconsideration of the original proposal. The applicant must also give written notice of his intentions to the Secretary of State.

1 Insolvency Rules 1986, r 5.25.

Chapter 7

IMPLEMENTATION AND SUPERVISION OF THE ARRANGEMENT

7.1 Requirements of the Act and Rules

7.1.1 Introduction

There are few provisions in the Act[1] and Rules[2] on this subject. The absence of any really substantive statutory provisions is not surprising, since the whole question of implementation and supervision will turn on the specific provisions of the proposal. The debtor, creditors and supervisor must therefore examine the proposal to ascertain the arrangements made for implementing the scheme and the extent of the supervisor's role, obligations and responsibilities.

---

1 Insolvency Act 1986, s 263.
2 Insolvency Rules 1986, rr 5.20–5.28.

7.1.2 Reports to Secretary of State [1]

As soon as the chairman of the creditors' meeting has filed in court his report of the creditors' meeting, he must report certain details to the Secretary of State.

---

1 See para 6.1.20.

7.1.3 Supervisor's accounts and reports

Where the arrangement authorises or requires the supervisor:

(a) to carry on the debtor's business or to trade on his behalf or in his name; or
(b) to realise assets of the debtor or, in a Case 1 matter, belonging to the estate; or
(c) otherwise to administer or dispose of any funds of the debtor or the estate;

the supervisor must keep accounts and records of his acts and dealings in and in connection with the arrangement, including in particular records of all receipts and payments of money.[1]

This provision will normally relate to most arrangements. Whilst it will be rare for a supervisor to carry on the debtor's business or trade on the debtor's behalf or in the debtor's name,[2] the supervisor will frequently be involved even indirectly in the realisation of assets and will in almost every case be concerned in the administration or disposal of funds. In anything other than the most unusual circumstances, it will be quite unwise for the supervisor to carry on the business in his own name. To do so will involve the incurring of a personal liability which is clearly not envisaged by the status of supervisor. Supervision implies the concept of supervising something which is done by someone else.

Once every 12 months, beginning with the date of his appointment, the supervisor must prepare an abstract of receipts and payments, and send copies of the abstract accompanied by his comments on the progress and efficacy of the arrangement to the court, the debtor and all creditors bound by the arrangement. If, in any period of 12 months, he has made no payments and had no receipts, he must at the end of that period send a statement to such categories of persons to that effect.[3]

This imposes on the supervisor an obligation to keep all those concerned with the arrangement informed as to progress. There appears to be no requirement for the court to take any action other than, presumably, to file the abstract that it receives. However, if the court has any queries on the content of the abstract, it may have power under its inherent jurisdiction to summon the supervisor before it for an explanation and then give directions. It is more likely, however, that any points arising from the supervisor's report will lead to an application by the debtor or any creditor.[4]

The supervisor should give the fullest possible account of material developments, and any problems and difficulties which have arisen. The proposal may impose on him an obligation to report more frequently than annually and, if this is the case, he must comply with the reporting conditions set out in the proposal as well as those contained in the Rule. The creditors are entitled to expect cogent reasons to be given for delay and, in particular, difficulties which arise in the realisation of assets or any particular difficulties that the supervisor may be experiencing with the debtor. This may give rise to default proceedings.[5] In appropriate cases and subject to the provisions of the proposal, the supervisor may be required to call a meeting of the creditors' committee, if any, or a meeting of creditors.

Since a voluntary arrangement is based on trust and co-operation, the supervisor must maintain the trust and co-operation of the debtor and creditors and he should always be able to demonstrate that he is maintaining the trust and co-operation of the debtor. His report should be full and frank. Experience shows that, if reasons for delay and the nature of difficulties are explained to creditors, they are far more likely to be understanding and co-operative than if they are kept in the dark or if they perceive that they are being kept in the dark. It is all too easy for a situation to arise whereby creditors subsequently come to the conclusion that the arrangement exists primarily for the benefit of the debtor, if not the supervisor.

The abstract to which the Rule refers must relate to a period beginning with the date of the supervisor's appointment or, as the case may be, the day following the end of the last period for which an abstract was prepared; copies of the abstract must be sent out as required by the Rule within two months following the end of the period to which the abstract relates. The court may, on application by the supervisor, vary the dates on which the obligation to send abstracts or reports arises.[6]

In the rare case where the supervisor is not authorised to carry out any of the duties specified above, he must, at least once every 12 months beginning with the date of his appointment, send to the specified categories of persons a report on the progress and efficacy of the arrangement.[7]

1 Insolvency Rules 1986, r 5.26 (1).
2 This degree of activity will certainly involve the supervisor in personal liability and the arrangement in considerable expense.
3 Ibid, r 5.26 (2). If there have been no financial transactions in a 12-month period, the fullest possible explanation should be given to the creditors.
4 Insolvency Act 1986, s 263 (3).
5 Ibid, s 276; see generally Chapter 8.
6 Insolvency Rules 1986, r 5.26 (3)–(5).
7 Ibid, r 5.26 (4).

7.1.4 General statutory provisions

The main provision relating to implementation and supervision of an approved voluntary arrangement[1] applies where a voluntary arrangement approved by a creditors' meeting has taken effect.[2]

The person who for the time being is carrying out in relation to the voluntary arrangement the functions conferred by virtue of the approval on the nominee (or his replacement) is known as the supervisor. In most cases, the supervisor and the nominee will be one and the same person, but this is not invariably the case.

1 Insolvency Act 1986, s 263. This provision continues to apply in the event of the death of the debtor, subject to the modification referred to in note 1 to para 7.1.5 below.
2 Ibid, s 263 (1).

7.1.5 Applications to the court by the debtor, creditors and others

If the debtor, any of his creditors or any other person is dissatisfied by any act, omission or decision of the supervisor, he may apply to the court. On such an application, the court may:

(a) confirm, reverse or modify any act or decision of the supervisor;
(b) give him directions; or
(c) make such other order as it thinks fit.[1]

It is interesting to note that those entitled to apply under this subsection include not only the debtor and any creditor (which does not appear to be limited to a creditor bound) but also any other person, thereby envisaging that, in appropriate circumstances, applications may be made by creditors who are not bound or by third parties who may be aggrieved by an act, omission or decision of the supervisor. This last category could include, for example, a creditor not bound who wishes to be bound and whom the supervisor is unwilling to include or a third party against whom, under the terms of the proposal, the debtor is making a claim or a third party bringing a claim against the debtor whose claim is being resisted.

This subsection would also appear to allow a procedure for the agreement of claims. If a creditor lodges his claim with the supervisor and no agreement is reached, the supervisor may, following the procedure analogous to bankruptcy, reject the claim in whole or in part. The subsection would appear to allow the aggrieved creditor to apply to the court for the level and quantum of his claim to be determined.

The power of the court in dealing with such an application is discretionary. Clearly it must be satisfied that the application concerns an act, omission or decision of the supervisor and not of any other party. Subject to this, however, the power of the court is extremely wide and a determination of its precise extent must await judicial decision. It must be borne in mind that the court is exercising a power in relation to the implementation and supervision of the arrangement, and so any application falling outside either implementation or supervision must, it seems, fail. It is doubtful if the court would have power to vary the terms of the proposal or, for example, extend the duration of the arrangement. Certainly, the court is unlikely to be persuaded to make any such order without first directing a meeting to be held of all the creditors bound by the arrangement. Similarly, it is unlikely that, under this section, the court would be willing to adjudicate on any application brought by a creditor or other person for a direction that the supervisor institute bankruptcy proceedings against the debtor. Such a decision is clearly a matter for the supervisor to take in accordance with any provisions in the proposal, and it seems that a court would generally be unwilling to direct a supervisor to bring a petition when that court itself would in all probability have to adjudicate on the petition itself. Finally, the subsection may not be used as a back-door method to bring a challenge under s 262 where the time-limit under that section has expired.

---

1 Insolvency Act 1986, s 263 (3). Where the individual dies after the arrangement has been approved, this provision continues to apply, subject to the words "debtor, any of his" being replaced by "personal representative of the deceased debtor, any of the deceased debtor's"; the supervisor must also give notice of the death to the court: Administration of Insolvent Estates of Deceased Debtors Order 1986, Part III, para 5.

7.1.6 Application to the court by the supervisor [1]

The supervisor may apply to the court for directions in relation to any particular matter arising under the arrangement.[2] The role of the court is apparently limited to giving directions on matters relating to implementation and supervision, although no provision is specifically made as to the nature of the order that the court may make.[3] It seems that this subsection is limited to enabling the supervisor to seek the assistance of the court for a situation which is not envisaged by the proposal itself and which, for whatever reason, cannot be determined either by the supervisor exercising his own professional judgment or by reference, if the proposal so provides, to a meeting of the creditors' committee or a meeting of the creditors themselves. Clearly, the particular matter is likely to be one of substance. The court does not exist to carry out the supervisor's duties and responsibilities. The supervisor must exercise his own judgement and proper discretion.

---

1 See note 1 to para 7.1.5 above. Compare with Insolvency Act 1986, s 303 which provides that the bankruptcy court can exercise general control over the trustee. The provisions are similar in form. Section 263 (4) is wider than the equivalent provision under the 1914 Act

which used the term "person aggrieved", implying a wrongful act complained of. It seems that the word "dissatisfied" in s 263 (3) may mean no more than "disagrees with", but the onus will be on the applicant to show not only that the supervisor is wrong in what he is doing or not doing but also that relief should be given.

2 Insolvency Act 1986, s 263 (4).

3 Otherwise, the legislature would surely have extended the scope of order which could be made under s 263 (4) to bring it in line with s 263 (3). In accordance with the wording of subsection (3), there is a difference between an order which confirms, reverses or modifies a direction and "such other order as it thinks fit". It follows that a direction is relief in itself and it is likely to constitute the answer to a specific question relating to the implementation and supervision of the arrangement.

7.1.7 Appointment and removal of supervisor

The proposal itself may contain provision as to the procedure to be followed in the event of a vacancy in the office of supervisor. However, vacancies may arise in arrangements where there is no specific provision or, alternatively, a situation may arise where either the debtor or the creditors wish to have a new supervisor appointed. The court has a discretionary power to make an order appointing a person who is qualified to act as an insolvency practitioner in relation to the debtor, either in substitution for the existing supervisor or to fill a vacancy, in the following circumstances: where it is expedient to appoint a person to carry out the functions of the supervisor and it is inexpedient, difficult or impracticable for an appointment to be made without the assistance of the court.[1] The very wording of the section shows that it is to take effect and be used where there is no provision in the proposal, or where a situation arises which is not envisaged by the proposal.

The question of the removal of a supervisor is always likely to be a difficult one and will depend largely on the facts. The court will need to be satisfied that, for whatever reason, the supervisor is not discharging his duties and it is right that he should be removed and another supervisor appointed. Clearly the consent of any replacement supervisor, who must be qualified to act, will be needed before any order is made appointing him.

1 Insolvency Act 1986, s 263 (5) which is expressed to be without prejudice to the Trustee Act 1925, s 41 (2) which relates to the power of the court to appoint trustees of deeds of arrangement. This suggests a voluntary arrangement is a trust, but this will not necessarily be the case. The supervisor is certainly not a trustee, per se, unless the proposal so provides; see also *Re Naeem* [1990] 1 WLR 48 at p 51A, per Hoffman J: "He/the supervisor has never been a trustee".

7.1.8 Debt avoidance

Relief in respect of transactions defrauding creditors is available under the Act.[1] If the victim of the transaction is bound by a voluntary arrangement, the application may be brought by the supervisor or the victim.[2] This reference to a person bound can only mean the debtor. Whilst creditors are undoubtedly bound,[3] it is illogical to suggest that a creditor, if a victim, can have his application brought by the supervisor.

1 Insolvency Act 1986, s 423.

2 Ibid, s 424 (1) (b).

3 Ibid, s 260 (2) (b).

7.2 General Considerations

7.2.1 The proposal

The proposal itself should set out the basis on which the arrangement is to be implemented and supervised, so stressing again the necessity of careful consideration being given to the preparation and completion of the proposal.

7.2.2 Supervisor's powers generally

In appropriate cases, specific powers may be conferred on the supervisor by reference to the statutory powers of an administrator or administrative receiver or trustee in bankruptcy as contained in the Act.[1] If such provisions are incorporated into the proposal with appropriate amendments, then, as between the supervisor on the one hand and the debtor and the creditors bound on the other, the supervisor will, as a matter of contract, be entitled to exercise such powers. This will not necessarily be the case as regards third parties not bound by the arrangement. However, such schedules can be conveniently adapted, but in each and every proposal the nominee should have given specific consideration as to whether such powers are necessary and desirable and whether or not the supervisor will be willing to incur the potential liability which will inevitably attach to the exercise of such powers. The more powers that are taken by a supervisor, the greater the degree of responsibility and liability that will fall on him. This underlines the importance of the nominee thinking through with care exactly what powers he will need in any given proposal: he must be certain in his own mind that he will have sufficient powers to ensure that he is able to supervise the particular arrangement and, insofar as he is able, to carry it through to a successful conclusion. It seems unlikely that, once the proposal has been approved by the creditors, a court can subsequently confer on a supervisor any powers and responsibilities which were not contained or envisaged in the proposal itself.

---

1 See Appendix 1, p 140, SC 11.

7.2.3 Decision-making

The decisions which need to be made will vary from one proposal to another. If there is property to be sold, the supervisor will have to make the decisions as to the mode of sale and asking price and, when an asset is sold, the terms of sale. In a difficult property market, a supervisor may find himself in a position of having to agree the sale of an asset for a sum considerably less than that envisaged in the proposal. He must think out the implications not only for the creditors but also for the debtor. In a properly worded proposal, this will have been thought of in advance and will not give rise to default.

Most policy decisions and day-to-day decisions will fall to made by the supervisor. He will exercise his own professional judgement and discretion in accordance with the guidelines given to him in the proposal. It is his responsibility to ensure that it is the proposal which is implemented and not some alternative scheme. If difficulties arise, he can apply to the court.[1] Furthermore, he must keep creditors informed.[2] Where there is a creditors' committee, he should seek to involve that committee fully and as envisaged by the proposal. The frequency of creditors' committee meetings will depend on each arrangement, as will the matters on which a decision is necessary or guidance required by the supervisor.

1 See para 7.1.6 above.
2 See para 7.1.3 above.

7.2.4 Duties of debtor

The debtor has a general duty and obligation to do all that is necessary to ensure the successful implementation and carrying out of the proposal. This general duty is clearly implied in every proposal, and failure by the debtor to fulfil this duty may have serious consequences for him.

The proposal may also confer on the debtor certain specified or express obligations. It will fall to the supervisor to ensure that these are carried out and, in the event of failure, to determine whether or not a default petition should be brought.[1] The supervisor should ensure that he maintains regular contact with the debtor and has meetings with him as often as necessary to receive reports from the debtor on the progress he is making in carrying out his duties and, if required, to give directions to the debtor as to what he should or should not be doing. In appropriate cases, the supervisor should without hesitation give the debtor a formal direction as to what the debtor should do to assist in the realisation of an asset. If the debtor fails to co-operate, the supervisor must immediately warn him of the consequences. It will always be prudent for the supervisor to confirm such matters to the debtor in writing, and the debtor should always ensure that the supervisor is kept informed as to any change of address or change of occupation. If the debtor is under an obligation to make regular payments, and difficulties arise, the debtor should report the fact to the supervisor at once who will then take such steps as may be appropriate.

1 Insolvency Act 1986, s 276 (1) (a), (c).

7.2.5 Agreement of creditors' claims

The nominee will normally seek to agree creditors' claims prior to the creditors' meeting, but this will not always be possible. Immediately after approval of the proposal, the supervisor should write to each creditor to seek confirmation of the claim and obtain appropriate documentary proof. Where a claim is disputed, the supervisor should endeavour to agree the same as quickly as possible. He should go through all claims with the debtor to ensure that all relevant information is supplied and the debtor's views ascertained. Where the supervisor determines that a claim should be admitted for a sum less than that claimed or more than is agreed by the debtor, he should give notice in writing to the creditor or debtor, as appropriate. Any party who is still aggrieved can make an application to the court for the supervisor's decision to be modified or reversed, or the court may make such other order as it thinks appropriate.[1]

1 Insolvency Act 1986, s 263 (3).

7.2.6 Realisation of assets generally

The supervisor is generally obliged to oversee and supervise the realisation of assets, and such realisation must clearly be for the best possible price and in the most favourable manner. Since legal title to assets will remain vested in the debtor in the vast majority of cases, it will be for the debtor to effect the sale of assets and enter into any contracts, as appropriate. The proposal should have identified all assets, the way in which they are to be realised and the timetable envisaged, and will normally confer on the supervisor the right to appoint whatever agents and solicitors may be necessary. There will always need to be the closest possible liaison and co-operation between supervisor and debtor. Market conditions and timing will be all-important, as will the level of incumbrances charged against assets. The supervisor, upon advice where appropriate, must determine matters of policy.

In certain circumstances, the assets to be realised will be owned jointly by the debtor and another. It is always prudent to ensure that the joint owner's co-operation will be forthcoming, and this should have been established prior to the creditors' meeting. If there is likely to be difficulty in this respect, the problem should have been spelt out in the proposal, which should contain provisions as to the steps to be taken to secure the co-operation of the joint owner. If there is any prospect of the need for litigation, this should also be referred to in the proposal, together with some realistic estimate as to the likely time that will be involved and costs incurred.

7.3 Specific Considerations

7.3.1 General

The supervisor should, immediately after the creditors' meeting, meet with the debtor, go through the proposal in detail and agree with the debtor as to the steps which each of them is to take and the manner in which those steps are to be taken.

7.3.2 Hand-over of property

The Rules[1] provide that, as soon as the voluntary arrangement has been approved, the debtor in a Case 2 matter, and the official receiver or trustee in a Case 1 matter, must do all that is required to put the supervisor into possession[2] of the assets included in the arrangement. The position in Case 1 is dealt with generally elsewhere.[3] In the vast majority of arrangements, there will in fact be no question of the supervisor going into possession in the usual understanding of the word, since legal title to the debtor's assets will remain vested in the debtor unless the proposal provides otherwise. If assets are to be vested in the supervisor, the appropriate documents of transfer must be prepared immediately. This is rarely the case and will seldom be desirable. If the supervisor is to be granted a power of attorney to enable him to deal with the debtor's assets, this should be executed forthwith.

---

1 Insolvency Rules 1986, r 5.21.
2 What is meant by possession is open to a wide interpretation. It should be taken as meaning "the ability to deal with assets in accordance with the proposal".
3 See Chapter 9.

7.3.3 Marketing of assets

Freehold or leasehold properties, and other immediately realisable assets, may have to be sold. The supervisor should agree with the debtor as to the agents and solicitors to be instructed and the appropriate methods of disposal. The supervisor should ensure that proper advice is taken and assets of whatever nature marketed in the best possible way. He should ensure that the debtor regularly prepares reports and keeps him up to date with all progress that is being made. When agents are instructed, the supervisor should ensure that he keeps in regular contact with the agents to ensure that the asking price is realistic and appropriate, and any necessary adjustments are made, having regard to the market and other circumstances. The debtor should not be left to his own devices, even though he retains legal title to the assets. The supervisor must supervise and be willing and able to give directions, guidance and advice to the debtor, who should be entitled to rely on the supervisor's general business and professional experience in all matters.

7.3.4 Book debts and work in progress

Immediate steps should be taken to call in book debts, and the proposal will specify the person to whom the responsibility falls. If it is the supervisor, he should write at once to all debtors, setting out the amount due, and enclose a copy of the relevant account or invoice requesting payment within a specified period of time. Inevitably, disputes will arise, and the supervisor should take the debtor's instructions and, where appropriate, professional advice. If the proposal so provides, legal proceedings should be instituted for recovery. It will frequently be the case that professional assistance will be required to measure and agree work in progress before steps can be taken for its realisation. The proposal should make provision for the supervisor to be empowered to agree, or concur in agreeing, to a compromise or settlement of disputed issues.

7.3.5 Litigation

It will generally be in the interests of all those concerned with the arrangement to avoid litigation, either by or against the debtor. Experience shows that ongoing litigation will often only serve to reduce the available assets, lengthen the duration of the arrangement and, as often as not, lead to a potential default or failure situation. Nevertheless, there will be instances where litigation cannot be avoided.

It will normally be unwise for any proposal to commit the debtor irrevocably to undertaking litigation. A proposal may, however, depend entirely on funds being generated as a result of the successful conclusion of either pending or proposed litigation, but such a proposal should be viewed with immense caution, if not scepticism. Where there is such a proposal, the creditors must be given, in the proposal and at the creditors' meeting, as much information as possible as to the nature of the litigation and its merits. Particular care needs to be taken if the proposed defendant to any such action is a creditor. Where legal advice has been taken or counsel's opinion obtained on the merits of a claim, the nominee should be in a position, at least at the creditors' meeting, to give a proper précis or summary of that advice. If funds held are in way to be put at risk through the prosecution of litigation, the creditors must have been informed.

Claims by the debtor may arise in a large number of different instances, but will normally relate to the realisation of assets. The debtor may be owed book debts or work in progress which cannot be allocated with litigation. Claims in professional negligence or breach of contract may lie against former advisers. If litigation is envisaged, this must have been spelt out in the proposal, together with all implications. Unless the debtor's assets are vested in the supervisor, any litigation will be by the debtor and, where the concurrence of another party is required, the creditors must be satisfied through the proposal that such concurrence is forthcoming. Litigation will be conducted by the debtor and this may include the continuation of litigation already commenced at the time of the creditors' meeting. The supervisor's role will be limited. The supervisor should carry out a watching brief, meeting as frequently as is appropriate with the debtor and his solicitors and counsel to receive reports on progress and offer such advice and guidance as may be appropriate.

If the settlement of a claim is proposed, the supervisor's view should be taken, especially if the settlement is adverse to the proposal or produces less funds than were envisaged. In such circumstances, the supervisor must consider the effect of the settlement on the proposal and report as appropriate to the creditors and the court.

The supervisor will also have to consider the costs of litigation, both the debtor's and any adverse order costs, for which provision should have been made in the proposal. If litigation is funded out of the arrangement, the supervisor must be satisfied as to the level of costs being incurred and will frequently insist that the legal advisers instructed are of his choice. The basic assumption must always be against involving the arrangement in litigation which is likely to be lengthy or expensive. Even if the litigation is conducted by the debtor with the benefit of legal aid, the supervisor is on risk for an order for adverse costs, although in many cases this risk may not be regarded as particularly serious.[1]

Where possible, the debtor should seek legal aid. However, he may not qualify financially, in which case the supervisor has to be quite certain that proper provision in accordance with the terms of the proposal can be made for costs, including adverse costs. Even if the debtor qualifies for legal aid and the case is such as would normally merit legal aid, the Legal Aid Board may nevertheless refuse a certificate on the basis that, in all the circumstances, it is proper for the creditors and not the taxpayer to fund the litigation, since it will normally be the creditors who benefit. To avoid such a point being taken, it may well be desirable to show that the debtor personally and in a financial sense will benefit himself directly from the litigation as opposed to the creditors. This may be achieved by providing that he personally retains the benefit of part of the fruits of the litigation. If, for example, the claim to be pursued is for personal injuries, then it may be quite proper to provide in the proposal that the debtor retains the whole or part of the damages which are attributable to pain and suffering, the creditors taking that part which relates to economic loss. The debtor should not be left to his own devices, and the supervisor must determine the level of his own involvement in accordance with the general requirements of the proposal.

Where litigation is of a more routine nature, such as the collection of book debts and work in progress, this will normally be overseen directly by the supervisor. However, supervisors will generally be well advised to avoid any involvement in areas of litigation notorious for their unsatisfactory outcome, such as building disputes or disputes relating to rights of way and boundaries.

Finally, the debtor may be involved in matrimonial proceedings. If the debtor is separated from his spouse, the spouse may bring claims relating to capital assets, seeking property adjustment or lump sum orders. Likewise, the debtor may wish to bring such claims against his or her spouse. Such a situation should be envisaged in the proposal and provision made for how such litigation is to be conducted and funded, and the proposal should take into account a realistic assessment of the likely order that will be made and its overall effect on the arrangement.[2]

Matrimonial proceedings which were not envisaged at the time of approval of the arrangement but which arose subsequently may well result in default or failure.[3]

---

1 *Aiden Shipping Co Ltd v Interbulk Ltd* [1986] AC 965, [1986] 2 All ER 409, HL.
2 See generally Chapter 11.
3 See generally Chapter 8.

7.3.6 Land law matters

Many proposals will envisage the sale of leasehold or freehold premises.

Leasehold premises attract their own peculiar difficulties. Prior to the creditors' meeting, the supervisor, in his nominee capacity, will have carried out an investigation into the value of the leaseholds, likely realisable values (taking into account any claims by secured creditors) together with an assessment of other encumbrances, such as arrears of rent, potential breaches of covenant or dilapidation claims. The attitude of the landlord to an assignment of a lease may also have been ascertained. If such steps have not been taken, they must be taken immediately, since the supervisor will have no power to disclaim.[1] If the supervisor concludes that a leasehold is of an onerous nature, he may seek to negotiate a surrender so as to determine the ongoing liability for rent and other matters under the lease.[2] If the proposal envisages the maintenance of leasehold premises for any period of time, the supervisor must be certain that, in accordance with the terms of the proposal, provision can be made for the payment of the rent and other outgoings. In dealing with the landlord, the supervisor must ensure that he negotiates as agent and not as principal and incurs no personal liability.

Generally, as regards leaseholds and freeholds, the supervisor will ensure that the co-operation of joint owners is obtainable. He will oversee the marketing of the property, including the instruction of agents and solicitors.[3] He should agree the asking price and subsequent sale price and should consider the effect on the arrangement if the property sells for less than was envisaged. He should ensure that any secured creditor's debt is serviced and, if it is not to be serviced, the effect on the proposal of the possible erosion of the equity. He should be satisfied that, before any binding contract is entered into, possession can and will be given.

In the case of the debtor's own home, the supervisor should be satisfied that the debtor is aware of the consequences of giving voluntary possession and the possible effect of the debtor being deemed to have rendered himself, his spouse and family deliberately homeless.[4]

The supervisor should maintain regular contact with selling agents and should be involved in any decision to lower the asking price or to change the agents. He should also be satisfied as to the terms on which agents and solicitors are instructed, including the level of professional charges to be made by them.

Likewise, the supervisor should keep in regular contact with secured creditors so as to monitor the level of indebtedness and any failure on the part of the debtor to keep to agreed payments. Where a secured creditor is exercising its own right of sale, the supervisor should ensure that the equity rising on any sale which is payable to the debtor is paid to him as supervisor.

---

1 For the position in bankruptcy see Insolvency Act 1986, ss 315–321.
2 But care must be taken to ensure that this does not constitute default.
3 However, as against the joint owner, he will have no right to do so.
4 See generally Housing Act 1985, Part III, as amended by Housing and Planning Act 1986.

7.3.7 Ongoing trading

Although individual voluntary arrangements have only been available for a short period of time, experience already shows that ongoing trading can cause the greatest of difficulties and will often lead to the failure of the arrangement.

The usual justification for ongoing trading is that the debtor will be able to make contributions to the creditors out of trading receipts. Such a proposal should normally be viewed with scepticism. If a business has already failed, then creditors are likely to need some persuading that, if they allow it to continue, the debtor can not only produce a reasonable living for himself and his family, and avoid further liabilities accumulating, but he can also produce sufficient profit to enable past liabilities to be discharged. Accordingly, if the proposal contains such a proposition, it needs to be given the most careful consideration.

The supervisor will have ascertained the likely attitude of the Inland Revenue and Customs and Excise if there exist past VAT and PAYE liabilities. It will rarely be safe to agree a proposal where ongoing trading would involve further credit facilities. If this is proposed, the Rules provide that the proposal must give full details of such further credit facilities and how the debts so arising are to be paid;[1] normal practice is for them to be paid out of trading receipts. If new creditors arise as a result of continued trading, they will not be bound by the arrangement; if unpaid, they will be free to pursue remedies against the debtor.

The proposal must contain the fullest possible details and explanation as to how the business is to be conducted during the course of the arrangement. The debtor will continue to trade in his own name. The supervisor's role must be carefully defined so as to avoid any suggestion that the debtor is trading on an agency basis for the supervisor or vice versa. The debtor will remain liable for all the liabilities of the business, including trade liabilities, VAT in respect of employees,[2] income tax, rates and all other outgoings and liabilities relevant to the particular business.

The supervisor's role should be supervisory. In a normal case it would be far too expensive for the supervisor to maintain a continuing presence at the business. He should ensure that he meets regularly with the debtor to review the progress of the business and should be provided with regular written reports and management accounts. The supervisor should ensure that the general purpose of the arrangement is being met and that default does not arise. The supervisor himself will be anxious to avoid a second insolvency of the same debtor.

The debtor will generally wish to continue trading by utilising the stock that existed at the time the arrangement was proposed. The proposal itself will refer to stock as an asset and, if that stock is to be utilised for trading purposes as opposed to being immediately sold, this must be made clear in the proposal;[3] otherwise, the creditors may be misled.

The proposal will normally provide for the debtor to make payments to the supervisor on a periodic basis, normally monthly. If payments at the agreed amount are not regularly received at the agreed time, the supervisor should as soon as there has been a single default seek an explanation from the debtor and, if appropriate and taking into account the general terms of the proposal, report the same to the creditors. Whilst a single such default in theory would justify a petition for default, in practice this is not likely to be the case unless there has been continued default over a reasonable period of time and it is clear to the supervisor that there is no hope of the arrears being made good and the terms of the proposal fulfilled.

---

1 Insolvency Rules 1986, r 5.3 (2) (n).
2 It would appear that a voluntary arrangement does not terminate contracts of employment, and there will be continuation of employment through the period of supervision.
3 Such stock would constitute 'excluded' assets under ibid, r 5.3 (2) (a) (iii).

Chapter 8

DEFAULT AND FAILURE

8.1 Introduction

The legislation envisages two different procedures whereby a voluntary arrangement can be attacked: first, there is the possibility of a challenge of the decision of the creditors' meeting,[1] and, secondly, a bankruptcy petition may in certain circumstances be brought against the debtor.[2]

The term 'failure of the scheme' or 'failure of the arrangement' is commonly used, but is not to be found anywhere in the Act or Rules.

---

1 Insolvency Act 1986, s 262; see generally paras 6.3.1–6.3.11 above.
2 Ibid, ss 264 (1) (c), 276.

8.2 Default

The Act permits a number of categories of persons to petition for the bankruptcy of an individual.[1] The categories include the supervisor of, or any person (other than the individual) who is for the time being bound by, a voluntary arrangement proposed by the individual and approved under the Act.

It will be seen, therefore, that the debtor himself cannot petition for his own bankruptcy whilst he is subject to a voluntary arrangement.[2] The court, on hearing a debtor's petition, may not make a bankruptcy order if it appears to the court that, within the period of five years ending with the presentation of the petition, the debtor has neither been adjudged bankrupt nor made a composition with his creditors in satisfaction of his debts or a scheme of arrangement of his affairs.[3]

---

1 Insolvency Act 1986, s 264 (1).
2 See generally paras 10.8.1–10.8.5 below.
3 Ibid, s 273 (1) (c).

8.3 Statutory Considerations

8.3.1 General

The general power of the court to make a bankruptcy order is discretionary.[1] In the case of a petition by a supervisor or creditor bound by a voluntary arrangement, the court may not make a bankruptcy order unless it is satisfied that one of three grounds exists:

(a) the debtor has failed to comply with his obligations under the voluntary arrangement; or

(b) information which was false or misleading in any material particular or which contained material omissions:

   (i) was contained in any statement of affairs or other document supplied to any person by the debtor under Part VIII of the Act, or

   (ii) was otherwise made available by the debtor to his creditors at or in connection with a meeting summoned under that Part; or

(c) the debtor has failed to do all such things as may for the purposes of the voluntary arrangement have been reasonably required of him by the supervisor of the arrangement.[2]

---

1 Insolvency Act 1986, s 264 (2).
2 Ibid, s 276.

8.3.2 Failure to comply with obligations [1]

This must relate to the obligations on the part of the debtor set out either expressly or by implication in the proposal. If, for example, the debtor, as part of his proposal, agrees to pay to the supervisor periodic sums of money either out of his future earnings or trading receipts and fails to do so, that is clearly such a failure to comply. Similarly, if the debtor undertakes to realise certain assets or, indeed, to do any particular act and fails to do so, he is liable to have a petition brought against him. In theory at least, the smallest failure to comply with obligations could be sufficient for the bringing of a petition but, where the failure is de minimis, the court may, in the exercise of its general discretion, decline to make a bankruptcy order. The bankruptcy court will clearly be entitled to have regard to the extent of the failure and its effect on the arrangement as a whole. If a failure is capable of remedy and does not threaten to destroy the arrangement as a whole, the court may be reluctant to make a bankruptcy order. It seems that some degree of culpability is required.

---

1 Insolvency Act 1986, s 276 (1) (a).

8.3.3 False or misleading information [1]

The debtor is under a clear duty to provide his creditors with a full, frank and honest disclosure of his financial position. If he fails to do so, whether intentionally or unintentionally, this is liable to constitute false or misleading information. There is no need to prove intent or culpable dishonesty on the part of the debtor. The relevant test would appear to be, "Had the correct situation been known, would this have materially affected the attitude of the creditors and the approval of the arrangement?" The court hearing the bankruptcy petition is entitled to give the fullest consideration to the situation that exists at the time that the petition comes before the court. If the default is de minimis, the petition may not succeed. If, however, the debtor has grossly understated his liabilities or overstated the value of his assets, a bankruptcy order is likely to be made, depending on the particular circumstances. The term "otherwise made" would seem to include a verbal statement made at the creditors' meeting.

---

1 Insolvency Act 1986, s 276 (1) (b).

8.3.4 *Failure to co-operate* [1]

A voluntary arrangement can only succeed if the supervisor has the fullest possible co-operation of the debtor. A debtor cannot enter into a voluntary arrangement and then abandon his responsibilities. Equally, the supervisor's requests for co-operation must be reasonable and they must be directly connected with the implementation of the arrangement. The supervisor or petitioning creditor must therefore be able to demonstrate to the court not only that the requests have been reasonable and that the debtor has failed to comply but that the requests were directly essential to the implementation of the scheme.

---

1 Insolvency Act 1986, s 276 (1) (c).

8.3.5 *Evidence*

Whether or not a case can be made out under s 276 of the Act is almost entirely a matter of evidence turning on the facts of each individual case. The petitioning creditor must be able to establish with clarity the particular allegations that are made.

8.3.6 *Initial procedure*

The supervisor or other petitioning creditor should first take into account whether any procedure is specified in the proposal itself. For example, the proposal may provide that, where default has arisen, notice is to be given to the creditors and no petition may be presented until the creditors have had an opportunity of meeting and expressing their views. If there is such a provision, it must be complied with. The debtor should in most circumstances be given a reasonable opportunity to explain his alleged default not only to the supervisor but also to the creditors.[1]

---

1 See, for example, Appendix 1, p 137, SC 5.4.

8.3.7 *Formal procedure*

The bankruptcy petition must be prepared in a specified form.[1] Details of the default must be set out with sufficient particularity so that the debtor knows exactly what is alleged. Otherwise, the general rules relating to bankruptcy procedure apply.[2] The petition must be supported by an affidavit in pre-scribed form as to the truth of the statements in the petition.[3] In most cases it will be desirable for the affidavit, which is normally sworn by the supervisor, to be rather fuller than a "standard affidavit of truth", and it should contain sufficient evidence to justify the allegations of default contained in the petition. The relevant documentation should be exhibited. If it is alleged that a particular document was false or misleading, that document should be exhibited. If the debtor has failed to do what is reasonably required of him, relevant letters between the supervisor and the debtor and, where appropriate, notes of meetings and conversations should be exhibited.

---

1 Statutory Form 6.10; see Appendix 2, p 178.
2 See generally Insolvency Rules 1986, rr 6.6–6.36.
3 Ibid, r 6.12 and Form 6.13.

8.4 Effect of Bankruptcy Order on Arrangement

See paras 10.1–10.7 below.

8.5 Failure

If the concept of failure is to be introduced into an arrangement, there must be specific provision in the proposal.[1] Otherwise, it seems that an arrangement can only be attacked under the specific statutory provisions mentioned above. In many instances, failure and default will be synonymous, although this will not always be the case. Much will depend on the terms of the proposal and precisely what is envisaged, and failure other than default must be defined.

A carefully worded proposal may provide that a particular property is to be sold and the documents provided to the creditors may give an estimated sale price and may indicate that, whilst it is hoped to fetch such a price, no guarantee is given. If the property is subsequently sold for less than was envisaged, it is difficult to see that such facts give rise to default. The matter is arguable, but such a situation would normally be regarded as failure. Failure is commonly regarded as being an end result other than that envisaged by the proposal. In such circumstances, the creditors may wish to bring the arrangement to a conclusion so that they can then pursue other remedies, but they will only be able to do this if the concept of failure is recognised in the proposal itself and the proposal contains a mechanism for determining the proposal. Such termination is then a matter of contractual considerations.

---

1 See Appendix 1, p 141, SC 15.

8.6 Completion of Arrangement[1]

The rules envisage a situation whereby an arrangement is completed essentially in accordance with what was proposed. Not more than 28 days after the final completion of the arrangement, the supervisor must send to all creditors who are bound and to the debtor a notice that the arrangement has been fully implemented. Clearly such a notice can only be given where there has been full implementation. Notwithstanding this, with the notice there must be sent a copy of a report by the supervisor summarising all receipts and payments made by him in pursuance of the arrangement and explaining any difference in the actual implementation of it, as compared with the proposal as approved by the creditors' meeting. Where the difference in implementation is to the detriment of creditors, it is difficult to see that the arrangement has been fully implemented. There may be a default situation or, alternatively, failure.

The proposal may itself contain other provisions relevant to its completion. The effect of supervening bankruptcy on an arrangement is dealt with elsewhere.[2]

1 Insolvency Rules 1986, r 5.29.
2 See Chapter 10.

8.7 Setting Aside

The Act and Rules do not allow for an approved arrangement to be set aside and it is doubtful whether the court would have such a power.[1] The proposal itself may provide for a mechanism to set aside, since there is seemingly no limit to the matters on which the debtor and his creditors, as a matter of contract, can agree. In such circumstances, provision could be made to the effect that the creditors are no longer bound.[2] Subsequent bankruptcy will not of itself set aside the arrangement.[3]

1 Eg under Insolvency Act 1986, s 263 (3) or (4).
2 See Appendix 1, p 141, SC 15.2.
3 See generally paras 10.1–10.7 below.

8.8 Frustration

Frustration, as a matter of law, is a term of art. In the context of a voluntary arrangement, facts which in contract law might give rise to frustration are likely to result in either default or failure.

8.9 Criminal Liability

The Rules[1] provide that the debtor commits an offence if he makes any false representation or commits any other fraud for the purpose of obtaining the approval of his creditors to a proposal for a voluntary arrangement. A person guilty of such an offence is liable on indictment, to seven years' imprisonment or a fine or both and, on summary conviction, to six months' imprisonment or the statutory maximum or both.[2]

The Rule does not provide that intent must be proved, but this would appear to be implicit so that an innocent misrepresentation is unlikely to constitute an offence. However, the term 'other fraud' clearly involves intent.

The existence of this rule and the provisions relating to default[3] emphasise the necessity for careful preparation of the proposal and supporting documents and the necessity for a completely frank, open and honest account of the debtor's affairs.

1 Insolvency Rules 1986, r 5.30, made pursuant to Insolvency Act 1986, s 412 in conjunction with ibid, Sch 9, para 32.
2 Insolvency Rules 1986, Sch 5.
3 Insolvency Act 1986, s 276.

Chapter 9

SPECIAL CONSIDERATIONS WHERE THE DEBTOR IS AN UNDISCHARGED BANKRUPT

9.1 Introduction

Under the Rules,[1] where the debtor is an undischarged bankrupt, the arrangement constitutes a Case 1 matter and, where he is not, it constitutes a Case 2 matter. Generally speaking, the Act and Rules apply with similar effect to both cases, although there are special considerations relating to Case 1 arrangements which it is convenient to summarise.

---

1 Insolvency Rules 1986, r 5.1 (2).

9.2 Application for Interim Order

The Act[1] provides that, if the debtor is an undischarged bankrupt, the application for the interim order may be made by the debtor, the trustee of his estate or the official receiver; in practice, applications by an official receiver are rare. As a general rule, an application will be made in a Case 1 matter where it is clear to either the debtor or the trustee that a voluntary arrangement is likely to produce, financially, a more beneficial result to creditors, in particular having regard to the saving on DTI fees, reduced professional fees generally, speedier realisation of assets and possibly third party assets being made available, which would not be the case in bankruptcy.

---

1 Insolvency Act 1986, s 253 (3) (a).

9.3 The Interim Order

In a Case 1 matter, the wording of the order itself will be slightly amended[1] so as to provide that no further bankruptcy petition relating to the debtor may be presented or proceeded with.

---

1 See Appendix 2, p 169, note 1.

9.4 Declaration as to Existence of Bankruptcy

The debtor must declare in his affidavit in support of the application for the interim order that he is an undischarged bankrupt.[1]

1 Insolvency Rules 1986, r 5.5 (1) (c).

9.5 Further Provision in Interim Order

The interim order may contain provision as to the conduct of the bankruptcy and the administration of the bankrupt's estate during the period for which the order is in force.[1] Such provision may include orders staying proceedings in the bankruptcy or modifying any provision of the Act relating to insolvency of individuals and bankruptcy and any provision of the Rules in their application to the debtor's bankruptcy.[2] The interim order may not, in relation to a bankruptcy, make any provision relaxing or removing any of the requirements unless the court is satisfied that that provision is unlikely to result in any significant diminution of, or in the value of, the debtor's estate for the purposes of the bankruptcy.[3]

Furthermore, notice of the application, if by the debtor, must be given to the official receiver and, if there is one, the trustee of the debtor's estate,[4] since the interim order may affect their administration of the debtor's estate. It is not altogether clear how and in what sense the court may modify provisions in the Act or Rules in relation to an individual bankrupt; the only specific instance which is given as to the extent and limitation of the power is that the court must not significantly diminish the quantum or value of the bankrupt's estate. It seems, therefore, that the general effect of these provisions is to ensure that, in the event of the proposal not being accepted, nothing has been done which is likely to be prejudicial to the interests of the creditors.

1 Insolvency Act 1986, s 255 (3).
2 Ibid, s 255 (4).
3 Ibid, s 255 (5).
4 Insolvency Rules 1986, r 5.5 (3).

9.6 Effect of Approval

In a Case 1 matter, the approval of the voluntary arrangement does not automatically annul the bankruptcy. Until it is annulled the bankruptcy remains in full force and effect. In Case 1, the court may do one or both of the following, namely:

(a) annul the bankruptcy order by which the debtor was adjudged bankrupt; or

(b) give such directions concerning the conduct of the bankruptcy in the administration of the bankrupt's estate as it thinks appropriate for facilitating the implementation of the approved voluntary arrangement.[1]

1 Insolvency Act 1986, s 261 (1). In the event of the death of the debtor, the whole section ceases to apply on or after the death of the individual: Administration of Insolvent Estates of Deceased Debtors Order 1986, Part III, para 4.

9.7 Annulment

The Act makes specific provision for annulment outside the general provisions.[1] The court cannot annul a bankruptcy order at any time before the end of the period of 28 days beginning with the day on which the report of the creditors' meeting is made to the court under s 259 or at any time when an application under s 262 or an appeal in respect of such an application is pending or at any time in the period within which such an appeal may be brought.

Notwithstanding this mandatory provision, some courts adopt the practice of making an order for annulment at the time of consideration of the report under s 259. This would appear to be wrong: such orders are made purportedly on a suspended basis or on a basis that they are not to take effect until the expiry of the statutory period or are to lie on the table until the expiry of the statutory period. This may be convenient and may well save expense and unnecessary applications to the court, but the practice is clearly wrong in principle. The legislation specifically provides that the order itself is not to be made before the end of the specified period.[2]

1 Insolvency Act 1986, s 282. Subsection (4) applies to annulment under s 261; by virtue of Insolvency Rules 1986, r 6.212A, rr 6.206–6.212 apply to such annulments.
2 Insolvency Act 1986, s 261 (2).

9.8 Directions[1]

It may be the case that the court cannot both annul a bankruptcy order and at the same time give directions as to its further conduct. Although the Act provides that the court 'may do one or both' of the acts specified, the two acts appear to be mutually exclusive. The alternative appears to envisage that, in certain circumstances, the bankruptcy may continue, even though a voluntary arrangement has been approved. If there is the remotest possibility of this happening, this must be spelt out in the proposal so that the creditors are aware of the implications. Such a situation is, however, likely to be rare indeed, and there would have to be some very good reason. It may be that a trustee in bankruptcy has already instituted proceedings which, if the bankruptcy were to be annulled, would automatically be brought to an end. In such a case, it may be desirable for the trustee to be able to continue the proceedings and it seems, therefore, that this would be acceptable under this provision. The reality of the situation is that, if a trustee is well advanced into the administration of the estate, it is probably undesirable to seek to establish a voluntary arrangement since the principal beneficial considerations would be unlikely to be attained.

1 Insolvency Act 1986, s 261 (1) (b).

9.9 Specific Provisions in the Rules

Notice of the hearing to consider the application for an interim order must be given to the official receiver and the trustee.[1] It will always be wise for the nominee to liaise closely with the official receiver and any trustee to ascertain his attitude and any material considerations which may be unknown to the nominee.

If the debtor has already delivered a statement of affairs,[2] he need not deliver a further statement unless so required by the nominee with a view to supplementing or amplifying the formal one.[3]

The debtor is bound to inform the nominee if he has previously been adjudged bankrupt or entered into an arrangement with his creditors.[4]

1 Insolvency Rules 1986, r 5.5 (4).
3 Ie under Insolvency Act 1986, s 272 or 288.
3 Insolvency Rules 1986, r 5.8 (1).
4 Ibid, r 5.9 (2) (b).

9.10 Categories of Creditor

All the debtor's creditors in the bankruptcy will be entitled to claim in the voluntary arrangement and will be creditors for the purpose of the arrangement; this applies equally to any creditors who may have arisen since the making of the bankruptcy order. Inevitably, if such a situation exists, it is unlikely that a voluntary arrangement will be appropriate. The greatest possible care must be taken in the preparation of the proposal to ensure that the bankruptcy creditors are not prejudiced. Special consideration must also be given to the proper treatment of preferential creditors, since two separate sets of preferential creditors could arise because of the different relevant dates.[1]

1 See Insolvency Act 1986, s 386, Sch 6.

9.11 Hand-over of Property[1]

Following the approval of the voluntary arrangement, and apparently after the annulment,[2] the official receiver or trustee must do all that is required to put the supervisor into possession of the assets included in the arrangement. This will not involve an actual vesting of assets in the supervisor unless the proposal so provides.[3] On taking possession of the assets, the supervisor must discharge any balance due to the official receiver and the trustee by way of remuneration or on account of fees, costs, charges and expenses properly incurred and payable under the Act or Rules[4] and any advances made in respect of the insolvent estate, together with interest at the prescribed rate. Alternatively, the supervisor must before taking possession give to the official receiver or trustee a written undertaking to discharge any such balance out of the first realisation of assets. The official receiver or trustee has a charge on the assets included in the voluntary arrangement in respect of any sums so due until they have been discharged, subject only to the deduction from realisations by the supervisor of the proper expenses of realisation. Sums due to the official receiver take priority over those due to a trustee. The supervisor must from time to time out of realisations discharge all guarantees properly given by the official receiver or the trustee for the benefit of the estate and must pay all their expenses.

---

1 See generally Insolvency Rules 1986, r 5.21.
2 Because until then the bankruptcy still subsists, there may be a challenge and the debtor's property will still be vested in the trustee under Insolvency Act 1986, s 306.
3 Following annulment, the assets will revest in the debtor.
4 See, for example, Insolvency Rules 1986, r 5.28.

9.12 Opposition to Application for Interim Order by Official Receiver or Trustee

Nothing in the Act or Rules prohibits the official receiver or the trustee from appearing either at the hearing of the application for the interim order or the hearing for the consideration of the nominee's report for the purpose of opposing the making of the interim order or the order directing that a creditors' meeting be held. However, very careful consideration should be given before imposing any such restriction, because the court, notwithstanding the fact that it must at all times act judicially, is likely to proceed on the basis that ultimately it is the creditors who should decide whether or not the voluntary arrangement is to proceed. Nevertheless, the official receiver and the trustee will in many instances know the debtor better than the nominee. For example, they may be aware of matters which are detrimental to the likely success of a voluntary arrangement, such as the concealment of assets, uncooperative behaviour and other matters which indicate that a voluntary arrangement might be doomed to fail. It is perfectly proper for the official receiver or the trustee to point out errors, omissions or discrepancies in the proposal and other relevant documentation prepared for the proposal generally. Any opposition should be well founded, and the official receiver or trustee will be entitled to be legally represented at either hearing and may file with the court a report or affidavit in opposition. If at either hearing the court considers that there is substance in the opposition, it will normally adjourn the hearing so that proper consideration can be given to the matters raised. It does not seem that either the official receiver or trustee is entitled to attend the creditors' meeting, but the chairman would generally be unwise to prevent this.

9.13 Pending Bankruptcy Petition

Where there is a pending bankruptcy petition, the matter is Case 2 and not Case 1, as a pending petition does not result in the debtor being an undischarged bankrupt. The application for the interim order must be served on any creditor who, to the debtor's knowledge, has presented a bankruptcy petition against him.[1] This would not include a creditor who has merely served a statutory demand, but the existence of such a demand must clearly be referred to in the debtor's affidavit in support. The petitioning creditor will be entitled to attend the hearing of the application for the interim order and subsequent hearing for consideration of the nominee's report and will be entitled to put forward observations or oppose the making of the interim order.

To a large extent, the same considerations will apply as those discussed in the preceding paragraphs. Once an interim order is made, it has the effect that no bankruptcy petition relating to the debtor may be presented or proceeded with. Since an application for an interim order will normally be made to the same court as that where the bankruptcy petition is pending, it will be the practice of most courts to list the application for the interim order at the same time as the appointment for the hearing of the bankruptcy petition or the adjourned hearing thereof. The effect of approval of a voluntary arrangement on proceedings on a bankruptcy petition which have been stayed by an interim order, is that once the interim order ceases to have effect, the petition is deemed to have been dismissed, unless the court otherwise orders.[2] Since the whole of the relevant procedure is based on a creditors' meeting with no specific order of the court giving legal effect to the approval, it is by no means clear how the deemed dismissal of the petition takes effect as a judicial act. It would seem to require the act of some party or court official in order to bring the petition proceedings to an end, particularly having regard to the need to vacate the registration of the petition under the Land Charges Rules. In the circumstances, it may well be prudent to have a hearing under s 259 to seek a specific order for the dismissal of the petition and vacation of land charge entries.

---

1 Insolvency Rules 1986, r 5.5 (4) (b).
2 Insolvency Act 1986, s 260 (5).

Chapter 10

EFFECT OF BANKRUPTCY PROCEEDINGS

10.1 Introduction

Notwithstanding the approval of a voluntary arrangement, bankruptcy proceedings may be brought against the debtor in two quite different sets of circumstances. First, there may be a petition based on default.[1] Otherwise, a petition may be brought against the debtor by a creditor who either was not bound by the voluntary arrangement or whose debt arose after the voluntary arrangement was approved. In both instances, it is necessary to have regard to the effect on the voluntary arrangement of the making of a subsequent bankruptcy order.

Alternatively, a petition for a bankruptcy order may be made by the individual himself.

---

1 Insolvency Act 1986, s 276; see generally Chapter 8.

10.2 Void Transactions[1]

Where a person is adjudged bankrupt, any disposition of property made by that person in relation to which the section applies is void except to the extent that it is or was made with the consent of the court or is or was subsequently ratified by the court. This provision applies to a payment whether in cash or otherwise just as it applies to a disposition of property and, accordingly, where any payment is void, the person paid must hold the sum paid for the bankrupt as part of his estate. This provision applies to the period beginning with the day of the presentation of the petition for the bankruptcy order and ends with the vesting of the bankrupt's estate in a trustee. Saving provisions exist.

Consequently, if a supervisor presents a default petition or becomes aware of a petition having been presented by either a creditor bound or a creditor not bound, he must take the greatest possible care to ensure that the debtor does not dispose of property without the consent of the court. The application to the court for consent would be made to the court in which the bankruptcy petition is pending. The Act specifically refers to any disposition of property made by the debtor. This would not appear to affect dispositions made by the supervisor of the debtor's property; however, if the supervisor decides to dispose of the debtor's property, after having decided to petition, it would be in his best interests to do so before presenting the petition or else after obtaining the sanction of the court.

10.3 Effect of Bankruptcy Order on the Arrangement

The Act is by no means clear as to what happens to the voluntary arrangement itself if the debtor is subsequently made bankrupt. As has already been seen, there are no express provisions for a voluntary arrangement to be undone. On the face of it, the making of a bankruptcy order has no effect on the existing approved arrangement which it seems may continue and be implemented so far as is possible subject, of course, to any relevant provisions in the proposal. In short, there is nothing in the Act or Rules which provides for revocation. If, therefore, the mere making of the bankruptcy order does not revoke or avoid the arrangement, consideration must be given as to whether there is any other way, outside the specific terms of the proposal, which determines the arrangement.

Provisions relating to void transactions[1] cannot be applicable since the arrangement came into effect before the petition was presented. Learned authors[2] have suggested that the arrangement might in the subsequent bankruptcy be attacked as being a transaction at an undervalue, a voidable preference or a transaction in fraud of creditors, but this seems an extremely remote possibility. The court's general power to review and rescind its orders[3] will be of no assistance, since the very essence of an arrangement is that the approval or agreement takes effect without any order of the court, so there is no court order to be reviewed or rescinded.[4]

It is possible to conceive of an argument that the arrangement, being a contract, could be set aside at common law on the grounds of misrepresentation or inadequate disclosure or as a result of a fundamental breach of contract in relation to its terms. However, as has been rightly pointed out,[5] it would not seem possible to harmonise such a remedy or remedies with the statutory structure nor, indeed, would it seem possible for some creditors, but not others, to seek to set the arrangement aside on such grounds.

It might be argued that the very point of a default petition[6] is to bring the arrangement to an end. The logic of such argument is understandable but not clear. Whilst the argument is supported by the statutory provision that, where a bankruptcy order is made on a petition by a supervisor or a creditor bound,[7] any expenses properly incurred as expenses of the administration of the voluntary arrangement in question shall be a first charge on the bankrupt's estate, this cannot in any sense be regarded as conclusive, despite the fact that it implies that the voluntary arrangement comes to an end. Certainly it seems that this is what is envisaged by the subsection. This provision is, however, the only statutory provision which seems to suggest that the arrangement in some way or another becomes void or statutorily set aside or otherwise terminated.

The general situation is clearly unsatisfactory and must await judicial consideration. Until then, it would be sensible for the supervisor in such a situation to make an application to the court for directions. He should serve either the official receiver or any trustee in bankruptcy who is appointed and it would seem that the court would then be able to determine on a practical basis such matters as fail to be resolved. What is manifestly clear is that, until this uncertainty has been resolved, it is essential for the proposal to contain specific provision for the procedure in the event of a supervening bankruptcy[8] so that all concerned will know exactly what is to happen and what their position will be.

---

1   Insolvency Act 1986, s 284; see para 10.2 above.
2   *Muir Hunter on Personal Insolvency* (Stevens, 1987), paras 3-118, 3-119.
3   1986 Act, s 375 (1).
4   Except possibly the interim order itself but, since the arrangement takes its authority from the creditors' meeting, this would seem to be a futile move.
5   *Muir Hunter on Personal Insolvency* (Stevens, 1987), paras 3-118, 3-119.
6   1986 Act, s 276; see generally Chapter 8.
7   Ibid, s 264 (1) (c).
8   But such provisions cannot bind a third party.

10.4 Bankrupt's Estate

Difficulties may arise for the creditors in the arrangement if the debtor is subsequently adjudged bankrupt and more liabilities have been incurred without the creation of further assets since the arrangement came into existence; in such a case, the only assets available are those in the arrangement, and the creditors' return by way of dividend will be much less. It seems that this can be overcome by a provision in the proposal to the effect that the debtor holds his assets on trust for the creditors of the arrangement. This would appear to take those assets outside the bankrupt's estate for the purpose of his bankruptcy and leave them available for the arrangement creditors.[1] This is another reason for presupposing that it is conceivable for an arrangement to survive subsequent bankruptcy.

---

1   Insolvency Act 1986, s 283 (3) (a).

10.5 Preferential Creditors[1]

For the purpose of an individual voluntary arrangement, the relevant date (being the date which determines the existence and amount of a preferential debt) is, in relation to a debtor who is not an undischarged bankrupt, the date of the interim order.[2] In relation to a bankrupt, subject to where an interim receiver has been appointed, the relevant date is the date of the making of the bankruptcy order. It is clear, therefore, that two categories of preferential creditors can arise, one of which is relevant to the voluntary arrangement and the other to the subsequent bankruptcy. If the voluntary arrangement preferential creditors are not protected, they may be seriously prejudiced by the making of a subsequent bankruptcy order in that, in the bankruptcy, if that is where their claim falls to be dealt with, they may lose their preferential status and rank equally with the unsecured creditors and behind a new category of preferential creditor. To protect the preferential creditors' position, and indeed that of the unsecured creditors, in the arrangement, it is desirable for the supervisor to settle, agree and pay the preferential creditors as early as possible. If a bankruptcy petition is presented it would seem possible for the supervisor to make an application to the court for leave to pay those creditors subject to there being any question of the assets being held on trust; in a proper case, the court may accede to such an application.

---

1 See Insolvency Act 1986, s 386, Sch 6 for definition.
2 Ibid, s 387.

10.6 Unsecured Creditors

If a bankruptcy order is made and there is no question of the voluntary arrangement remaining in existence or the assets being held on trust for the arrangement creditors, it seems that the remaining assets in the arrangement form part of the bankrupt's estate for the general purposes of his bankruptcy and the unsecured creditors in the arrangement will be entitled to prove in the subsequent bankruptcy, although they will rank equally with any further unsecured creditors who exist outside the arrangement.

10.7 Appointment of Trustee

Where the supervisor petitions for bankruptcy, he may seek to be appointed trustee of the debtor's estate. The petition must contain a request for the appointment of the supervisor as trustee, and the person whose appointment is sought must, not less than two days before the day appointed for hearing of the petition, file in court a report including particulars of: (a) the date on which he gave written notification to creditors bound by the arrangement of his intention to seek such appointment as trustee, such date to be at least 10 days before the day on which the report is filed; and (b) details of any response from creditors to that notice, including any objections to his appointment.[1]

---

1 See generally Insolvency Rules 1986, r 6.10 (6).

10.8 Proceedings on a Debtor's Petition for Bankruptcy

10.8.1 General

A petition for a bankruptcy order may be made by the individual himself.[1] Such a petition may be presented to the court only on the grounds that the debtor is unable to pay his debts.[2] The petition must be accompanied by a statement of the debtor's affairs containing particulars as to his creditors, debts, other liabilities and assets.[3]

The petition will be heard almost at once and may lead the court to apply special statutory provisions which may, in turn, lead the debtor to enter into a voluntary arrangement with his creditors. The court must not make a bankruptcy order if it appears:

(a) that if a bankruptcy order were made the aggregate amount of the bankruptcy debts, so far as unsecured, would be less than the small bankruptcies level;[4]

(b) that if a bankruptcy order were made the value of the bankrupt's estate would be equal to or more than the minimum amount;[5]

(c) that within the period of five years ending with the presentation of the petition the debtor has neither been adjudged bankrupt nor made a composition with his creditors in satisfaction of his debts or a scheme of arrangement for his affairs;[6] and

(d) that it would be appropriate to appoint a person to prepare a report under section 274.[7]

---

1 Insolvency Act 1986, s 264 (1) (b).
2 Ibid, s 272 (1).
3 Ibid, s 272 (2).
4 Ibid, s 273 (1) (a); the 'small bankruptcies level', which may be altered periodically, is presently £20,000: Insolvency Proceedings (Monetary Limits) Order 1986, SI 1986/1996.
5 1986 Act, s 273 (1) (b); the 'minimum amount' is £2,000: SI 1986/1996.
6 1986 Act, s 273 (1) (c).
7 Ibid, s 273 (1) (d).

10.8.2 *The four conditions*

The four conditions set out in the preceding paragraph must be satisfied before bringing the special provisions into operation.[1] The first three are objective and the fourth is subjective, in the sense that the court has to consider the appropriateness of appointing a person to prepare a report. There are no guidelines. In the absence of authority, it would seem that the test to be applied by the court is whether the debtor and the creditors would benefit from a voluntary arrangement as opposed to a bankruptcy.[2]

At this initial stage, since the petition is brought by the debtor, there is no involvement by the creditors, and they will only be consulted if a meeting of creditors is held. There is no question of creditors coming into the proceedings at this stage either to support or oppose, which is in marked contrast to the provisions relating to a creditors' petition.[3]

---

1 They are clearly cumulative, ie all four must be satisfied.
2 The general 'balancing' consideration which applies to all arrangements.
3 See Insolvency Rules 1986, r 6.23.

10.8.3 *The report*

Once the four conditions are satisfied, the court must appoint a qualified insolvency practitioner to prepare a report[1] and, subject to the statutory provisions relating to modifications,[2] to act in relation to any voluntary arrangement to which the report relates, either as trustee or otherwise,[3] for the purpose of supervising its implementation.

The nature of the report is prescribed.[4] The person appointed must enquire into the debtor's affairs and, within such period as the court allows, submit a report to the court, stating whether the debtor is willing for the purposes of Part VIII of the 1986 Act to make a proposal for a voluntary arrangement.[5]

The report, if it states that the debtor is willing, must also state:[6]

(a) whether in the opinion of the person reporting a meeting of the debtor's creditors should be summoned to consider the proposal; and

(b) if, in that person's opinion, such a meeting should be summoned, the date on which and time and place at which he proposes the meeting should be held.

---

1 Insolvency Act 1986, s 273 (2).
2 Ibid, s 258 (3).
3 Ie to act as supervisor.
4 Ibid, s 274.
5 Ibid, s 274 (1).
6 Ibid, s 274 (2).

10.8.4 *Consideration of report*

When the court considers the report, it may without any application make an interim order if it thinks that it is appropriate to do so for the purpose of facilitating the consideration and implementation of the proposal or, if it thinks it would be inappropriate to make such an order, to make a bankruptcy order.[1]

Any interim order so made ceases to have effect at the end of such period as the court specifies so that the proposal may be considered by the creditors in accordance with the provisions of Part VIII.

Where it has been reported to the court under these provisions that a meeting of the debtor's creditors should be summoned, the person making the report must, unless the court otherwise directs, summon the meeting for the time, date and place which he has proposed in his report. The meeting is then deemed to have been summoned under s 257 and the relevant provisions of the Act apply, as do ss 258 to 263.[2]

---

1 Insolvency Act 1986, s 274 (3).
2 Ibid, s 274 (5).

10.8.5 *Effect of bankruptcy petition*

The short effect of these provisions, if a voluntary arrangement comes into being, is to bring the bankruptcy proceedings to an end and convert them into a voluntary arrangement.[1]

---

1 The purpose of these provisions is to allow the court, on hearing a debtor's petition, to investigate the desirability and possibility of a voluntary arrangement. Debtors may file petitions without being aware of the provisions of Part VIII of the 1986 Act.

Chapter 11

MATRIMONIAL CONSIDERATIONS

11.1 Introduction

Financial difficulties will often lead to matrimonial difficulties and vice versa. Voluntary arrangements can, therefore, be affected by matrimonial proceedings pending at the time the proposal is prepared, and also by matrimonial proceedings that arise after the acceptance of the proposal by creditors. Furthermore, due consideration has to be given to the position of the debtor's spouse, whether or not matrimonial proceedings arise and, in particular, as regards the position concerning the matrimonial home.

11.2 Position of the Spouse Generally

Even if there are no matrimonial proceedings and the debtor and spouse are in agreement, the position of the debtor's spouse must be considered at the time of preparation of the proposal. If the proposal includes provision for the realisation of jointly owned assets, the nominee should ensure that the spouse will co-operate and give the appropriate consents. For reasons which are discussed below, the spouse should seek independent advice. As assets that belong beneficially to the spouse cannot form part of the debtor's estate for the purpose of bankruptcy, there is no reason for such assets to be included in the proposal unless the spouse specifically agrees. This the spouse might be willing to do, after taking proper advice, for the purpose of facilitating the proposal and avoiding the bankruptcy of the debtor. The spouse must, therefore, be fully advised. He or she must be aware of their rights and the nature of any commitment or obligation they are to enter into. Whilst financial pressures can be acute within the context of a marriage, the spouse should not be put under pressure or coercion.

In some cases, it may be better, from the family's point of view, for the debtor to enter into bankruptcy rather than a voluntary arrangement, and each case must be considered on its own merits. Personal considerations may sometimes outweigh financial ones. If a voluntary arrangement is likely to place on the family too great a strain and in itself lead to matrimonial proceedings, it would seem desirable for the proposal to be taken no further. Accordingly, the nominee has to have regard not only to financial but also to personal circumstances and considerations. The nominee should never take for granted what the debtor may say to him about the co-operation and concurrence of the spouse, and should always seek and obtain independent verification of the attitude of the spouse, especially where the proposal contains a commitment on the part of the spouse. In certain circumstances, having regard to the nature of liabilities, it may be necessary for the spouse also to enter into a voluntary arrangement. There can be no objection, as such, for a nominee dealing with both proposals, which should be separate documents,[1] but clearly he should be aware of any possible conflict of interest.

1 See para 2.3 above.

11.3 Matrimonial Proceedings Pending at the Time of Preparation of the Proposal and Application for the Interim Order

The nominee should seek to ascertain the nature and extent of such proceedings and the extent to which they may affect the debtor's assets. The effect of an interim order would appear to operate as a stay in respect of matrimonial proceedings which concern the debtor's property.[1] This would not affect proceedings on a petition itself for a decree of divorce or matrimonial proceedings relating to the custody of children. Generally, claims that might be brought by a spouse against a debtor for a matrimonial order would not seem to be affected in the long term, as it is difficult to see how the spouse could be constituted a creditor for the purpose of being bound by the approval. If the spouse is in fact a creditor, the proposal is entitled to treat that spouse in exactly the same way as if the debtor were in bankruptcy. The spouse cannot then complain of unfair prejudice. Otherwise, the spouse's claims would appear in general terms to be regarded as proprietary rights putting him or her on the same footing as a landlord or secured creditor.[2]

Matrimonial proceedings which affect the debtor's property are likely to have material effect on the proposal, and there will in most instances be such a degree of uncertainty as to the outcome of matrimonial proceedings that it will be difficult, if not impossible, to frame a proposal which has any reasonable degree of certainty.[3]

1 Insolvency Act 1986, s 252 (2) (b).
2 For the position as regards secured creditors and landlords see ibid, s 258 (4) and *Re Naeem (No 18 of 1988)* [1990] 1 WLR 48 respectively.
3 The powers of matrimonial courts are discretionary and wide. A spouse whose rights are purported to be restricted may be able to challenge the decision approving the proposal under the 1986 Act, s 262; see generally paras 6.3.1–6.3.11 above.

11.4 Matrimonial Proceedings Arising after an Arrangement has been Approved

The extent to which any such proceedings materially affect the proposal will depend, first, on the nature of the proceedings and, secondly, on the terms of the proposal. If the proceedings are merely by way of a petition for a decree of divorce or custody, these proceedings will have no material effect. Likewise, proceedings which are limited purely to maintenance for either the spouse or children are likely to have no material effect, subject to whatever provision is made in the proposal as to the application of the debtor's income for the period of the duration of the arrangement.[1] Proceedings which affect other assets of the debtor will almost certainly be material. For the reasons previously mentioned, the spouse cannot be precluded from bringing such proceedings. If the proposal purports to bar her from bringing such proceedings, it is considered that such a bar would be unenforceable. Such proceedings are, therefore, likely to result in either default or failure.[2] This in itself is likely to have an adverse effect on the spouse, who will need to be advised as to the consequences for him or her of taking proceedings that jeopardise the voluntary arrangement with the possible result of the bankruptcy of the debtor.

---

1 See para 3.2.13 above.
2 See generally Chapter 8.

11.5 Matrimonial Home

11.5.1 General

In personal insolvency, the debtor's beneficial interest in the matrimonial home will often comprise the single most important asset. Before the Insolvency Act 1986 came into force the courts were asked on a number of occasions to adjudicate on the conflicting interests between the bankrupt's creditors as represented by the trustee on the one hand and the co-owning spouse on the other hand; the general effect of the decided authorities was that the creditors' interests prevailed unless there were exceptional circumstances.[1]

The 1986 Act has introduced a framework of statutory provisions[2] which essentially covers three quite separate situations:

(1) where the legal estate to the property is vested solely in the debtor;[3]
(2) where the property is jointly owned;[4]
(3) in either event, where the property is occupied by a person under the age of 18.[5]

The general effect of the statutory provisions is to confer on the non-debtor party certain rights of occupation which can only be varied or terminated by order of the court. Applications for possession and sale have to be made to the bankruptcy court, and the court has to take into account all relevant circumstances.[6]

Where the application, which would be made by the trustee, is made after the end of the period of one year beginning with the first vesting of the bankrupt's estate in a nominee, the court must assume, unless the circumstances of the case are exceptional, that the interests of the bankrupt's creditors outweigh all other considerations.[7] Having regard to the pre-1986 authorities, it seems that there will be few cases where the interests of the creditors are outweighed by any others.

Without judicial authority to assist, there can only be speculation as to the circumstances in which much other interests might arise. They may possibly include a situation where the house in question has, at public or charitable expense, been specifically adapted to cater for the needs of a severely handicapped child. Other special circumstances might include the fact that the equity arising in the hands of the trustee would not produce any funds for creditors, as opposed to the administration expenses of the estate; alternatively, all the creditors may be large commercial institutions who could not argue that, by not receiving any dividend that might be payable, they would suffer financial hardship. However, such a proposition is entirely speculative.

The spouse should always be given an opportunity to acquire the debtor's beneficial interest in the property. The 12-month rule appears to exist so as to mitigate the immediate hardship to the debtor's family of the bankruptcy and to afford the debtor's spouse and family some opportunity to settle their affairs and lives generally prior to having to face up to a sale of the property.

---

1 See, for example, *Boydell v Gillespie* (1970) 216 EG 1505; *Re Solomon* [1966] 3 All ER 255, [1967] Ch 573, [1967] 2 WLR 172; *Re Turner* [1975] 1 All ER 5, [1974] 1 WLR 1556; *Re Bailey* [1977] 2 All ER 26; [1977] 1 WLR 278; *Re Holliday* [1980] 3 All ER 385, [1981] Ch 405, [1981] 2 WLR 996, CA; *Re Lowrie* [1981] 3 All ER 353. Although not reported until 1990, *Re Citro* [1990] 3 All ER 952, was an 'old Act' case and seems to imply, per Nourse LJ at p 963G, that the courts applying 'the new law' will very much follow the approach of the 'old Act' cases.
2 Insolvency Act 1986, ss 336, 337.
3 Ibid, s 336 (1), (2).
4 Ibid, s 333 (3).
5 Ibid, s 337.
6 See ibid, ss 336 (4), 337 (5).
7 Ibid, s 336 (5), (6).

11.5.2 Application to voluntary arrangements

The considerations stated above in relation to bankruptcy apply equally to a voluntary arrangement, in the sense that the creditors should not, without good reason, be expected to receive from the property anything less than would be received if the debtor's affairs were to be administered in bankruptcy. It follows, therefore, that the proposal should generally provide for the sale of the house, although a provision preventing sale for a period of 12 months from the date of approval would not be unreasonable. Likewise, the debtor's spouse should be given an opportunity to acquire the debtor's interest.

In some circumstances, the debtor's spouse may be willing to concur in the proposal by granting to the creditors an enhanced benefit as compared to that which would accrue in bankruptcy.

This might include:

(1) an earlier sale than would be the case in bankruptcy;[1]
(2) the waiver of exoneration rights;[2]
(3) a contribution to the arrangement of part of her entitlement in the proceeds of sale.

If the debtor's spouse is to make such a contribution, then it is clear that she must be given the fullest possible independent advice as to her position and rights.

---

1 Because of the '12-month rule' discussed in the preceding paragraph.
2 See para 11.6 below.

11.5.3 Enforcement of the sale of the property

In bankruptcy, an application is made to the bankruptcy court under either the Matrimonial Homes Act 1983, s 1 or the Law of Property Act 1925, s 30.[1]

The relevant considerations are discussed above. In a voluntary arrangement, the question of enforcement should not arise as such, although it may do so in two sets of circumstances.

First, the debtor himself may have a change of heart and refuse to concur in the sale; this would clearly constitute default.[2] It might, depending on the circumstances, be inappropriate to take the matter any further; alternatively, it is arguable that a supervisor could be constituted in the proposal as 'a person interested', within the meaning of s 30 of the 1925 Act, and could make an application directly.[3]

Secondly, the spouse may have a change of heart. This could be connected with matrimonial proceedings, which would greatly complicate the situation, or it could be for other reasons. In such a case, the debtor himself would have to make an application to the court and, if he did not do so, he would be likely to fall foul of the default provisions.

A material consideration in the preparation of the proposal and in the advice given to the debtor is the risk that the debtor and his spouse may take in agreeing voluntarily to sell the property. If they are able to arrange alternative accommodation, no problem would arise. However, if they are looking for local authority accommodation, there is a substantial risk that the local authority will consider that they have rendered themselves voluntarily homeless. Accordingly, it may be necessary to build into the proposal a provision whereby the supervisor is empowered to take proceedings to secure the possession of the property. There is still the risk that the local authority would regard this as a sham, but the consideration of homeless persons generally is outside the scope of this work.

---

1 Insolvency Act 1986, ss 336 (3), 337 (4).
2 See generally Chapter 8.
3 There is as yet no authority for this proposition.

11.6 Other Considerations as regards the Spouse

In addition to the question of whether or not the spouse should agree a sale and whether or not he or she should make available to the arrangement part of his or her beneficial interest in the property, two principal considerations arise.

First, there is the question of quantifying the spouse's beneficial interest in the property. Any such considerations will be governed outside the context of discretionary matrimonial powers unless, of course, matrimonial proceedings are pending. If the property is vested in joint names, it seems unlikely that the spouse will be able to establish a beneficial interest greater than 50 per cent. If the property is vested solely in the debtor's name, general principles of trust law will apply and, if it is to be conceded that the spouse has a beneficial interest, this must be set out in detail in the proposal and a full explanation given. It is essential that a matter such as this be resolved and agreed between the debtor and his spouse prior to the presentation of the proposal to the creditors.[1]

Secondly, the question of exoneration may be relevant. In essence, this arises where jointly owned property is charged to secure the debt of only one of the joint owners. If this is the case, then under the doctrine and in the absence of any evidence suggesting that the parties intend otherwise, the other joint owner (in the position of a surety) is entitled not only as between the two joint owners but also as between himself and the creditor to have the secured indebtedness discharged so far as possible out of the debtor's interest in the property, thereby enhancing the value of the other joint owner's share of the property.[2] This may in some cases have a dramatic effect on the debtor's actual beneficial entitlement in the property. This situation will most commonly arise where a second mortgage is granted to a bank to secure the debtor's business liability. Sometimes it is necessary to examine the relevant bank account in detail to ensure that the whole of the liability is genuinely attributable to the business.

The debtor's spouse should not be permitted to concede a claim in exoneration without full legal advice. In appropriate cases, she may be prepared to concede this so as to enhance the funds available in the arrangement. If this is the case, the general principles discussed before most clearly apply.

---

1 See generally *Re Gorman* [1990] 1 All ER 717.
2 For a modern application of this doctrine see *Re Pittortou* [1985] 1 All ER 285. See also *Re Woodstock* unreported, November 1979 where an 'exoneration' claim was refused on the basis that the wife's claim related in fact to a debt.

11.7 Debts due to Spouses

The Act[1] as it relates to bankruptcy provides for the postponement of debts due to spouses. Such debts rank in priority after preferential and other unsecured liabilities. It would seem equitable to apply similar provisions to a voluntary arrangement.

---

1 Insolvency Act 1986, s 329.

11.8 Provable Claims

The Rules[1] provide that, in bankruptcy, all claims by creditors are provable whether they are present or future, certain or contingent, ascertained or sounding only in damages. In bankruptcy, neither a fine imposed for an offence nor any obligation arising under an order made in family or domestic proceedings is provable, nor any obligation arising under a confiscation order made under the Drug Trafficking Offences Act 1986, s 1. The terms 'fine', 'domestic proceedings' and 'family proceedings' have the meanings given by the Insolvency Act 1986, s 281 (8) (which applies the Magistrates' Courts Act 1980 and the Matrimonial and Family Proceedings Act 1984). There cannot, therefore, be any objection to treating such debts in similar fashion in a voluntary arrangement. On the other hand, there is nothing, on the face of it, to prevent such debts being allowed to be proved; if this is to be the case, however, the creditors would need to be satisfied that they are not prejudiced. To do otherwise might result in a successful challenge. A spouse is an associate.

---

1 Insolvency Rules 1986, r 12.15.

Chapter 12

VALUE ADDED TAX AND OTHER TAX CONSIDERATIONS

12.1 Introduction

Considerations relating to the Inland Revenue and HM Customs and Excise are always likely to be important in the construction of the proposal. Detailed consideration of matters relating to taxation are outside the scope of this work and reference should be made to specialist text books on the subject.

12.2 Status as Preferential Creditors

Certain debts due to the Inland Revenue and HM Customs and Excise are preferential debts.[1] For the purpose of s 387, "the relevant date" in determining a preferential claim is the date of the interim order. However, where the debtor is an undischarged bankrupt, the relevant date is the date on which any interim receiver was first appointed after the presentation of the bankruptcy petition and, in cases where there is no interim receiver, the date of the making of the bankruptcy order.

As discussed elsewhere,[2] the rights of preferential creditors cannot be altered without their agreement. This is unlikely ever to be the case as regards either the Inland Revenue or HM Customs and Excise, unless the proposal is one where the entire fund available for creditors is to be provided by a third party or comprises assets which would not be available at all in bankruptcy.

---

1 Insolvency Act 1986, s 387, Sch 6.
2 See (c)(i) at page 20 above.

12.3 Attitude of the Taxation Authorities

As regards the Inland Revenue, consideration of proposed voluntary arrangements is a matter for the Enforcement Office and not the local collector or inspector. The Revenue will not be motivated purely by commercial considerations and the extent of the estimated dividend. The Revenue will take into account "the way in which the taxpayer has attended to his tax obligations, the level of uncertainty over assets and liabilities and whether a voluntary arrangement is the appropriate course for the Revenue to approve as a creditor". The debtor's history will, accordingly, be relevant. If any investigation is in progress or likely, the Revenue is unlikely to support the proposal. There is, however, no obligation on the Revenue to give reasons for its refusal to support a proposal. In certain cases, the Enforcement Office may conclude that the greater investigatory power in bankruptcy and the general effect of bankruptcy proceedings, for example in determining any trading activities, take precedence over pure commercial or economic considerations touching on dividend prospects.

Similar considerations are generally adopted by HM Customs and Excise. Voluntary arrangement cases are not dealt with by local offices but are administered by a specialist team in Bootle.

12.4 VAT Considerations

12.4.1 Trading

Although it appears that HM Customs and Excise will not regard the supervisor as being responsible for accounting for VAT either during the period from which he was first involved as nominee or as regards the period from the date of the creditors' meeting, the supervisor should nevertheless ensure that proper records are kept, returns made and VAT fully accounted for. If trading continues, the position regarding VAT should be specified in the proposal so that HM Customs and Excise has no doubt as to what is being proposed and the basis on which trading is to continue.

12.4.2 Disposal of assets

Where the payment of VAT is involved, the supervisor must account for VAT arising on behalf of the debtor. Accordingly, it is important for the supervisor to maintain strict control over the disposal of assets in all circumstances.

12.4.3 Set-off

HM Customs and Excise considered previously that it was entitled to handle a refund under one accounting period for VAT so as to offset it against a payment in the previous accounting period.[1] This rule was applied, notwithstanding the fact that the commencement of an insolvency had intervened. Accordingly, this had the effect of making HM Customs and Excise pre-preferential if the supervisor were to make a repayment claim and there were either preferential or non-preferential VAT liabilities for periods prior to the commencement of the insolvency. The position now adopted by HM Customs and Excise as regards individual voluntary arrangements is to apply the same rules as relate to compulsory or voluntary liquidations. This has the effect that any repayment claims arising after the start of the arrangement will be due for payment in full, notwithstanding the fact that HM Customs and Excise may have, or have had, a claim either as a preferential or non-preferential creditor. However, if at the date of the interim order there is both a VAT liability and a refund due in respect of separate accounting periods, HM Customs and Excise is entitled to apply set-off.

---

1 Finance Act 1988, s 21.

12.4.4 Bad debt relief

This is always a matter of importance to creditors. Before the Finance Act 1990 came into force, creditors in a voluntary arrangement were able to obtain bad debt relief.[1] This provision in fact did not relate to creditors in a company voluntary arrangement. The Finance Act 1990 introduced a new regime which is not dependent on the insolvency process.[2] The principal requirement is that a business is entitled to bad debt relief where the debt is more than one year old and it has been written off. Accordingly, creditors in both individual and corporate voluntary arrangements are now able to obtain bad debt relief, provided they have written off the irrecoverable portion of their debt and have allowed one year to elapse. Where the bad debt accrued prior to 26 July 1990, the old regime applies and the supervisor will normally supply the creditor with the appropriate form to reclaim the VAT element on the bad debt. Where a creditor receives a dividend, he must account to HM Customs and Excise for the VAT portion of that dividend.

---

1 Value Added Tax Act 1983, s 22 (2) (a).
2 Finance Act 1990, s 11 as amended by Finance Act 1991.

12.4.5 *VAT returns*
If VAT returns are outstanding as at the date of the creditors' meeting, the proposal should provide for these to be completed and lodged with HM Customs and Excise within a specified period of time. If the proposal does not contain such a provision, HM Customs and Excise, in the event of them supporting the proposal, is almost certain to make it a condition of its support that such a provision be included by way of modification to the proposal.

12.4.6 *Registration*
HM Customs and Excise has no right to cancel the debtor's registration because of the arrangement and, accordingly, the same registration will continue.

12.5 Other Tax Considerations

12.5.1 *General*
In order to agree tax liabilities provable in the arrangement either as pre-ferential or unsecured, liabilities should be agreed as at the date of the interim order. This will often be difficult where there is an absence of returns and outstanding assessments which may often bear little resemblance to the debtor's actual tax liability position. Nominees should always treat with caution estimates given by debtors as to their tax liability and should always secure early confirmation of the position from the Inland Revenue. Where appropriate, the assistance of the debtor's accountants should also be sought. Fortunately, since the vast majority of nominees and supervisors are ac-countants, they will have available to them within their own firms specialist tax departments able to deal with and answer all points arising on taxation.

A conflict could arise between the debtor and supervisor, possibly in relation to capital gains tax roll-over relief. If, for example, the debtor sold a hotel prior to the interim order and then bought another, he would 'roll over' the gain on the second acquisition. If after the interim order the second hotel is sold, there arises a post interim order liability which must be taken into account.

Another problem can arise where there are outstanding accounts. It may be uneconomical to complete them and the best solution may be to agree a "no loss, no gain" situation. The danger is that, if the arrangement envisages ongoing trading, any losses are not then available for the benefit of the future trading.

It must also be remembered that accounting periods are not terminated by virtue of the interim order, so a single accounting period might straddle the date of the interim order.

12.5.2 Capital gains tax
Any liability for capital gains tax as at the date of the interim order is not preferential. The principal point arises on the liability for capital gains tax on assets disposed of during the course of the administration of the arrangement. It is arguable that the supervisor acquires a responsibility as a quasi-agent of the debtor. If there is merit in this argument, then two points clearly arise. First, the proposal must set out precisely who is to be responsible for the realisation of assets and the payment of tax thereon. The Inland Revenue, if a creditor, will of course see the proposal and will be bound by its provisions, but this will not be the case if the Inland Revenue is not a creditor at the date of the creditors' meeting. Secondly, the supervisor must ensure that all funds realised come into his hands so that he can be responsible for the calculation and agreement of tax arising and can be satisfied that it is paid in due course. This will sometimes mean that the arrangement has to be left open for longer than might otherwise be envisaged. As regards capital gains tax if, for example, the interim order is made in January of one year and a disposal made in September of the same year, the tax will not become payable until 1 December of the following year.

12.5.3 Personal tax
Income tax arising on the debtor's income during the period of the arrangement will remain the liability of the debtor alone. Where the debtor's income is subject to PAYE, this will normally give rise to no particular difficulties. Where the debtor remains self-employed, the Inland Revenue may regard the future with some suspicion. The supervisor should not assume any responsibility, either expressly or by implication, for the debtor's tax affairs other than as expressly provided for in the proposal.

12.5.4 Future PAYE liability
Where the proposal envisages the continuation of trading, the debtor may retain staff. Such staff will be subject to the PAYE regime, and the Enforcement Office is likely to require the supervisor to ensure that PAYE is correctly operated during this period. Furthermore, the Enforcement Office will generally insist that proper arrangement is made to pay all taxation liabilities which result from the proposal.

12.5.5 Tax consequences generally
The question sometimes arises, as regards a creditor, whether, by entering into a voluntary arrangement and agreeing to be bound by it, the creditor permits a

sum of money due to him to be released. This will largely depend on the terms of the proposal and the dividend prospect. If there is any question of such a release, the point arises as to whether the amount so released falls to be taxed as a trading receipt arising in the period in which the release is effected by the debtor. This only arises where for tax purposes, the profits or gains of a trade deduction has previously been allowed for the debt. The creditor may not necessarily be entitled to a deduction on the release of the debt. It may be the case that the funds available for creditors are restricted to make provision for the tax due on the debt released, unless the debtor has trading losses sufficient to absorb the deemed trading income. This could put the arrangement in great danger. Any taxation liability resulting from any such deemed income will not fall to be discharged as an expense of the arrangement but will be added to the debtor's liabilities, and this may be material in some arrangements. The Enforcement Office is unlikely to support any proposal which does not make provision for any liabilities arising from the arrangement to be paid.

For creditors who wish to claim a reduction in respect of their "released portions of their debt," a deduction may only be allowed for bad debts proved to be such and doubtful debts to the extent that they are estimated to be bad. This means that the mere inability of a creditor to recover part of what is due to him may not be sufficient for obtaining a deduction for that part. It seems that the Inland Revenue takes the view that the allowable write-off cannot exceed the amount which would have been irrecoverable in a bankruptcy. The position is by no means clear. It seems that the fact of an approved arrangement cannot in itself constitute a formal waiver. Otherwise, the position of an assenting creditor might be different from that of a dissenting creditor who nevertheless finds himself bound because of the 75 per cent majority.

Appendix 1

DRAFT PROPOSAL AND RELATED MATERIALS

		Page
DRAFT PROPOSAL (AND REPORT OF THE NOMINEE)		125

STANDARD CONDITIONS

1, 2	Interpretation	136
3	Approval	136
4	Warranty	136
5.1	Effect of Approval (General)	136
5.2	Duration	137
5.3	Completion	137
5.4	Default Petition	137
6	General Power to Call Meetings	137
7.1	Debtor's Obligations (to execute deeds etc)	137
7.2	Declaration of Trust	138
7.3	General Obligations	138
7.4	After-acquired Assets	138
8	Continuation of Business	138
9	Taxation	139
10	Third Parties	139
11	Supervisor's Powers	140
12	Application of Bankruptcy Provisions	140
13	Wrongdoing	140
14	Completion of the Arrangement	141
15	Failure	141
16	Directions	142
17	Expenditure on Assets	142
18	Agreement of claims	142
19	Priority of Payments	143
20	Payments to Creditors	143
21	Bank Account Costs and Expenses	143
22	Health of Debtor	144
23	Termination	144
24	Vacancy in Office	145
25	Ambiguity	145
26	Amendment	146

SPECIFIC PROVISIONS FOR INCLUSION IN PROPOSAL

	Introductory Comment	147
1–4	Assets, Trust Property etc	148
5–7	Valuation – Freehold	149
8	Sale of Property – Co-owner's Concurrence	149
9	Leasehold – Nil Value	149
10	Stock – Subject to Possible Reservation of Title Claims	150
11–14	Excluded Assets	150
15, 16	Third Party Obligations	151
17, 18	Secured Liability	151
19	Preferential Creditor – To be treated Pari Passu with Unsecured Creditors	151
20	Secured Creditor – Possession Order	152
21	Landlord – Forfeiture – Surrender	152
22	Lease – Surrender	152
23	Claims – Contingent and Disputed	152
24–26	Undervalue	153
27	Preference	154
28	Existing Bankruptcy to Continue	154
29	Guarantee	155
30	Duration – Extension of Time	155
31–33	Distributions	155
34	Trading – Further Credit – Guarantee to be Given	156
35	Further Credit	156
36	Book Debts	156
37	Building Contract	157
38	Shares in Private Company	157
39	Freehold Property – Jointly Owned – Third Party Interest	157
40, 41	Life Policies	158
42, 43	Motor Car – Sale – Personalised Number Plate	158
44	After-acquired Assets	158
45	After-acquired Income	159
46	Standard Conditions	159
47	Supervision Powers	159
48	Supervisor's Liability	160
49	Assets held on Trust	161
50	Power of Attorney	161

DRAFT PROPOSAL (AND REPORT OF THE NOMINEE)

IN THE   COUNTY COURT   No   of 19

IN BANKRUPTCY

RE:

PROPOSAL FOR VOLUNTARY ARRANGEMENT WITH CREDITORS PURSUANT TO PART VIII OF THE INSOLVENCY ACT 1986[1]

INTRODUCTION

This is the proposal of   of   for the purposes of Part VIII of the Insolvency Act 1986 and the Insolvency Rules 1986 as amended. As appears from the summaries of assets and liabilities annexed hereto as appendices 1 and 2 respectively and also from the estimated outcome and comparison shown as appendix 3, it is clear that I am insolvent[2] in that I am unable to pay my debts as and when they fall due and my liabilities, including prospective and contingent liabilities, exceed my assets.

In the circumstances there are two alternatives available to me. I may either petition for my own bankruptcy or seek to enter into a voluntary arrangement with my creditors.[3]

For the reasons set out below, I seek a voluntary arrangement which I believe will be acceptable to my creditors:[4]

1.[5]

2.

3. I believe that a voluntary arrangement will give rise to a more orderly quicker and more beneficial realisation of other assets.[6]

4. The administrative costs and charges of a voluntary arrangement are likely to be less than in a bankruptcy, as demonstrated in Appendix 3, and consequently there is likely to be a greater return to unsecured creditors.[7]

5. I will avoid the personal consequences of bankruptcy.[8]

PERSONAL HISTORY[9]

ASSETS[10]

Appendix 1 contains full particulars of my assets with an estimate of their respective values. The jointly owned freehold property has been professionally valued by Messrs   but other assets have not. A copy of the valuation is available for inspection.[11]

(1) The House

It will be seen that there is at present a small margin of equity in the freehold property. It remains to be seen, having regard to the current state of the property market and the level of secured indebtedness, whether there may in fact be a short fall as regards the secured creditor. If there should be a short fall upon completion of the sale then this will constitute an unsecured liability for the purpose of dividend. If the property is sold within the next six months then it is likely that there will be a margin of equity, one half of which will be available for purposes of this arrangement. The property is currently being offered for sale by Messrs   at the price of £
The figure shown in Appendix 1 is £   which represents an estimate of what the property is in fact likely to realise. Until sale I anticipate that Housing Benefit will cover the cost of the mortgage instalments.[12]

(2) My Van

My delivery van is subject to a hire purchase agreement and has only a nominal equity. It is in any event proposed that the delivery van should be excluded from assets available for the purposes of voluntary arrangement together with all other assets as are defined by Section 283 (2) of the Insolvency Act 1986.[13]

(3) Other Assets[14]

(4) Cash Injection by Third Party[15]

DEBTORS[16]

My debtors are shown in Appendix 1. Whilst it is believed that the figure for debtors is correct and accurate, it will be seen that the individual amounts due are of a comparatively small amount and, in the event of there being difficulty as regards recovery, it is not anticipated that any individual claim will justify the expense of litigation.

LIABILITIES[17]

My unsecured liabilities are set out in Appendix 2. As regards my lorry, it will be seen that this is subject to a leasing agreement in favour of   and there will be no equity. In the event of the lorry being repossessed and sold for a sum less than that shown as being currently due, then   will be entitled to prove in the voluntary arrangement for their unsecured balance which is estimated at £

ESTIMATED OUTCOME AND COMPARISON[18]

There is shown in Appendix 3 an estimate of the likely outcome of the voluntary arrangement and a comparison with the situation as it is likely to be in bankruptcy. The principal factor in the comparison is the voluntary injection of third party funds, coupled with the saving on professional fees, charges and the Department of Trade and Industry ad valorem duty.

Save as otherwise stated, all figures for assets and liabilities are estimated to the best of my knowledge.[19]

NOMINEE AND SUPERVISOR[20]

The nominee under the proposal is Mr   of   who is a Chartered Accountant and, so far as I am aware, qualified to act as an insolvency practitioner in relation to this proposal and voluntary arrangement. It is proposed that for the purposes of the Act and Rules, Mr   should be the sole supervisor.

If appointed supervisor, Mr   will exercise the functions set out in the Act and Rules and as set out in this proposal. He will act as supervisor and not trustee. No assets will vest in Mr   . No liability will fall upon him and he will not enter into any contract or other arrangement in a position so as to incur any personal liability.

GENERAL CONDITIONS

(1) Secured Creditors[21]

It is not proposed that anything in this proposal should affect the rights of any secured creditor to enforce its security.

(2) Preferential Creditors[22]

Any preferential debt will be paid in priority to all unsecured liabilities. Preferential debts will be calculated in accordance with the provisions of the Act and Rules.

(3) Voidable Transactions[23]

So far as I am aware, no claim could arise in the event of my Bankruptcy under the following provisions of the Act:

Section 339 (Transactions at an undervalue)
Section 340 (Preferences)
Section 343 (Extortionate Credit Transactions).

(4) Guarantees[24]

No guarantees have been given in respect of any of my liabilities by any other person other than my Wife who is jointly liable with me in respect of the secured liabilities charged against our house.

(5) Duration[25]

It is proposed that the voluntary arrangement should last for   from the date of the Creditors' Meeting. In that period of time it is anticipated that the supervisor will have been able to realise all assets, agree all claims and make a final distribution.[26]

(6) Proposed Dates of Distributions[27]

It is proposed that there will be a single distribution to creditors within the time specified above as soon as all assets have been realised and the liabilities quantified. No specific date can be given because the quantification of liabilities will depend so far as   [28] and   are concerned on the realisation of their assets and the calculations of any short fall.

(7) Fees to Nominee[29]

The nominee will be entitled to a fee of £   plus VAT at 17.5% and, from such fee, the nominee will discharge all legal costs relating to the application of the interim order and other ancillary legal work.

(8) Supervisor's Remuneration[30]

It is proposed that the Supervisor should be remunerated on the basis of work undertaken and time spent. It is estimated that his fees will not exceed £   plus VAT. In addition, the supervisor will be entitled to retain out of the general funds of the arrangement such sums as may be necessary to defray his reasonable expenses and any costs incurred by him by virtue of the employment of any Solicitor or other Agent.

(9) Guarantees to be offered[31]

No guarantees are to be offered by any other person and no security is to be given or sought.

(10) Funds[32]

All funds shall be held by the supervisor who shall open such account as he may consider necessary with a United Kingdom Bank in his name as supervisor of the arrangement. The supervisor will pay into such account all funds received or realised by him under the terms of the arrangement. Any funds held by the supervisor which, in his opinion, are not required for the immediate purposes of the arrangement may be placed by him on deposit with any recognised bank in the United Kingdom or invested in short dated United Kingdom Government Securities.

(11) Continuation of Business[33]

It is not proposed that my business should be continued save for the purpose of realising assets and agreeing liabilities.

(12) Further Credit Facilities[34]

None are proposed.

(13) Functions to be Undertaken by the Supervisor[35]

In his supervisory capacity the supervisor will oversee my realisation of assets and will directly agree all liabilities. The supervisor will have complete control of realisations. I will co-operate as fully as possible with him in order that the best possible value may be achieved.

(14) Quantification of Assets and Liabilities[36]

If any asset is realised for a sum less than that proposed in this proposal and the appendices thereto or if any liabilities shall exceed the estimated figure then that shall not constitute a default within the meaning of Section 276 of the Act and shall not entitle any creditor to seek relief from the Court either by way of Bankruptcy proceedings or otherwise.

(15) Conditions[37]

This proposal should be deemed to incorporate the standard conditions annexed hereto as Appendix 4 with the exception of Standard Conditions . . . .

....

Dated ....

APPENDIX 1

PRESENT FINANCIAL POSITION[38]

ASSETS

£   £

(Values are estimated by the debtor except where
otherwise indicated)

Freehold Property (professionally valued)

Less

Secured Creditor –   ———
Costs of Sale   ———   ———

Less

Spouse's interest in property   ———   ———

Other Assets

Delivery van
Lorry
Office equipment
Stock
Voluntary Contribution

Total assets available for Creditors

LIABILITIES

Preferential Creditors:

HM Customs & Excise – VAT
Inland Revenue (estimated)   ———

Trade and other unsecured Creditors[39]   ———

Deficiency as regards Creditors   ———

APPENDIX 2

Schedule of Liabilities

Secured Creditors

Preferential Creditors

HM Customs & Excise
Inland Revenue (Schedule D tax estimated)

Unsecured Creditors

as per separate schedule annexed[40]

APPENDIX 3

POSSIBLE OUTCOMES[41]

	BANKRUPTCY		VOLUNTARY ARRANGEMENT	
	£	£	£	£
Estimated Realisations				
Interest in Freehold Property	2,250		2,250	
Trade Fixtures & Fittings	250		750	
Stock	200		200	
Interest in racehorse	3,000		4,000	
Voluntary Contribution	–		5,000	
Total estimated realisable Assets		5,700		12,200
Estimated Administration Expenses				
Nominee's Fee	–		1,250	
Supervisor's Fee	–		1,500	
Trustee's Fee	873			
Department of Trade Fees @ 15%	855			
Petition Costs	650			
Official Receiver's Costs	1,000			
Solicitor's Fees	500		1,500	
Agent's Fees	500		1,000	
Out of pocket expenses	350		350	
		4,728		4,350
		972		7,850
Amount available for creditors				
Preferential Creditors	2,500		2,500	
		2,500		2,500
		(1,528)		4,350
Unsecured Creditors		12,000		12,000
Estimated Surplus/Deficiency		(13,528)		(7,650)
Dividend available to Unsecured Creditors		NIL		36p in the £

Note The figures are included for example purposes only.

IN THE   COUNTY COURT   No   of 19

IN BANKRUPTCY

RE:

IN THE MATTER OF A PROPOSAL FOR
A VOLUNTARY ARRANGEMENT PURSUANT TO PART VIII OF
THE INSOLVENCY ACT 1986

REPORT OF THE NOMINEE
PURSUANT TO SECTION 256 OF THE INSOLVENCY ACT 1986

The debtor   of   has submitted to me a proposal, a copy of which is attached. The debtor's proposal contains a summary of his statement of affairs.

The debtor's proposal sets out a proposed voluntary arrangement with creditors which allows for the possibility of:
(1) modest assets being made available which would not otherwise be available in bankruptcy;
(2) a quicker and more economical realisation of assets than would be the case in bankruptcy;
(3) the avoidance on the part of the debtor of the consequences of bankruptcy.

I have assisted[42] the debtor in the preparation of the proposal and I am of the opinion that a meeting of creditors should be summoned in order that the creditors may consider this proposal.

I have the following additional comments to make to the Court:

(*a*)   Having regard to the nature of the assets no professional valuation has been carried out. I have not independently checked the extent of the liabilities but have relied upon invoices and other documents produced to me by the debtor. I have however spoken with   plc and   Ltd and am satisfied as to the extent of their claim. I have communicated with Messrs   and am satisfied that £   is a fair asking price for the freehold property. They were not however able to give any time table as to a likely sale and advise me that house prices generally are falling.

(*b*)   Should any preferential creditor materialise who has not so far been allowed for, then that preferential creditor as a matter of law would be entitled to payment in full ahead of any dividend of the unsecured creditors.

(*c*)   The payment of a dividend will inevitably be delayed until the unsecured claim on the part of the   is known and quantified.

(*d*)   I have had a brief interview with   . I believe she will co-operate in the sale of the house. She has not received any independent legal advice.

(e)　I am holding the £　　to be made available by　　on the terms specified in the proposal.

In the circumstances I propose that a meeting of creditors be held:

at:

on:

time:

for the purposes of considering the proposal.

Dated　　　　　　　　　1991

_____

Nominee

1　No pro forma draft can ever hope to cover all the possible variations which may arise in a proposal. This draft is 'basic' and merely seeks to give an idea as to what a proposal might look like. It is not essential to include the court heading but desirable.

2　See Insolvency Act 1986, s 255(1)(b). The debtor must be in a position to petition for his own bankruptcy.

3　Strictly there is a third option, namely for a creditor to petition.

4　See Insolvency Rules 1986, r 5.3(1) and para 2.5 in the text.

5　Here briefly set out why an arrangement is likely to be acceptable to creditors.

6,7　Such paragraphs are commonly found in proposals and may need to be justified.

8　This is largely a benefit to the debtor but, if a benefit will accrue to the creditors if the debtor avoids bankruptcy, this should be stated.

9　This should be brief and relevant (see 1986 Rules, r 5.3(1) and para 3.1.3 in the text).

10　All assets must be disclosed (see ibid, r 5.3(2) and para 3.1.3 et seq in the text).

11　It is important for creditors to know the basis on which valuations are arrived at.

12　Creditors will want to know how the mortgage is to be financed until sale so as to avoid the equity being eroded.

13　As to exclusion of assets see ibid, r 5.3(2)(a)(iii) and para 3.1.3 in the text.

14　Here deal fully with all other assets.

15　If such is intended, the terms must be set out.

16　Particular considerations or likely problems with assets or their realisation should be made clear.

17　See generally ibid, r 5.3(2)(c) and para 3.1.3 in the text.

18　This is essential and must be realistic.

19　See note 11 above; as much care must be taken with the quantification of liabilities as with assets, especially since they are likely to increase.

20　See 1986 Rules, r 5.3(2)(p).

21　See 1986 Act, s 258(4).

22　See ibid, s 258(5).

23　See 1986 Rules, 5.3(2)(c), as amended.

24　See ibid, r 5.3(2)(d).

25　See ibid, r 5.3(2)(e).

26　If the duration is to be capable of extension, specific provision must be made.

27　See ibid, r 5.3(2)(f).

28　This will cover, for example, possible shortfalls on secured claims.

29　See ibid, r 5.3(2)(g). If the fee has been paid in advance, this should be specified.

30　See ibid, r 5.3(2)(h). The basis of the fee must be clearly stated.

31　See ibid, r 5.3(2)(j).

32　See ibid, r 5.3(2)(k), (l).

33 See ibid, r 5.3(2)(m).
34 See ibid, r 5.3(2)(n).
35 See ibid, r 5.3(2)(o). The role of the supervisor and his powers must be made clear so that neither debtor nor creditor is in any doubt as to who is to do what (see ibid, r 5.3(2)(n) and paras 3.1.3 and 3.3 in the text and generally Chapter 7.
36 This is a reasonable safeguard for the debtor, but it will not allow for, or protect against, the shoddy or negligent preparation of the proposal.
37 See generally paras 1.7 and 3.3 in the text.
38 The position will be as at the date of the proposal and does not include costs.
39 If this includes contingent claims, this should be specified.
40 A detailed list should be supplied.
41 See notes 6,7 above.
42 If this is not the case, this fact should be stated.

STANDARD CONDITIONS[1]

Interpretation

1 (*a*) These conditions are an integral part of the proposal. Should there be, in any respect, any conflict or ambiguity as between the proposal and these conditions, then the proposal shall prevail.

(*b*) "The proposal" means the document annexed hereto and signed by the debtor together with any amendments that may be made thereto, provided that any such amendments shall be in writing signed by the debtor or made pursuant to Section 258(2) of the Act.[2]

(*c*) Where the arrangement is co-dependent upon the proposal of any other debtor,[3] then these conditions shall apply to all such proposals.

---

1 For the use of standard conditions generally, see para 3.3 in the text.
2 See paras 3.1.2 and 3.3.8 in the text.
3 For example, in the case of partners or spouses; see para 2.3 in the text and generally Chapter 2.

---

2 In the proposal and these conditions, except where the context otherwise demands:

(*a*) "the Act" means the Insolvency Act 1986;

(*b*) "the Rules" means the Insolvency Rules 1986 and the Insolvency (Amendment) Rules 1987;

(*c*) "the arrangement" means the proposal and these conditions read together.

Approval

3 The approval[1] by creditors of the arrangement pursuant to the Act and the Rules shall be deemed to include approval of and acceptance of these conditions in all respects.

---

1 See generally paras 6.1.1–6.1.20 and 6.2.2 in the text.

Warranty

4 The debtor warrants[1] that he has disclosed to the Nominee full and complete particulars of:

(*a*) all matters without exception relating to his assets and liabilities whether actual or contingent;

(*b*) all matters which are required of him under the Act and the Rules and further warrants that the contents of the proposal are in all respects accurate and true.

---

1 Special care must be taken to ensure that the debtor is aware of the effect of this warranty. See generally Chapter 8.

Effect of Approval (General)

5.1 From the approval of the debtor's proposal pursuant to the provisions of the Act[1] and the Rules:

(*a*) the arrangement shall come into effect;

(*b*) the Supervisor shall exercise the functions[2] given to him by the arrangement and under the Act and Rules.

Duration

5.2 The arrangement shall continue for such period of time as is set out in the proposal[3] provided that such a period of time may be extended by agreement of all parties bound by the proposal in accordance with Section 260(2) of the Act. If it is decided to so extend the arrangement, this shall be done by the Supervisor calling a meeting of creditors and in respect of such a meeting the provisions of Rules 5.14, 5.15, 5.17 and 5.18 (1) shall apply.[4]

Completion

5.3 On completion of the arrangement, the Supervisor shall in writing notify the creditors accordingly.[5]

Default Petition

5.4 The Supervisor shall not present any petition pursuant to Section 264(1)(c)[6] of the Act unless such has first been agreed upon by a meeting of creditors called pursuant to the provisions of the Rules and these conditions. The debtor shall be given notice of any such meeting and shall be entitled to attend the same.[7]

---

1 See generally para 6.2 in the text.
2 See generally Chapter 7.
3 See Insolvency Rules 1986, r 5.3(2)(e).
4 Without such a provision, it seems that the period of duration cannot be extended. In the alternative, this power can be conferred on the creditors' committee, if there is one, or even the supervisor alone, whose decision could then be challenged on an application under Insolvency Act 1986, s 263(3).
5 See also 1986 Rules, r 5.29.
6 See generally Chapter 8.
7 The effect of bankruptcy may be considerable (see paras 10.1–10.7 in the text) so, in most cases, the creditors should be allowed to have their say. The debtor should be allowed to make representations.

General Power to Call Meetings

6.1 Rule 6.81[1] shall apply to the arrangement with the following amendments:
    (*a*) for "the official receiver" or "trustee" read "the supervisor";
    (*b*) for "the bankruptcy" read "the arrangement";
    (*c*) for "the bankrupt" read "the debtor";
    (*d*) for "the statement of affairs" read "the proposal".
6.2 If at any meeting so held the supervisor is dissatisfied with any resolutions so passed, he[2] may apply to the court for directions pursuant to Section 263 of the Act and the decision of the court shall be final. There shall be no obligation upon the supervisor to give notice of any such application to any creditor or the debtor unless the court orders otherwise.[3]

---

1 The Rule deals with the general power to call meetings. The time-limits contained in the Rule need consideration and can be reduced.
2 The debtor and, indeed, the creditors will have this right in any event.
3 Notice should normally be given.

Debtor's Obligations (to execute deeds etc)

7.1 The debtor shall at the request of the supervisor execute upon such terms as the supervisor shall require such deeds, transfers, conveyances, deeds of trust and powers of attorney as may be required by the supervisor for the implementation of the scheme and the sale of assets and getting in of assets and the protection of the debtor's property included in the proposal provided that the debtor shall not be obliged to execute any power of attorney or deed of trust save in favour of the supervisor unless otherwise so directed by the court.[1]

Declaration of Trust

7.2 The debtor declares that all property comprised in the proposal is held by him on trust for the supervisor for the purposes of the proposal.[2]

General Obligations

7.3 For the general implementation of the arrangement, the debtor shall at the request of the supervisor, unless the court otherwise directs:[3]

(*a*) do all things that the supervisor shall require;

(*b*) institute or defend any legal proceedings which touch or concern the arrangement;

(*c*) apply for legal aid for such proceedings;

(*d*) attend upon the supervisor when required;

(*e*) deliver to the supervisor upon receipt any communication received by him (save from the supervisor) which may touch upon or concern the arrangement.

After-acquired Assets

7.4 If prior to the completion of the arrangement the debtor shall become possessed of assets or property (of whatever nature) which are not included in the proposal and the existence of which could not or could not reasonably have been known or envisaged at the date of the creditors' approval of the arrangement, then the debtor shall forthwith disclose the same to the supervisor and make available to the supervisor such part of such assets or property as shall allow the supervisor to pay in full all the liabilities of the debtor with interest at the rate applicable to bankruptcies.[4]

---

1 Generally this is to ensure that the debtor will co-operate fully in the realisation of assets.
2 Alternatively, the trust can be expressed to be in favour of the creditors.
3 Clearly the debtor must do all things that the proposal envisages. Failure so to do may result in default (see Chapter 8).
4 This seeks to apply provisions which are applicable to after-acquired assets to an arrangement (see generally para 4.12 in the text).

Continuation of Business

8.1 The following conditions[1] shall only apply if the debtor's business is to be continued either for:

(*a*) the purpose of eventual sale and the distribution of the sale proceeds to the creditors under the arrangement; or

(*b*) to make funds available for the creditors calculated by reference to the debtor's future income from his business.

8.2 The debtor shall continue his business on his own account[2] and:

(*a*) in his own name; or

(*b*) if applicable, in the name or names in which it was conducted immediately before the date of the interim order.

8.3 Until such time as the arrangement has been completed and the provisions of Rule 5.29 complied with, the debtor shall not:[3]

(*a*) enter into any contract or agreement or undertaking for the sale of his business without the consent of the supervisor;

(*b*) dispose of the goodwill of his business or any assets forming part of or essential to such goodwill without such consent as aforesaid;

(*c*) make any other material changes to the extent, nature or place of his business except:

    (1) in accordance with any provisions of the arrangement;

    (2) with the written agreement of the supervisor;

    (3) if bound by law to do so.

8.4 Until completion of the arrangement or such time as the debtor ceases to carry on his business, whichever is the earlier, the debtor shall:

(*a*) submit such accounts to the supervisor as the supervisor may require;

(*b*) consult the supervisor as often as the supervisor may require on the conduct and management of his business and keep the supervisor informed on any material developments relating thereto.

8.5 For the avoidance of doubt, it is hereby stated that:

(*a*) the debtor shall carry on his business as principal and shall be solely responsible for any liabilities incurred therein after the approval of the arrangement;

(*b*) notwithstanding the provisions of the arrangement, the creditors shall be at liberty to commence and continue legal proceedings against the debtor in respect of any liabilities incurred by him after the approval of the arrangement.[4]

---

1 These conditions apply when the debtor's business is to be continued (see generally para 3.3.13 in the text).

2 The conditions make it clear that the debtor will trade in his own name; he is not an agent for the supervisor, and the supervisor must make it clear that the debtor is not his agent.

3 A sale contrary to the provisions of the proposal would clearly constitute default.

4 The creditors are not bound as regards liabilities arising after the proposal has been approved.

Taxation

9 The debtor alone shall be responsible for the payment of any taxation liabilities (including any liability for value added tax) arising from the continuation of his business after the approval of the arrangement. Any reference in the proposal to the profits of his business means the profits of his business calculated on generally accepted accounting principles before any deduction or provision for tax.[1]

---

1 This provision relates to tax liabilities arising after the approval of the proposal (see generally Chapter 12).

Third Parties

10 Where the proposal includes any obligation whatsoever on the part of a third party:[1]

(*a*) such third party shall sign the proposal and thereby agree to be bound by the obligation and its due performance;[2]

(*b*) such obligation shall be enforceable, at the direction of the supervisor, by the debtor;[3]

(*c*) the failure of such obligation shall be deemed to constitute a failure of the debtor's obligations within the meaning of Section 276(1)(a) of the Act and a failure by the debtor to do all such things as may be reasonably required of him within the meaning of Section 276(1)(c) of the Act;[4]

(*d*) any assets transferred to the supervisor by any such third party shall be held by the supervisor on trust for the purposes of the arrangement.[5]

---

1 As to third parties, see generally Insolvency Rules 1986, r 5.3(2)(b), (j) and para 3.1.3 in the text. Obligations on third parties must be carefully explained to them.
2 This is to satisfy the creditors that the third party will comply.
3 It seems the supervisor would have no direct power to sue.
4 See generally Chapter 8. If a third party defaults, the supervisor will be able to petition.
5 See condition 7.2 and note 2 above. Any conditions attaching to third party obligations must be made clear in the proposal.

Supervisor's Powers

11.1 The powers of the supervisor[1] shall be those set out in the proposal and these conditions and, subject thereto, the supervisor shall have all the powers conferred upon an administrative receiver by virtue of Schedule 1 to the Act,[2] provided that the supervisor shall be under no obligation to exercise such powers unless expressly so required by the arrangement.[3] The powers set out in the said Schedule shall be read and construed as if the same applied to individuals and not bodies corporate.

Paragraphs 8, 15, 16, 19, 21 and 22 of the said Schedule shall not apply.[4]

11.2 The supervisor may delegate to his firm and any partner, servant, employee or agent of his any or all of his duties hereunder save those which by law he is bound to perform personally.

---

1 See generally Insolvency Rules 1986, r 5.3(2)(n) and paras 3.1.3 and 3.3.4 and Chapter 7. In general, the proposal must set out the supervisor's role and powers.
2 See Appendix 3, p 222. Alternatively, the powers conferred on a trustee by virtue of Insolvency Act 1986, Sch 5 could be applied.
3 The supervisor should not be forced to accept a greater responsibility or liability than that envisaged by the proposal.
4 These powers cannot have any relevance to an arrangement.

Application of Bankruptcy Provisions

12 Unless otherwise provided for in the proposal or the context of the proposal otherwise demands, the following provisions of the Act shall apply to the proposal:

Sections 322–326 inclusive.[1]

Sections 328, 329 and 330 with such modifications as shall be appropriate to make and render the same relevant to the proposal, provided that unless the proposal so provides no creditor's claim shall carry interest for any period commencing with the day on which the proposal is approved by the creditors' meeting. Creditors' claims shall be calculated as at such date.[2]

---

1 Insolvency Act 1986, ss 322 (Proof of debts), 323 (Mutual credit and set-off), 324 (Distribution by means of dividend), 325 (Claims by unsatisfied creditors) and 326 (Distribution of property in specie).
2 Ibid, ss 328 (Priority of debts), 329 (Debts to spouses) and 330 (Final distribution).

Wrongdoing

13 Unless disclosed in the proposal, if, before the completion of the arrangement, the supervisor becomes aware of any matter which in the context of a bankruptcy would constitute a prior transaction under Sections 339, 340 or 343 or a wrongdoing under Sections 353 to 362 inclusive, then he shall forthwith report the same to the creditors,

convene a creditors' meeting and, subject to the right of the debtor to apply to the court,[1] propose at such meeting the failure of the arrangement.[2]

1 Insolvency Act 1986, s 263(3).
2 As to failure generally, see SC 15 and Chapter 8. Insolvency Act 1986, s 339 deals with transactions at an undervalue, s 340 with preferences and s 343 with extortionate credit transactions. These must be declared in the proposal. See also Insolvency Rules 1986, r 5.3, as amended by Insolvency (Amendment) Rules 1987, r 83. Failure to disclose may also constitute default. The inclusion of the wrongdoing sections (ss 353–362) is to afford the creditors further protection.

Completion of the Arrangement

14 The term 'completion of the arrangement' shall be defined in accordance with the proposal.

Failure

15.1 The term 'failure of the arrangement'[1] shall mean any of the following events:

(a) any matter which would entitle any person to petition for the bankruptcy of the debtor under Sections 264(1)(c) and 276 of the Act;[1]

(b) any bankruptcy petition being filed in respect of the debtor in respect of any liability arising after the approval of the arrangement;[2]

(c) the failure of the debtor to comply with any of the terms of the arrangement;

(d) any act or thing which in the opinion of the supervisor renders the implementation of the arrangement impossible or frustrated unless such act or thing is envisaged or catered for in the proposal, provided that the sale of an asset or realisation of an asset for a sum less than that estimated in the proposal shall not constitute an act or thing within the meaning of this provision unless such is caused by the act or default of the debtor or by someone on his behalf other than the supervisor;[3]

(e) the failure of any matter set out in the proposal and stated to be a condition precedent of the arrangement;[4]

(f) the passing of a resolution pursuant to condition 13 hereof relating to wrongdoing.

15.2 Where the arrangement has failed within the meaning of condition 15.1 hereof then:

(a) the supervisor shall report such fact to the creditors and shall issue a certificate of non-compliance pursuant to condition 23 of these conditions;

(b) the supervisor may[5] call a meeting of creditors pursuant to condition 5.4 hereof;

(c) any creditor bound by the arrangement shall no longer be bound and shall be entitled in respect of his debt to proceed against the debtor as he sees fit.[6]

(d) the supervisor shall disburse such funds in his hands in accordance with the provisions of the arrangement unless he is prevented by law from so doing.[7]

15.3 It is hereby declared that the failure of any person, including the debtor, to do any act or thing or to refrain from doing any act or thing within a specified period of time shall not constitute a failure of the scheme unless in the proposal such specified period of time is expressed to be of the essence. Any condition precedent shall be 'of the essence' unless otherwise provieed for in the proposal.[8]

1 See generally Chapter 8.
2 See paras 10.1–10.7 in the text.
3 The debtor should be protected from 'innocent default', such as acceptable failure to realise an asset for a projected sum, provided no culpability exists.

4 If there are to be condition precedents, these must be set out. They may involve third party obligations.
5 In all probability he should do so.
6 Since an arrangement is, in essence, a contract, such a provision seems possible if it is a contractual term.
7 For example, in the event of supervening bankruptcy (see paras 10.1–10.7 in the text).
8 This is to avoid 'de minimis' defaults destroying the arrangement.

Directions

16 If the supervisor is for whatever reason uncertain as to what action he should take in any situation,[1] he shall within his own discretion:

(a) seek the advice of the creditors' committee (if any);

(b) seek the advice of the creditors;

(c) apply so far as is possible the Act and Rules as they relate to bankruptcy and, subject thereto,

(d) apply to the court for directions.[2]

1 Although this should not arise with a well-drawn proposal.
2 See Insolvency Act 1986, s 263(4).

Expenditure on Assets

17 The supervisor shall only spend any funds in his hands for the purposes of repairing, completing or altering any asset held by him or by the debtor on trust for the purposes of the arrangement if:

(a) he is of the opinion that, as a result, the asset or assets concerned are likely to become more readily saleable or increase in value by an amount greater than that of the expenditure thus incurred;

(b) if so bound to do by the terms of the proposal.[1]

1 Such a situation is unlikely to occur, but this will protect the supervisor from undue pressure by the debtor.

Agreement of Claims

18.1 As soon as possible after the approval of the debtor's proposal (provided no application under Section 262 is pending), the supervisor shall send a notice to each person shown in the debtor's proposal or statement of affairs as a creditor requiring him/her or it to provide such details as the supervisor thinks fit of the amount claimed to be due from the debtor.[1]

18.2 The supervisor shall:

(a) send a similar notice to any other person to whom he believes the debtor may be indebted;[2]

(b) be entitled but not obliged to insert a similar notice in such newspapers as he considers appropriate;[3]

(c) be entitled to ask for any further details or documentation he thinks necessary for the purpose of establishing the amount due to any person claiming to be a creditor.

18.3 No creditor shall be entitled to receive any payment or dividend from the supervisor or any other person under the terms of the arrangement unless:

(a) he is bound by the arrangement by virtue of Section 260 or by an undertaking to that effect; or (*b*) the supervisor has admitted his claim for the purpose of participation in any payment or dividend under the arrangement, provided that the supervisor may, if he thinks fit, admit the claim of any other person to whom the debtor appears to be indebted as at the date of the creditors' meeting save that, if the aggregate of such indebtedness exceeds £1,000, then prior to admission the supervisor shall notify all creditors bound. No such further claim shall be so admitted unless the creditor undertakes to be bound by the arrangement.[4]

18.4 Unless otherwise agreed by the creditors in general meeting or otherwise provided for in the proposal, no creditor shall be entitled to participate in the arrangement unless that creditor's debt is one provable in bankruptcy within the meaning of the Act and Rules.[5]

---

1 The supervisor must have as much information as possible to allow him to agree claims.
2 See generally para 7.2.5 in the text.
3 The debtor must be made aware of this provision and the adverse publicity it might bring.
4 This provision must be modified in the light of each individual proposal, having regard to the effect that such admission may have on dividend prospects.
5 See Insolvency Rules 1986, r 12.3 and para 3.3.22 in the text.

Priority of Payments

19 The funds held by the supervisor shall be applied strictly in accordance with the terms of the proposal but, subject thereto, in the order of priority as would apply in bankruptcy.[1]

---

1 See Insolvency Act 1986, s 328.

Payments to Creditors

20.1 The supervisor shall not make any payment to creditors until at least 28 days have elapsed since the date of the creditors' meeting approving the arrangement. Subject thereto and provided no application under Section 262 or 263(3) is pending, he shall make payments or distributions to creditors:

(*a*) at the time or times specified in the arrangement;

(*b*) if no other provision is made, at such time or times as he considers appropriate.

20.2 If any dividends remain unclaimed on completion of the arrangement, then:

(*a*) the supervisor shall pay the amounts thereof by way of dividend amongst the remaining creditors;

(*b*) the supervisor shall have no further duties, obligations or liabilities to those creditors not claiming a dividend.

20.3 Section 325(1)[1] of the Act shall apply for the purpose of the arrangement.

---

1 This deals with claims by unsatisfied creditors.

Bank Account Costs and Expenses

21.1 The supervisor shall open one or more accounts with a United Kingdom branch or branches of a recognised bank in his name as supervisor of the arrangement and pay into such account or accounts all the funds received or realised by him under the terms of the arrangement. Any funds held by the supervisor which in his opinion are not required for the immediate purposes of the arrangement may be placed by him on deposit with any recognised bank in the United Kingdom or invested in short dated United Kingdom Government securities.

21.2 The supervisor shall be authorised to pay from funds under his control:

(*a*) the fees and disbursements set out in the proposal;

(*b*) any expenses properly incurred by him in pursuance of the arrangement including, without prejudice to the generality of the foregoing,:

(1) the fees of any solicitors appointed to assist the debtor or the nominee in connection with the application of the interim order and proceedings related thereto, if any;

(2) the fees of any valuer or agent retained by the supervisor to value or dispose of any of the assets assigned to the supervisor or held by the debtor on trust for the purpose of the arrangement pursuant to condition 7.2 above;

(3) unless the court orders otherwise, the cost of any action to which the supervisor is a party wherein costs are incurred by him or awarded against him in his capacity as supervisor;

(4) any tax assessable on the supervisor in his capacity as such;

(5) the costs of complying with any obligation laid upon the supervisor by virtue of the arrangement, the Act, the Rules or any other rules, regulations or orders made thereunder;

(6) such other sums as he shall be authorised or required to pay by virtue of the arrangement or any rule of law.[1]

21.3 There shall be paid to the nominee, whether or not he is the supervisor, such fees and disbursements as are specified in the arrangement.

21.4 Subject to any contrary provision in the arrangement, the amount to be paid to the supervisor for his services shall be:

(*a*) as provided for in the proposal and subject thereto;

(*b*) determined by the creditors' committee;

(*c*) if no committee is established or the committee does not determine the amount, then as determined by the creditors in general meeting;

(*d*) if not determined by the committee or the creditors, then calculated according to the scale applicable to the Official Receiver when he is acting as trustee in bankruptcy.

If he is dissatisfied by the amount determined as above, the supervisor, the debtor or any creditor may apply for the amount to be determined by the court, but any such application must be made within 28 days of the applicant becoming aware of the amount.

21.5 The supervisor may draw sums on account of his fees and disbursements from time to time as he thinks fit.

---

1 Generally the proposal must be explicit in detail as to the quantum and basis of fees to be paid to the supervisor.

Health of Debtor

22 Should the debtor die before the completion of the arrangement, the arrangement shall be binding on his personal representatives.[1]

---

1 See para 7.1.5 in the text.

Termination

23.1 The arrangement shall cease to have effect[1] once:

(*a*) there are no further funds or assets held by the supervisor or the debtor on trust for the purposes of the arrangement; or

(*b*) the supervisor has issued a certificate of due completion or a certificate of non-compliance.

23.2 The issue of a certificate of non-compliance shall:

(*a*) not release the debtor from any obligation placed upon him under the arrangement;

(*b*) not prejudice the supervisor's rights to exercise any of the powers given to him under the arrangement, including the power to realise any of the assets under his control and to distribute any funds in his hands in accordance with the terms of the arrangement.

23.3 When he issues a certificate of due completion or a certificate of non-compliance, the supervisor shall forthwith give notice of that fact to the debtor and all known creditors.

---

1 See generally Chapter 8 and SC 15 above.

Vacancy in Office

24.1 Should a vacancy[1] arise in the office of supervisor by death or otherwise, that vacancy may be filled by the creditors at a meeting:

(*a*) convened for the purpose by:

(1) any creditor;

(2) any person acting as a representative of any member of the creditors' committee (if any);

(3) any person who is in partnership with the supervisor immediately before the vacancy occurred;

(*b*) and chaired by:

(1) the convenor;

(2) any person qualified to act as an insolvency practitioner in relation to the debtor;

(3) a partner or senior employee of the former supervisor's firm experienced in insolvency matters.

---

1 See Insolvency Act 1986, s 263(5) and paras 3.3.26 and 7.1.7 in the text.

Ambiguity

25 Where any part of these conditions incorporates any provisions of the Act or Rules and such incorporation gives rise to an ambiguity or inconsistency, then the supervisor shall within his own absolute discretion resolve such ambiguity or inconsistency as he shall think fit and the exercise of such discretion shall not be open to any challenge by legal proceedings or otherwise by any creditor bound by the arrangement or by the debtor or by any person on their or his behalf.[1]

---

1 The very wording of such a clause indicates the danger in lengthy standard conditions and the making of arrangements or sophisticated, non-statutory bankruptcies. A proper balance must be struck between a simple, workable proposal and one that has too many loopholes and discrepancies.

Amendment

26 No amendment or variation of the terms of the arrangement shall be permitted after the approval of the arrangement unlesss so agreed at a general meeting of creditors called pursuant to condition 6 hereof and, at such meeting, Rule 5.18(1) shall apply. No amendment or variation shall be made without the consent in writing of the debtor and any third party affected thereby.[1]

---

1 Without this, no arrangement can be varied after approval unless provided for in the proposal itself.

SPECIFIC PROVISIONS FOR INCLUSION IN PROPOSAL

Introductory Comment

Set out below are 50 draft Clauses that may be suitable for inclusion in Proposals.

Draft specific provisions must contain just as strong a warning as Standard Conditions. The draftsman of any Proposal must not be slave to precedents found in a book, and must always consider the individual requirements of each and every Proposal.

It is certainly not possible to draft, in a book of this size, Clauses to cover each and every possibility and alternative. It is hoped that the Clauses which follow may, either in their set form or in such varied form as may be appropriate, be of general assistance.

A specific warning must be given as regards some of the Clauses: Clauses 10 (stock subject to possible reservation of title claim), 23 (claims – contingent and disputed), 26 (undervalue), 27 (preference) and 36 (book debts) all envisage a possible claim against a third party which might not be pursued. It may well be the case that the Proposal and Notice of the Creditors' Meeting are sent to the third party if that third party is, or is likely to be, a creditor. From the point of view of tactics, careful consideration must always be given as to the desirability of advising in advance a party against whom a claim may be made, that the claim will not or may not be pursued, or may be compromised.

A provision such as that found in Clause 28 (existing bankruptcy to continue) must be approached with the greatest care and caution. See generally Chapter 9.

The question of Supervisor's powers (Clause 47) must always be thought through with care. In many Arrangements, extensive powers such as those set out in this Clause will be quite unnecessary. The Supervisor must only take such powers as are necessary for the purpose of the Arrangement, but on the other hand must ensure that he has adequate powers. He must also bear in mind that, if he takes more powers, his responsibilities and potential liability will consequently be greater.

Whilst it must always be desirable to include provision limiting the liability of the Supervisor (as in Clause 48), it is unlikely that such a Clause will excuse the Supervisor from negligence. Clearly, it cannot excuse him for dishonesty. Such a provision should, however, excuse him from personal liability in contract although, in any specific contract into which he enters, special provision should be included to exclude liability.

Clause 49 provides for assets to be held on trust (see generally para 3.3.3 in the text). The Trustee in every specific case must think through the implications.

Any Power of Attorney granted pursuant to Clause 50 may be in general terms or, preferably, in limited terms to meet specific requirements.

The Provisions

Assets, Trust Property etc

1   I am an Executor of the estate of . . . . deceased, jointly with . . . . and . . . . As such, I am the owner with the other Executors of the legal estate of all the assets in this estate. I do not, however, have any beneficial interest whatsoever in any of the assets of the estate.

2   I am a Trustee of the assets of the Charity known as . . . . I have no beneficial interest whatsoever in any of the assets. I have disclosed to my Co-Trustees that I am seeking a Voluntary Arrangement and they are willing for me to continue as Trustee [OR] I have agreed with them that immediately the Voluntary Arrangement is approved, I will resign as a Trustee.

3   On the . . . . day of . . . . 19. . the freehold property known as . . . . was conveyed into my sole name. The reason for this is that the property is the private residence of my son, ... who, at the time of purchase, was resident abroad. Due to unforeseen circumstances, it had not been possible to arrange for my son to give a Power of Attorney to enable the property to be purchased in his name. The whole of the deposit, the costs of purchase and all subsequent Mortgage instalments have, in fact, been paid by my said son. I hold the property on trust for my son absolutely and have no beneficial interest in the property whatsoever. I understand that it has been suggested that I am the beneficial owner of this property. I confirm that I am not. Messrs. . . . . acted as Solicitors in connection with the transaction and I understand that they have expressed their willingness to make their file of papers relating to the purchase available to my Nominee. I confirm that my Nominee will carry out his own independent check of all matters relating to this transaction and the ownership of this property.

4   I am a beneficiary under the Will of my late Great Aunt . . . . who died on . . . . I do not have a copy of any of the documentation relating to my Great Aunt's estate and at the time of the preparation of this Proposal, I am unable to state with any certainty as to the precise nature of my interest in the Trust or whether or not at the present time my interest has any realisable value. I believe that my interest is subject to at least one prior life interest, and that it is possible that my interest may be subject to defeasance. Accordingly, for the purpose of my Statement of Affairs and assets generally, my interest in this estate has been shown as nil. If the Arrangement is approved by my creditors, then I confirm that I will co-operate to the full with the Supervisor to investigate and clarify the precise nature of my interest in the Trust and if it is possible, realise, for the benefit of the creditors, my interest provided that the same is, in fact, realisable, to the extent that there will be made available to my creditors such sum of money as would be realisable in the event of my being made Bankrupt. In the event of my interest falling in during the duration of the Arrangement, then the full sum received less costs and any liability for Tax of any description, will be made available for creditors.

Valuation – Freehold

Based on formal valuation

5   The property known as . . . . has been valued by Messrs. . . . . and a copy of their Valuation is annexed hereto as Appendix . . . No guarantee is given that the property will, in fact, be sold for such sum. I confirm that my wife and I will co-operate as best we can to achieve the earliest possible sale of the property at the best possible price, and that one half of the net proceeds of sale will be made available for the purposes of the Arrangement.

Based on asking price

6   The Valuation of the property known as . . . . is based on the current asking price of the property, discounted by £. . . . . . I am advised by Messrs. . . . ., the Estate Agents dealing with the sale, that the property is unlikely to sell for at least . . . . months. The Estate Agents cannot give any indication as to when the property is likely to sell, having regard to current market conditions and the fact that there are a number of other properties in the same road on the market for sale, some of which frankly are in a better condition than my property. Accordingly, it may well be the case that, when the property eventually is sold, there will be no equity available for the general purposes of the Arrangement.

No equity

7   As regards the property . . . . as will be seen from my Statement of Affairs, the current sums owing to the secured creditors . . . . and . . . . exceed the likely sale price of the property. Accordingly, it is unlikely that there will be any equity available for the general purposes of the Arrangement. In the event of there being a shortfall as regards the secured creditors, then such shortfall will constitute a further unsecured liability in the Arrangement.

Sale of Property – Co-owner's Concurrence

8   As regards the property . . . . my wife will fully co-operate in the sale of the property and, notwithstanding the fact that she may have a claim in exoneration, is content that one half of the net proceeds of sale will be made available for the general purposes of the Arrangement. A copy of a letter from my wife's Solicitors, confirming her agreement to this, is annexed hereto as Appendix . . .

Leasehold – Nil Value

9   As regards the leasehold property known as . . . . this is held by me on a Lease from . . . . at a current rate of £. . . . . . per annum and the Lease presently has . . . . years to run, though I am advised that in the normal course of events, I would be entitled to a renewal pursuant to the provisions of the Landlord and Tenant Act 1954. Unfortunately, there are rent arrears of £. . . . . . and I anticipate a dilapidations claim which is presently unquantifiable. The Landlord has indicated his intention to seek a forfeiture of the Lease on the grounds of breaches of covenant on my part, particulars of which are set out in the letter annexed hereto as Appendix . . . I am advised that it is most unlikely that I will ever be in a position to remedy these defects. Accordingly, whilst the leasehold property is in a favourable commercial position, and in normal circumstances would attract a considerable premium on sale, in the circumstances set out I am advised that it is prudent to proceed on the basis of a nil realisable value. If my Arrangement is approved by creditors, then the Supervisor will seek to negotiate with the Landlord

a period of grace to enable the property to be marketed and hopefully sold for the benefit of creditors, but no guarantee can be given that the Landlord will agree or that a beneficial sale will be negotiated.

Stock – Subject to Possible Reservation of Title Claims

10   My Statement of Affairs shows stock to the value of £. . . . . . I have obtained stock from a number of different suppliers and I understand that some, if not all, are likely to suggest that their stock is subject to reservation of title claims. Accordingly, whilst I consider the stock to have a value of £. . . . . . it should be understood that it is likely that this sum will be reduced considerably in the event of reservation of title claims being established. As soon as is reasonably possible after the Creditors' Meeting, the Supervisor will investigate each and every reservation of title and it will be solely within his discretion as to whether or not such claims should be conceded and the stock in question returned to the supplier. My Supervisor will be at liberty to expend such reasonable sum as he considers appropriate for the purpose of taking legal advice. In the event of my Supervisor determining that any such claim is either doubtful or without merit, there will be no obligation upon me having regard to the size of any individual claim to contest the same through the Courts. My Supervisor will have full power to compromise claims on the best possible terms, and furthermore will be at liberty to concede a claim, even if he thinks it is bad, on the basis that it will not be in the interest of the creditors for large sums of money to be expended on litigation, having regard to the fact that no individual reservation of title claim exceeds £. . . . . . and all my suppliers are substantial commercial enterprises with far greater resources for the purposes of litigation than I. It follows that, if any reservation of title claim is conceded, then whilst this will deplete the assets available as shown in my Statement of Affairs, there will be a consequential reduction in unsecured liabilities.

Excluded Assets

11   There will be excluded from the Arrangement all assets as defined by s 283(2) of the Insolvency Act 1986.

12   Although I am advised that both my vehicles . . . . and . . . . are excepted items within s 283(2) of the Insolvency Act 1986, nevertheless, both vehicles will be sold immediately following the Creditors' Meeting. Any resulting equity after the discharge of the existing Hire Purchase arrangements will be made available for the general purposes of the Arrangement. In the event of there being a shortfall as regards the Hire Purchase liability, then such shortfall will constitute an additional unsecured liability for the purpose of the Arrangement.

13   There is excluded from the Arrangement my Premium Savings Bonds to a total of £100. If, during the duration of the Arrangement, any of my Premium Savings Bonds win a prize in excess of £50 on any one occasion, then such excess will be made available by me to the Supervisor. I have deposited my Bonds with the Supervisor and have signed a letter of authority to . . . ., notifying them that for the purposes of the Premium Savings Bonds, my address is . . . . Accordingly, should any prize be forthcoming, then the same will be sent to my Supervisor.

14   There is excluded from the Arrangement my . . . . because this is of immense sentimental importance to both me and my family. If, within 12 months of

the date of the Creditors' Meeting, my Supervisor determines that my other assets are likely to be insufficient to pay a dividend of . . . . . . pence in the pound to my unsecured creditors, then the said . . . . will be sold forthwith [OR] my Great Uncle . . . . will pay to the Supervisor the sum of £. . . . . ., this being the estimated valuation of the said . . . . A letter from my said Great Uncle, confirming this, is exhibited hereto as Appendix . . .

Third Party Obligations

15 My . . . . is willing to contribute the sum of £. . . . . . for the general purposes of the Arrangement as is evidenced by the letter annexed hereto as Appendix . . . In the event of my Bankruptcy, such money would not be available for my creditors. The terms upon which this money is made available is set out in the letter referred to and has, subject to the approval of this Proposal, already been paid to my Supervisor, who is holding the same on an interest bearing Account.

16 I am advised that my wife has a good claim in exoneration. She is willing to waive this claim if my Proposal is accepted. Her terms of waiver are set out in the letter annexed hereto as Appendix . . .

Secured Liability

Uncertain amount

17 The amount due to the . . . . Building Society in respect of its secured claim over my property is £. . . . . . I have not, however, received a statement from the Building Society for some months, and I know that during the course of the last 18 months, I have, on occasions, been unable to meet some monthly instalments. Accordingly, I am not certain as to the full extent of arrears and the precise balance due to the Building Society. This sum will be ascertained as quickly as possible by my Supervisor. Accordingly, it may be the case that the sums due to secured creditors are greater than is stated in my Statement of Affairs, with a resulting reduction in equity.

Increasing amount

18 Due to my general financial position as disclosed in this Proposal, neither I nor my wife nor anyone else on my behalf will be able to make any payments in respect of the secured liabilities in respect of our jointly owned property. Accordingly, until sale, the secured liability will increase as arrears accumulate. This will not only result in a substantial reduction of the anticipated equity in the property but also, if a sale is not achieved within . . . . . . months, may very well mean that there will be no equity whatsoever available. I undertake, as does my wife, to do all that we can to arrange our personal income and expenditure position so that some payments are made in respect of the secured liability, or alternatively, to obtain such benefits as may be available. No guarantee or assurance is given that we will be successful or that any payments will be made to the secured creditors.

Preferential Creditor – To be treated Pari Passu with Unsecured Creditors

19 In the normal course of events, preferential creditors would be paid in priority to non-preferential debts. However, as is demonstrated by my Statement of Affairs, I have no assets whatsoever and preferential liabilities of £10,000 and unsecured liabilities of £20,000. To avoid Bankruptcy, my employer/father is willing to make available the sum of £15,000. This, as is demonstrated from his letter annexed hereto as Appendix . . ., is strictly on the basis that all creditors of whatever

category, whether preferential or non-preferential, are treated the same and accordingly, for the purpose of this Proposal, I propose that preferential creditors are paid pari passu with unsecured creditors. My preferential creditors are in no way prejudiced by this proposal because, in Bankruptcy, which is the only viable alternative to this Proposal, they would, in fact, receive nothing at all, whereas by virtue of this Proposal, they will receive a dividend of . . . . . . pence in the pound. I am advised that as this, in effect, represents an unexpected windfall for the preferential creditors, there can be no question of prejudice within the meaning of the Act.

Secured Creditor – Possession Order

20 The . . . . Building Society has already obtained a Possession Order in respect of my property, such Order being capable of enforcement on . . . . I am advised that a more beneficial purchase price is likely to be obtained by a voluntary sale by myself and my wife, as opposed to a forced sale by the Building Society. Accordingly, with the assistance of the Supervisor, I will endeavour to negotiate an arrangement with the Building Society whereby I have from . . . . a period of six months or such other period as the Building Society may agree for the purpose of effecting the sale. At the expiration of that period of time, or in the event of the Building Society declining to co-operate in this way, my wife and I will vacate the property and surrender possession to the Building Society. It is not proposed that any funds will be made available for the purpose of an Application to the Court for any further suspension of the Possession Order.

Landlord – Forfeiture – Surrender

21 The Landlord of my leasehold property at . . . . has declined to waive or suspend his right to seek forfeiture. I am advised that in the circumstances, it would be uneconomic and generally a waste of money to expend funds on an Application to the Court for relief against forfeiture. Accordingly, I have vacated/will vacate the property forthwith and surrender possession to the Landlord.

Lease – Surrender

22 I am advised that, on a sale of my leasehold property known as . . . ., I could reasonably expect to obtain a premium of £10,000. Nevertheless, as is evidenced from the correspondence annexed hereto as Appendix . . ., the co-operation of my Landlord is unlikely to be forthcoming. As will be seen from the correspondence, he has offered to pay me the sum of £2,500 if I surrender the property forthwith. I am proposing to take that course of action, having been advised that taking into account all considerations, including economic ones, that is the sensible, practical and commercial course of action to take. It will also be seen that, in consideration of the surrender and the payment of the sum of £2,500, my Landlord has agreed to waive all other claims he may have against me for dilapidation, breach of covenant and non-payment of rent.

Claims – Contingent and Disputed

23 There is listed in Appendix . . . some . . . . . . claims against me which, for the reasons stated, are either contingent or disputed. At the present moment, it is quite impossible for me to state with any certainty as to whether or not these claims will be good for the purpose of the Arrangement and, if so, their quantum. For the purpose of voting at the Creditors' Meeting, these claims will be admitted for the

amounts shown. Immediately following the Creditors' Meeting, my Supervisor will use his best endeavours to agree these claims, but neither he nor I will be under any obligation whatsoever to expend any money on litigating the same to determine their validity or quantum. It will be entirely a matter of the discretion of my Trustee as to whether or not to admit these claims for the purposes of dividends. My Supervisor will be empowered to take such other professional advice as may be appropriate. If the Creditors listed are aggrieved by my Supervisor's decision, then clearly they will be at liberty to take such proceedings against me as they think fit and my Supervisor will then have an unfettered discretion as to whether or not to resist these proceedings. If my Supervisor decides to admit all or any of these claims for any sum whatsoever, then no other creditor will have any remedy to apply to the Court under s 263 of the Insolvency Act 1986.

Undervalue

24 On . . . . I transferred my interest in the matrimonial home to my wife. At the time, I did not consider myself to be insolvent, and certainly there was no question of any Bankruptcy proceedings being taken against me. Nevertheless, I am advised and accept that the transaction in question would be open to attack under s 339 of the Insolvency Act 1986. There are annexed hereto as Appendix . . . copies of the letters from the Building Society and the Bank, showing the amount of the secured liability at the time of the Transfer, together with a letter from Messrs. . . . ., indicating the value of the property at the time. Taking into the account the sum of £. . . . . . in respect of the notional costs of sale, I am advised and accept that my beneficial interest in the property at the time was of a value of approximately £5,000. I received nothing from my wife by way of monetary consideration in respect of the Transfer. As is evidenced from the letter herewith, my wife has agreed to pay into the Voluntary Arrangement the sum of £. . . . . . in the event of the Proposal being accepted. It is not proposed that any interest should be paid on this sum as since the date of Transfer, my wife has, from her own earnings, discharged all the instalments due to the Building Society and has also reached terms with the Bank for repayment of their Second Mortgage.

25 On . . . . I gave to my son . . . . and my holding of Shares in . . . . Plc. I am advised and accept that, at the date of the gift, the Shares were worth £. . . . . . The reason for the gift was that at the time, my son was getting married and this, in effect, constituted a wedding present. As the Shares were only of a value of £500 and are now valued at approximately £. . . . . ., it is not proposed that any steps should be taken to recover from my son the value of the said Shares.

26 On . . . ., an Order was made in matrimonial proceedings between myself and my former wife, ... which provided, inter alia, that I should transfer to my wife all my beneficial interest in the then matrimonial home at . . . . Under the terms of the Order, my wife undertook to accept sole responsibility for the Mortgage in favour of the . . . . Building Society. It will be seen that at the time, the equity in the property was to the value of £30,000. Whilst an Order was made for me to pay periodical payments in respect of my three children, I was relieved of any liability to pay periodical payments in respect of my former wife. I am advised that on the face of it, this transaction is likely to be held as being a transaction at an under-value within the meaning of s 339 and accordingly, if I were adjudged bankrupt, a Trustee in Bankruptcy might well be able to impeach this transaction and obtain relief for the benefit of creditors generally. No

definitive legal opinion has been given, but I am advised that my wife will be likely to have the benefit of Legal Aid and will almost certainly defend any action brought by a Trustee. Minimal funds would be available to a Trustee to prosecute such a claim, unless the creditors were willing to put up a fighting fund. In the circumstances, I am advised that it is by no means certain that a Trustee would prosecute the case and, in any event, some points of law do arise. I appreciate that this is a potentially valuable asset and I can do no more than bring the full facts to the attention of my creditors. There is annexed hereto as Appendix . . . a letter from Messrs. . . . ., Solicitors acting for . . . . to whom I am indebted in the sum of £. . . . . . They are aware of the matrimonial Order and have indicated that they will vote against this Proposal for the reason stated in their letter, namely that they wish to see a Bankruptcy Order made, so that a Trustee can be appointed to attack this Transfer. They do not indicate whether or not their Client is prepared to contribute to a fighting fund. On information currently available, the claim of £. . . . . . represents some 15% of my total liabilities, so their vote alone cannot defeat the Proposal. I understand that, in the event of the claim being successful, then on the footing that, net of costs, the sum of £. . . . . . was recovered, this is likely to enhance dividend prospects by . . . . . . pence in the pound, taking into account the increased expenses that would be involved in administering my affairs in bankruptcy.

Preference

27 On . . . ., I paid to . . . . the sum of £1,250 in full and final settlement of their claim against me. I am advised that, on the face of it, this could constitute a preference within the meaning of s 340 of the Insolvency Act 1986. I accept that I was insolvent at the time. I did not make this payment with the intention of putting . . . . in a better position than they would have been in in the event of my Bankruptcy. I made the payment for a number of reasons. First, they had served a Statutory Demand on me and I was anxious to avoid Bankruptcy proceedings. Secondly, they were making life very difficult for me in that not only were they sending me numerous threatening letters, but I was also receiving threatening telephone calls at work and at home, and this was causing my family great distress. Of the payment made of £1,250, £700 came from my own funds, and the balance of £550 was paid by my wife. I am advised that it is unlikely that a Trustee in Bankruptcy would pursue a claim against Messrs. . . . . to recover the whole or part of the sum paid.

Existing Bankruptcy to Continue

28 As I have mentioned in paragraph . . . hereof, I am already subject to a Bankruptcy Order. My Trustee in Bankruptcy has already commenced proceedings against . . . . in an attempt to recover the sum of £. . . . . . in respect of a transaction whereby I paid to . . . . the sum of £. . . . . . three months prior to the making of the Bankruptcy Order. The Trustee considers that this is a good case under s 340 of the Insolvency Act 1986. In the circumstances, it is proposed that, in the event of my Proposal being accepted by creditors, the Bankruptcy should not be annulled, but should continue so as to permit my Trustee to prosecute this action for the possible benefit of my creditors. My creditors in the Bankruptcy are identical to those in the proposed Arrangement. It is further proposed that the Supervisor should leave with the Trustee the sum of £. . . . . . in respect of his likely costs of the proceedings, such sum having been calculated to cover not only the Trustee's costs but also any possible Order for adverse costs. If

the action is successful, then the net proceeds after the payment of all costs, charges and disbursements will be paid by the Trustee to the Supervisor. The precise terms of the proposed agreement between the Trustee and the Supervisor are set out in the letter attached hereto as Appendix . . .

Guarantee

29 My liability to . . . . Bank in the sum of £. . . . . . is guaranteed by my father to the extent of £. . . . . . A formal demand has been made by the Bank against my father and, as is shown by the copy correspondence annexed hereto as Appendix . . ., my father has reached an agreement with the Bank that, in the event of the Bank not being paid £. . . . . . by . . . ., he will discharge the guaranteed liability in full, thereby reducing my unsecured liabilities to . . . . The correspondence also shows that my father has waived any claim that he may have against me in the Arrangement, by virtue of him discharging, either in whole or in part, the guaranteed liability.

Duration – Extension of Time

30 It is proposed that the Arrangement should last for a period of two years from the date of the Creditors' Meeting, it being anticipated that in this period it will be possible for the Supervisor to realise all my assets, agree all claims against me, including contingent claims, and pay the dividend envisaged. I am, however, advised that there could well be difficulties in realising my work in progress relating to the contract at . . . . and furthermore, given the current state of the property market, it is by no means certain that my property at . . . . will have been sold within the two-year period. Accordingly, it is proposed that, if at any time it becomes clear to my Supervisor that all matters under this Arrangement cannot be completed by the expiration of the two-year period, then the duration of the Arrangement can be extended by such further period as in the circumstances my Supervisor deems appropriate. This will be done by him writing to all creditors who are bound, notifying them that the Arrangement has been extended by the given period. My Supervisor's decision in this respect will be absolutely final, and will be entirely a matter of his discretion. His decision will not be open to challenge by any creditor by application to the Court under s 263 of the Act or otherwise. No such extended period will be in excess of 18 months.

Distributions

31 It is proposed that my Supervisor will make a first and final distribution to creditors on . . . .

32 It is proposed that there will be the following distribution to creditors:
  (i)   to preferential creditors on the basis of 100p in the pound not later than
        . . . .
  (ii) to unsecured creditors an interim dividend of 25p in the pound on . . . .
  (iii) to unsecured creditors a final distribution of not less than 10p in the pound on
        . . . .

33 In the event of the Supervisor not being in a position, for whatever reason, to make distributions on the dates mentioned above, this will not constitute default within the meaning of s 276 of the Act, unless my Supervisor certifies in writing to all

creditors bound that the reason why he has been unable to make distributions on these dates is because of default on my part within the meaning of the Section.

Trading – Further Credit – Guarantee to be Given

34 The success of my Proposal depends on my being able to continue trading for a period of . . . . from the date of the Creditors' Meeting, so as to enable me to complete the contracts mentioned in paragraph . . . above [OR generate the sums set out in paragraph . . . above], which are to be made available to the Supervisor. Such trading is only possible if I am able to maintain my present level of overdraft facility with . . . . Bank. The Bank have indicated that they are only willing for this to happen if a guarantee is given in respect of this overdraft by my . . . . My . . . . is willing to give a guarantee and has confirmed this to the Bank, as is evidenced by the letter exhibited hereto as Appendix . . . No security is sought in respect of the guarantee, and none is to be given.

Further Credit

35 To enable me to complete my obligations set out in paragraph . . ., it is necessary for me to obtain further credit in the sum of £. . . . . Bank Limited have agreed to give me such credit facilities, as is evidenced by the copy letter annexed hereto as Appendix . . . It will be observed that the total credit facility is in the sum of £8,000 plus interest. This sum will be repaid by me through the Supervisor from the first funds to be recovered by my Supervisor from the realisation of assets, together with all accrued interest. It is anticipated that this further credit facility will be repaid in full by . . . .

Book Debts

36 My Statement of Affairs shows book debts owing to me of £10,000 with an estimated realisable value of £9,000. The individual book debts are listed in Appendix . . . I anticipate that the whole of the debt due from AB is bad. I know that AB is himself in severe financial difficulties, and I am advised that it would be uneconomic to pursue any claim against him through the Court. I am not aware of any reason why the other book debts should not be recovered in full, and I confirm that none of them have been challenged by any of my own debtors. I have already passed to the Nominee all paperwork relating to these debts. As soon as the Proposal has been accepted by my creditors, then the Supervisor will write to each individual debtor, seeking payment of the sum due. In the event of any of the debts being disputed, I confirm that I will give the fullest possible co-operation to my Supervisor in resolving any disputes. My Supervisor will have full power within his own discretion to settle or compromise the debts in whatever sum he may feel appropriate. He will also have full power to instruct Solicitors and other relevant agents for the purpose of endeavouring to recover the book debts. If so requested by the Supervisor, I will agree to proceedings being instituted in my name for the recovery of the book debts. It is a term of my Proposal that the costs for the recovery of book debts, including any Orders for adverse costs, will be payable out of the general funds of the Arrangement as an expense of the Arrangement. In the event of my Supervisor recovering less than is anticipated in respect of the book debts, or in the event of nothing being recovered, then this will not constitute either the failure of the Proposal or default within the meaning of s 276, unless my Supervisor certifies in writing to all creditors bound that there has been default on my part within the meaning of the Section.

Building Contract

37 My principal asset constitutes a building contract in respect of work at . . . .
for which I am owed, in my opinion, the sum of £30,000. This is disputed by the
employer, who maintains that he has a counterclaim against me and a claim for
liquidated damages, particulars of which are set out in a letter annexed hereto as
Appendix . . . If my Proposal is accepted, then my Supervisor will, on my behalf,
negotiate with the employer to effect the best possible settlement of my claim. My
Supervisor will have full power to employ such Solicitors and Quantity Surveyors
and other experts as he considers appropriate and the basis of any settlement or
compromise will be entirely within his discretion. There will be no obligation on
either my Supervisor or myself to issue any proceedings, whether in a Court or by
way of arbitration. I specifically give no guarantee that any sum whatsoever will be
recovered in respect of this contract. I am advised that a very considerable amount
of investigation work will have to take place to ascertain the true position and come
to a conclusion as to the merits of my claim and the counterclaim. The Supervisor's
investigation of this matter will be funded from the realisation of the other assets in
my estate.

Shares in Private Company

38 I hold 1,000 Shares in . . . . Limited, which is a family Company. This
represents a minority interest and, at the time of the preparation of this Proposal, I
have not received any advice as to the value of these Shares. I understand that there
may well be difficulty in arriving at a valuation, having regard to the fact that this is
a family Company and that there are restrictions on the sale or transfer of Shares
pursuant to the Company's Articles of Association. The other shareholders of the
Company are all members of my family and I think it unlikely that any of them
would want to buy my Shares. I doubt if the Shares have any value on the open
market. Both I and my Supervisor will take such steps as we reasonably can to
realise these Shares, but this may not be possible. If, by . . . ., no purchaser
has been found for the Shares at a price which is acceptable to my Supervisor, then
subject to the provisions of the Articles of Association, I propose to sell the Shares to
my wife for £10.

Freehold Property – Jointly Owned – Third Party Interest

39 The freehold property known as . . . . is owned jointly with my wife
. . . . Our two children, who are aged respectively . . . . . . and . . . . . ., are
in occupation, as is my mother-in-law, Mrs. . . . . who contributed interest-
free, the sum of £. . . . . . towards the purchase of the property. It is agreed that the
property should be sold and after discharge of the Mortgage in favour of the
. . . . Building Society, and the repayment of the interest-free loan to my
mother-in-law, that one half of the net proceeds of sale should be paid to the
Supervisor for the general purposes of the Arrangement. Both my wife and mother-
in-law have agreed to the sale and to give vacant possession on completion and to
enter into the relevant Contract and Transfer to effect the sale. Evidence of this is
shown in letters annexed hereto as Appendix . . . and signed by them both. They
have both had independent legal advice. As is shown in the letters, both have agreed
that the Supervisor will have discretion as to:
1 the asking price and reductions therein;
2 the general terms of sale;
3 the Estate Agents to be instructed and the method of disposal;

4 the Solicitors to be instructed;

5 agreement as to the Estate Agents' commission and Solicitor's charges. Until sale, the instalments to the . . . . Building Society will be maintained. Alternative rented accommodation has already been secured for my family and mother-in-law.

Life Policies

40 I have a Life Policy Numbered . . . . . . with . . . . Assurance Company. The value of the Policy is . . . . as evidenced by a letter from the said Assurance Company annexed hereto as Appendix . . .

41 I have a Life Policy with . . . . . . Assurance Company which is charged to the . . . . Building Society as collateral security for my Mortgage. On completion of the sale of my property, it is anticipated that there will be sufficient funds to discharge the Building Society Mortgage in full. The Life Policy will then be free of charge and will be surrendered. I undertake to execute or sign all such Deeds and documents as may be necessary to procure and effect such surrender. The anticipated surrender value is £. . . . . . as evidenced by a letter from the said Assurance Company attached hereto as Appendix . . . My wife waives any claim that she may have against the Policy or its proceeds of sale, as is evidenced by a letter signed by her dated . . . . . ., a copy of which is annexed hereto as Appendix . . .

Motor Car – Sale – Personalised Number Plate

42 My motor car, registration number . . . . . ., will be sold immediately after the approval of this Arrangement by my creditors. Such sale will be arranged by the Supervisor through Messrs. . . . . The proceeds of sale will be utilised firstly by discharging the hire purchase in favour of . . . . Finance Company Limited, who have agreed to a sale in this manner, as is evidenced by a letter dated . . . . . ., a copy of which is annexed hereto as Appendix . . . The said letter also indicates the amount required to discharge the hire purchase agreement. The estimated sale price of the motor vehicle is £. . . . . . In conjunction with my Supervisor, I will arrange for the separate sale of the personalised number plate AA1 which has an estimated realisable value of £. . . . . .

43 Whilst my motor car registration number . . . . . . is not an excluded item within the meaning of s 283(2) of the Insolvency Act 1986, nevertheless I am advised that it has a realisable value of only £500. The current amount owing to . . . . Finance Company is £750, so it is proposed that the said motor vehicle be excluded from the Arrangement.

After-acquired Assets

44 It is proposed that any assets which are acquired by me after the date hereof and before the conclusion of the Arrangement should be made available to the Supervisor for the general purposes of the Arrangement insofar as the same could be claimed by a Trustee in Bankruptcy pursuant, and in all respects subject, to the provisions of ss 307–309 of the Insolvency Act 1986. I undertake within seven days of any such property devolving upon me to give notice of the same to the Supervisor and to co-operate with him fully as regards the realisation of the same. This is subject to the proviso that any such after-acquired assets will only be sold to the extent necessary to pay all my creditors in full.

After-acquired Income

45 At the present moment, my income is £. . . . . . per week gross from my employment with . . . . I suffer the following deductions at source, namely:
  1 PAYE
  2 National Insurance
  3 Other deductions (specify in detail).
  My wife is not in paid employment and we have three children aged 7, 5 and 3. Accordingly, I am not in a position to make any payments to the Supervisor out of income. I undertake, however, to notify my Supervisor of any change in my income and to do so within seven days of my being notified that my income is to alter. I also undertake to notify my Supervisor of any change of employment and to provide him immediately with full particulars of the terms of such changed employment. I undertake to pay to the Supervisor such weekly or monthly sum (depending on the frequency by which I am paid) as may be agreed, provided that in no circumstances shall my net income be reduced below what is necessary for meeting the reasonable domestic needs of myself and my family. In the event of there being a failure to reach agreement, then the Supervisor shall be at liberty to apply to the Court for an Order determining what sum shall be reasonable and the Supervisor may apply generally under the provisions of s 263(3),(4) of the Insolvency Act 1986. In the event of such an application being made, it is agreed that the Court will be requested to approach and resolve the matter as if it were an application under s 310 of the Act. Whilst the Court will have no power to make an Attachment of Earnings Order, nevertheless I undertake to provide the Supervisor with an authority addressed to my employer for the time being, authorising him to make such payments as may be agreed or ordered direct to the Supervisor in such manner as may be agreed between the employer and Supervisor. In the event of payments being made by me to the Supervisor under this provision, it is specifically agreed that such payments will end on the determination and conclusion of the Arrangement pursuant to paragraph . . . hereof. It is further agreed that if grounds exist, I and the Supervisor will be at liberty to apply to the Court under the provisions referred to above for a variation of any Order made.

Standard Conditions

46 The Standard Conditions annexed hereto as Appendix . . . form an integral part of my Proposal. Conditions . . . and . . . shall not be deemed to apply, and Condition . . . shall only apply with the following amendment or variation:
  . . . .

Supervision Powers

47 My Supervisor shall fulfil the duties, responsibilities and obligations and shall have the powers specifically set out or referred to in this Proposal and the Special Conditions annexed thereto and in addition will have the following powers insofar as the same can be lawfully conferred upon him. It is specifically agreed that the Supervisor shall not be under any obligation to exercise any of the powers hereinafter set out unless specifically obliged to do so under the general and specific provisions of this Proposal:
  1   power to carry on any business of mine so far as may be necessary either for its winding up beneficially, or for the general purposes of the Arrangement and, so far as he is able to do so, without contravening any requirement imposed by or under any enactment;

2 power to bring, institute or defend in my name any action or legal proceedings relating to the property comprised in my estate;

3 power to accept as the consideration for the sale of any property comprised in my estate a sum of money payable at a future time, subject to such stipulations as to security or otherwise, as may be deemed fit;

4 power to mortgage or pledge any part of the property comprised in my estate for the purpose of raising money for the payment of my debts;

5 power where any right, option or other power forms part of my estate to make payments or incur liabilities with a view to obtaining for the benefit of my creditors any property which is the subject of the right, option or power;

6 power to refer to arbitration or compromise on such terms as may be agreed on any debts, claims or liabilities subsisting or supposed to subsist between myself and any person who may have incurred any liability to me;

7 power to make such compromise or other arrangement as may be thought expedient with creditors or persons claiming to be creditors in respect of my debts provable in the Arrangement;

8 power to make such compromise or other arrangement as may be thought expedient with respect to any claim arising out of or incidental to my estate, made or capable of being made on my Supervisor or myself by any person or by the Trustee on any person;

9 power to sell any part of the property for the time being comprised in my estate, including the goodwill and book debts of any business;

10 power to give receipts for any money received by him, being receipts which effectually discharge the person paying the money from all responsibility in respect of its application;

11 power to prove, rank, claim and draw a dividend in respect of such debts due to me as are comprised in my estate.

For the purpose of or in connection with the exercise of any of the afore-mentioned powers or the powers specifically set out in the Proposal or implied thereby, my Trustee may, in his own name:

(a) hold property of any description;

(b) make contracts;

(c) sue and be sued;

(d) enter into engagements binding on himself and, in respect of my estate, on his successor in office;

(e) employ an agent;

(f) execute any Power of Attorney, Deed or other instrument

and he may do any other act which is necessary or expedient for the purpose of or in connection with the exercise of these powers and the general implementation and supervision of the Arrangement.

Supervisor's Liability

48 Neither my Supervisor, his firm, nor any of his agents, employees or servants shall, for any reason whatsoever, or in any manner whatsoever, incur any personal liability in respect of any act, deed, thing or omission carried out by him or any of them in connection with his acting as my Supervisor or in connection with the supervision and implementation of this Arrangement. The Supervisor will not enter into any contract or other arrangement in a position or manner so as to incur any personal liability.

Assets held on Trust

49 At all material times, all my assets of whatever nature, description, and where-·
soever shall remain vested in me. I declare that I hold all the assets listed in
Appendix . . . and the net proceeds of sale thereof and all rights and privileges
attaching thereto upon trust for the creditors bound by this Arrangement, subject to
the terms of this Arrangement.

Power of Attorney

50 If so required, I shall execute in favour of the Supervisor a Power of Attorney in the
form annexed hereto as Appendix . . .

Appendix 2

FORMS AND DRAFT LETTERS

FORMS

Number	Title (and Statutory Form Number, where appropriate)	Page
1	Application for Interim Order	165
2	Affidavit in Support of Application for Interim Order	166
3	Notice to Intended Nominee	167
4	Order Granting Stay Pending Hearing of Application for Interim Order (Form 5.1)	168
5	Interim Order of Court under Section 252 of the Insolvency Act 1986 (Form 5.2)	169
6	Interim Order – One-stage Procedure	170
7	Order extending Effect of Interim Order (Form 5.3)	171
8	Letter to Creditors giving Notice of Meeting	172
9	Notice of Meeting	173
10	Chairman's Report to Court	174
11	Supervisor's Report to Creditors	175
12	Supervisor's Notice to Secretary of State	176
13	Alternative Orders to be made at Hearing to consider Chairman's Report (Form 5.4)	177
14	Bankruptcy Petition for Default in Connection with Voluntary Arrangement (Form 6.10)	178
15	Debtor's Bankruptcy Petition (Form 6.27)	180
16	Statement of Affairs (Debtor's Petition) (Form 6.28)	182
17	Statement of Affairs (Creditor's Petition) (Form 6.33)	192
18	Order of Appointment of Insolvency Practitioner to Prepare a Report under Section 274(1) of the Insolvency Act 1986 (Form 6.29)	196
19	Proof of Debt – General Form (Form 6.37)	197
20	Affidavit of Debt (Form 6.39)	199
21	Originating Application (Form 7.1)	200
22	Ordinary Application (Form 7.2)	201
23	Proxy (Company or Individual Voluntary Arrangements) (Form 8.1)	202

DRAFT LETTERS

A   Nominee to Debtor   203
B   Nominee to Debtor's Spouse   205
C   Nominee to Creditor taking Proceedings   207
D   Nominee to Preferential Creditor   208
E   Nominee to Third Party willing to inject Funds   209
F   Nominee to Court to hear Charging Order   210

FORM 1: APPLICATION FOR INTERIM ORDER

IN THE   COUNTY COURT   No   of 19

IN BANKRUPTCY

RE:

IN THE MATTER OF
THE INSOLVENCY ACT 1986 PART VIII

NOTICE OF APPLICATION FOR INTERIM ORDER

TAKE NOTICE that   intends
to apply to the District Judge of this Court sitting at

on   day, the   day of   19   , at
     o'clock in the   noon for an Interim Order pursuant to Sections 252 and
253 of the Insolvency Act 1986 on the grounds that he intends to make a proposal to his
Creditors for a composition or scheme of arrangement within the meaning of Section
253 of the said Act.

AND FURTHER TAKE NOTICE that the Debtor seeks an Order pursuant to
Section 254 of the Act that, whilst any Interim Order is pending, all actions, executions
or other legal process against the property or person of the Debtor be stayed.[1]

AND FURTHER TAKE NOTICE that in support of this application there will be
read the Affidavit[2] of the Debtor sworn on

Dated

....

Ref:
Solicitors for the Debtor

To: The Court and[3]

---

1 This may be deleted if no such relief is sought.
2 See Form 2 at p 166 below.
3 See Insolvency Rules 1986, r 5.5(4).

FORM 2: AFFIDAVIT IN SUPPORT OF APPLICATION FOR INTERIM ORDER

IN THE   COUNTY COURT   No   of 19

IN BANKRUPTCY

RE:

IN THE MATTER OF
THE INSOLVENCY ACT 1986 PART VIII

I
the above named Debtor MAKE OATH and say as follows:[1]

1. I make this Affidavit in support of the application herein by myself for an Interim Order under Part VIII of the Insolvency Act 1986 and pursuant to Rule 5.5 of the Insolvency Rules 1986.

2. There is exhibited hereto and marked "1" a copy of my proposal.

3. There is exhibited hereto and marked "2" a copy of the notice to my intended Nominee under Rule 5.4 endorsed to the effect that he agrees so to act.

4. The reasons for making the application are set out in my said proposal.

5. No execution and other legal process has been commenced against me.[2]

6. I am able to petition for my own Bankruptcy.

7. No previous application for an Interim Order has been made by me or in respect of me in the period of twelve months ending with the date of this Affidavit.

8.   of
Chartered Accountant is a person qualified to act as an Insolvency Practitioner in relation to my affairs and is willing to act in relation to the proposal.[3]

Sworn at
in the County of
this   day of
            19

                    Before me

                    Solicitor

---

1 For the requirements of the affidavit generally see Insolvency Rules 1986, r 5.5(1).
2 If this process has been commenced, full particulars must be given.
3 Some courts may require proof.

FORM 3: NOTICE TO INTENDED NOMINEE[1]

RE:

IN THE MATTER OF
THE INSOLVENCY ACT 1986 PART VIII

To: of Messrs

Pursuant to Rule 54 of the Insolvency Rules 1986, I hereby give you notice of my proposal for a Voluntary Arrangement pursuant to Part VIII of the Act.

There is delivered herewith a copy of the proposal.

Dated:
Signed:[2]

I   of
                              do hereby confirm pursuant to Rules 5.4 and 5.5 of the Insolvency Rules 1986 that:

(1) On   day of   1991
    I did receive a copy of the above notice; and

(2) I agree to act as a Nominee.

Dated:
Signed:
        Intended Nominee

---

1 See Insolvency Rules 1986, rr 5.4, 5.5.
2 Debtor must sign in person.

FORM 4: ORDER GRANTING STAY PENDING HEARING OF APPLICATION FOR INTERIM ORDER

Form 5.1

Section 254

Order granting stay pending hearing of application for Interim Order[1]

(TITLE)

(a) Insert full name and address of applicant

Upon the application of (a)

And upon hearing

And upon reading the evidence

(b) Insert details of any action, execution or other legal process to be stayed

It is ordered that (b)

be stayed over the hearing of the application for an interim order pursuant to section 252 of the Insolvency Act 1986, namely the   day of   19   of over any adjournment thereof.

Date _____

---

1 See generally Insolvency Act 1986, s 254.

FORM 5: INTERIM ORDER OF COURT UNDER SECTION 252 OF THE INSOLVENCY ACT 1986

Form 5.2

Rule 5.7   Interim Order of Court under section 252 of the Insolvency Act 1986

(TITLE)

(a) Insert full name and address of applicant	Upon the application of (a)

And upon hearing

And upon reading the evidence

(b) Delete as applicable	(b) [And upon the application of , the nominee, for an extension of the period for which the interim order shall have effect pursuant to section 256(4) of the Insolvency Act 1986,]
(c) 14 days unless an extension is granted on the application of the nominee	It is ordered that during the period of (c) _____ days beginning with the day after the date of this order and during any extended period for which this interim order has effect:[1] (i) no bankruptcy petition relating to the above-named (d) _____

(d) Insert name of debtor	_____ (the debtor)
	   may be presented or proceeded with, and
	
	   (ii) no other proceedings, and no execution or other legal process, may be commenced or continued against the debtor or his property except with the leave of the court.

(e) Date to be 2 business days before the day on which the report is to be considered	And it is ordered that the report of the nominee be submitted and delivered by him to the court not late than (e) [And it is ordered that (f)[2]]
(f) Insert details of any orders made under section 255 (3) and (4) of the Insolvency Act 1986	And it is ordered that
(g) Delete if debtor is not a bankrupt or if he is a bankrupt but the applicant is the official receiver	(g) [And it is ordered that the applicant forthwith serve a copy of this order on the official receiver.][3]

Date _____

Time _____ hours

Place _____

be appointed for consideration of the nominee's report.

Dated _____

---

1 In a Case 1 application, this will read 'no further bankruptcy petition'.

2,3 These points relate to a Case 1 application (see generally para 9.5 in the text).

FORM 6: INTERIM ORDER – ONE-STAGE PROCEDURE[1]

IN THE   COUNTY COURT   No   of 19

IN BANKRUPTCY

RE:

IN THE MATTER OF
THE INSOLVENCY ACT 1986 PART VIII

ORDER

UPON THE APPLICATION of   of

AND UPON HEARING the Solicitors for the Applicant

AND UPON READING the evidence and the Court having this day considered the Report of the Nominee submitted pursuant to Section 256 of the Insolvency Act 1986 and filed on

IT IS ORDERED that during the period of   days beginning with the day after the date of this Order and during any extended period for which this Interim Order has effect:
  (i)   no Bankruptcy Petition relating to the above named   may be presented or proceeded with and
  (ii) no other proceedings and no execution or other legal process may be commenced or continued against the Debtor or his property except with the leave of the Court

AND IT IS FURTHER ORDERED that a meeting of the Applicant's Creditors be summoned to consider the Applicant's proposals, such meeting as proposed by the Nominee to be held on:
Date:
Time:
Place:

AND IT IS ORDERED that this application be adjourned to:

Date:
Time:
Place:

for consideration of the Report of the Chairman of the Creditors' Meeting

Dated   19

                   By the Court
                   District Judge

---

1 This is an adaptation of Form 5 at p 169 above (see generally para 5.8 in the text).

FORM 7: ORDER EXTENDING EFFECT OF INTERIM ORDER

Form 5.3

Section 256   Order extending effect of Interim Order

(TITLE)

(a) Insert full name and address of applicant

Upon the application of (a)

And upon hearing

And upon reading the evidence

And the court having this day considered the report of the nominee submitted pursuant to section 256 of the Insolvency Act 1986 and filed on (b)

(b) Insert date of filing

(c) Insert date

It is ordered that the period for which the interim order made on (c) _____ has effect be extended to (c) _____ to enable a meeting of the debtor's creditors to be summoned to consider the debtor's proposals, such meeting as proposed by the nominee to be held on:—

(d) Date to be not less than 14 days from date of filing of report under Rule 5.13 nor more than 28 days from date of consideration of report under Rule 5.12

Date (d) _____

Time (e) _____ hours

Place _____

(e) Time to be between 10.00 and 16.00 hours on a business day (Rule 5.14(2))

And it is ordered that this application be adjourned to:—

Date _____

Time _____ hours

Place _____

for consideration of the report of the chairman of the creditors' meeting.

Dated _____

FORM 8: LETTER TO CREDITORS GIVING NOTICE OF MEETING[1]

TO ALL CREDITORS

Dear Sirs
re:
> TRADING IN PARTNERSHIP AS:

Address:

I am acting as Nominee in respect of a proposal for a Voluntary Arrangement made by the above named debtor under the provisions of The Insolvency Act 1986.

In order that creditors might consider the proposal and either approve it, with or without amendment, or reject it, a meeting of creditors is to be held. I therefore enclose the following:

1. Notice of Meeting of Creditors
2. A Proxy Form
3. A copy of the Proposal
4. A copy of the Nominee's Report to the Court
5. A Statement of Affairs in summary form is included in the Proposal
6. A Schedule of the creditor's claims is appended to the Proposal

When returning your Proxy form, please enclose a statement of your claim against the debtor with sufficient documentary evidence as is available.

Yours faithfully

Nominee
Enc.

---

1 See generally Insolvency Rules 1986, r 5.13 and paras 6.1.1–6.1.20 in the text.

FORM 9: NOTICE OF MEETING[1]

IN THE   COUNTY COURT   No   of 19

IN THE MATTER OF THE INSOLVENCY ACT 1986
AND

NOTICE OF MEETING OF CREDITORS

I,   , Chartered Accountant, of
was appointed Nominee to act in relation to the above named Debtor's proposal for a
Voluntary Arrangement following the making of an Interim Order by the Court
on   upon the Debtor's application under Section 253 of the
Insolvency Act 1986.

NOTICE IS HEREBY GIVEN pursuant to Section 257 of the Insolvency Act 1986
that a meeting of the creditors of   will be held
on   199 at   am at   for the purpose
of considering the proposal for a Voluntary Arrangement made by the Debtor.

A Form of Proxy is enclosed.

The effect of Rule 5.18(1),[2] (3) and (4) of The Insolvency Rules 1986 is set out on the
attached sheet.

Dated this   day of   19

                          Nominee

---

1 See generally paras 6.1.1–6.1.4 in the text.
2 See para 6.1.16 in the text.

FORM 10: CHAIRMAN'S REPORT TO COURT[1]

Dear Sir

COUNTY COURT No   of 19

THE CHAIRMAN'S REPORT ON THE MEETING OF CREDITORS HELD AT
ON   , CONVENED PURSUANT TO SECTION 257
OF THE INSOLVENCY ACT 1986

APPROVAL OF THE PROPOSED ARRANGEMENT

I would inform you that at the Meeting of Creditors of   a
Resolution was passed approving the debtor's proposal with the following modifica-
tions[2] and also appointing Mr   as Supervisor of the Voluntary
Arrangement:

1. The Supervisor should retain sufficient funds to petition for the debtor's Bankruptcy
   in the event of default or in the event that the Arrangement should fail.

2. Should the debtor be the recipient of funds or assets not anticipated at the time of the
   approval of the Arrangement, then these funds/assets are to be made available to the
   Supervisor in order to make up any shortfall in the dividend to creditors.

3. If the sale of the assets realises sufficient funds, creditors shall receive   interest
   at   % from the date of the Interim Order.

4. All outstanding VAT returns shall be completed and rendered within three months
   of the date of the creditors' meeting.

5. All future VAT returns shall be rendered and paid by the due dates.

CREDITORS PRESENT OR REPRESENTED AT THE MEETING
AND HOW THEY VOTED ON THE RESOLUTIONS

	Amount		Percentage Value of Votes Cast
	£	£	%
Creditors Voting For Acceptance			
By way of Chairman's proxies:			
By way of Creditor in person:			
Creditors Voting Against Acceptance			

Therefore in accordance with rule 5.18(1) of the Insolvency Rules 1986 a majority in
excess of 75% (ie   ) in value of those creditors present in person or by proxy was
obtained in favour of the Resolution which was duly accepted.
Signed
          Chairman of the Meeting
          (Pursuant to Rule 5.15(2) of the Insolvency Rules 1986)

---

1 See Insolvency Rules 1986, r 5.22(1)–(4).
2 These are by way of example only.

FORM 11: SUPERVISOR'S REPORT TO CREDITORS

TO ALL CREDITORS

Dear Sir/s
– VOLUNTARY ARRANGEMENT

I am writing to inform you that at the Meeting of Creditors of the above debtor held on   , the proposal for a Voluntary Arrangement was accepted by the creditors and I was duly appointed Supervisor.

Enclosed with this letter at Appendix A is a copy of the Chairman's report on the Meeting of Creditors that was filed with the Court on   in accordance with Section 259 of the Insolvency Act 1986.[1]

I also enclose an acknowledgement of claim form which should be completed and returned in duplicate when submitting your claim. If you are VAT registered, this form will enable you to reclaim the VAT element of your claim under the provisions of the Value Added Tax (Bad Debt Relief) Regulations 1986. These provisions apply for debts accrued prior to 26 July 1990. For the provisions that apply after 26 July 1990 please see the enclosed leaflet which I hope will assist you on this occasion and in the future.[2]

Please note that the form should be completed even if you are not VAT registered since it also acts as formal acknowledgement of your claim in this matter.

If you have any queries regarding this report, please do not hesitate to contact me.

Yours faithfully

Supervisor
Enc.

---

1 See also Insolvency Rules 1986, r 5.22(4).
2 See generally Chapter 12.

FORM 12: SUPERVISOR'S NOTICE TO SECRETARY OF STATE[1]

The Secretary of State
Department of Trade and Industry
Insolvency Services HQ Birmingham Unit
9th Floor Commercial Union House
22 Martineau Square
Birmingham
B2 4UZ

Dear Sir

RE: VOLUNTARY ARRANGEMENT

Pursuant to Rule 5.24 of the Insolvency Rules 1986, I am writing to give you notice of my appointment as Supervisor in the above administration. I enclose my cheque for £35.00 in respect of the registration fee for the above Voluntary Arrangement.

Name and Address of Debtor:

Date on which Arrangement approved by the Creditors

Court where Chairman's Report Filed
            County Court

(Court Reference: County Court No   of 1992)

I trust this information is sufficient for your requirements, however, if I can be of further assistance please do not hesitate to contact me.

Yours faithfully

Supervisor
Enc.

---

1 See Insolvency Rules 1986, rr 5.23, 5.24.

FORM 13: ALTERNATIVE ORDERS TO BE MADE AT HEARING TO CONSIDER CHAIRMAN'S REPORT

Form 5.4

Sections 259, 260 and 261

Alternative orders to be made at hearing to consider chairman's report[1]

(TITLE)

(a) Insert full name and address of applicant

Upon the application of (a)

And upon hearing

(b) Delete as applicable

(b) [And upon reading the report of the chairman of the creditors' meeting that the said meeting had [approved the proposed voluntary arrangement with or without modifications] [declined to approve the debtor's proposal with or without modifications]]

[It is ordered that this application be [adjourned generally with liberty to restore] [adjourned to the   day of   19   to enable an application to be made to extend the time for filing the report of the chairman of the creditors' meeting]]

[And it is ordered that the time for filing the said report be extended to this day.]

[And whereas:
  (i) on the   day of   19   a bankruptcy petition No of 19   was filed by   against the above-named
                                              (the debtor) and
  (ii) by virtue of section 260(5) of the Insolvency Act 1986 the said petition is deemed, unless the court otherwise orders, to have been dismissed

This court makes no further order save that

(i) the registration of the petition as a pending action at the Land Charges Department of HM Land Registry on   under Reference No PA   may be vacated upon the application of the debtor under the Land Charges Rules.

(c) Insert any other orders made in respect of the petition

(ii) (c)   ]

Dated _____

NOTICE TO DEBTOR (where voluntary arrangement approved and there is a pending petition which is deemed to be dismissed).

It is your responsibility and in your interest to ensure that the registration of the petition at HM Land Registry is cancelled.

---

1 See generally paras 6.2.1–6.2.8 in the text.

FORM 14: BANKRUPTCY PETITION FOR DEFAULT IN CONNECTION WITH VOLUNTARY ARRANGEMENT

Rule 6.6   **Form 6.10**

Bankruptcy Petition for Default in Connection with Voluntary Arrangement [1]

IN THE MATTER OF THE INSOLVENCY ACT 1986

(a) Insert full name(s) and address(es) of petitioner(s).

I/We (a) _____

_____

_____

(b) Insert full name, place of residence and occupation (if any) of debtor

petition the court that a bankruptcy order may be made against (b) _____

_____

_____

(c) Insert in full any other name(s) by which the debtor is or has been known

[also known as (c) _____

_____

_____]

(d) Insert trading name (adding "with another or others", if this is so), business address and nature of business

[and carrying on business as (d) _____

_____

_____]

(e) Insert any other address or addresses at which the debtor has resided at or after the time the petition debt was incurred

[and lately residing at (e) _____

_____

_____]

(f) Give the same details as specified in note (d) above for any other businesses which have been carried on at or after the time the petition debt was incurred

[and lately carrying on business as (f) _____

_____

_____]

and say as follows:—

(g) Delete as applicable

1. That the debtor has for the greater part of six months immediately preceding the presentation of this petition (g) [resided at] [carried on business at] _

_____

(h) Or as the case may be following the terms of Rule 6.9.

within the district of this court (h)

(j) Insert date the debtor entered into voluntary arrangement

2. On (j) _____ a voluntary arrangement proposed by the debtor was approved by his creditors and I am (g) [a person who is for the time being

(k) Insert name of supervisor.

bound by the said voluntary arrangement and (k) _____

is the supervisor] [(k) _____ the supervisor of the said voluntary arrangement]

3. (I)²

(l) Give details of the default in connection with the composition or scheme, being the grounds under section 276(1) IA86 upon which the bankruptcy order is sought

---

Endorsement

This petition having been presented to the court on _____

it is ordered that the petition shall be heard as follows:—

Date _____

Time _____ hours

Place _____

and you, the above-named (m) _____ are to take notice that if you intend to oppose the petition you must not later than 7 days before the day fixed for the hearing:

(i) file in court a notice (in Form 6.19) specifying the grounds on which you object to the making of a bankruptcy order; and

(ii) send a copy of the notice to the petitioner or his solicitor.

The solicitor to the petitioning creditor is:— (n)

Name _____

Address _____

_____

Telephone Number _____

Reference _____

(m) Insert name of debtor

(n) Only to be completed where the petitioning creditor is represented by a solicitor.

PRINTED AND SUPPLIED BY
Jordans
JORDAN & SONS LIMITED
JORDAN HOUSE
BRUNSWICK PLACE
LONDON N1 6EE
TELEPHONE 01 253 3030
TELEX 261010

Member of
THE LAW SERVICES
ASSOCIATION

JBA10

---

1 See generally Chapter 8.
2 Full particulars of the default must be given; see also Insolvency (Amendment) Rules 1987, r 93 which amends Insolvency Rules 1986, r 6.10 as follows:

(1) In subparagraph (a) of paragraph (3) of Rule 6.10 the word "and" shall be omitted and there shall be added at the end of subparagraph (b) of that paragraph the following words:
"   , and
(c) If there is in force for the debtor a voluntary arrangement under Part VIII of the Act, and the petitioner is not the supervisor of the arrangement, one copy for him".

(2) After paragraph (5) of Rule 6.10 there shall be added the following paragraph:

"(6) Where a petition contains a request for the appointment of a person as trustee in accordance with section 297(5) (appointment of former supervisor as trustee) the person whose appointment is sought shall, not less than 2 days before the day appointed for hearing the petition, file in court a report including particulars of—
(a) a date on which he gave written notification to creditors bound by the arrangement of the intention to seek his appointment as trustee, such date to be at least 10 days before the day on which the report under this paragraph is filed, and

(b) details of any response from creditors to that notice, including any objections to his appointment.".

FORM 15: DEBTOR'S BANKRUPTCY PETITION

Rule 6.37   **Form 6.27**

Debtor's Bankruptcy Petition

IN THE MATTER OF THE INSOLVENCY ACT 1986

(a) Insert full name, address and occupation (if any) of debtor

I (a) _____

_____

_____]

(b) Insert in full any other name(s) by which the debtor is or has been known

also known as (b) _____

[lately residing at (c) _____]

(c) Insert former address or addresses at which the debtor may have incurred debts or liabilities still unpaid or unsatisfied

[and carrying on business as (d) _____

_____

_____]

(d) Insert trading name (adding "with another or others", if this is so), business address and nature of the business.

[and lately carrying on business as (e) _____

_____

(e) Insert any former trading names (adding "with another or others", if this is so), business address and nature of the business in respect of which the debtor may have incurred debts or liabilities still unpaid or unsatisfied

_____

_____

_____]

request the court that a bankruptcy order be made against me and say as follows:—

(f) Delete as applicable

1. I have for the greater part of six months immediately preceding the presentation of this petition (f) [resided at] [carried on business at] _____

_____

within the district of (f) [this court] [(j)   county court. I am presenting my petition to this court, as it is the nearest full-time county court to (j) county court, for the following reasons:

(g) State reasons

(g)

]

2. I am unable to pay my debts.

3. (f) That within the period of five years ending with the date of this petition:—

(i) I have not been adjudged bankrupt

OR

(h) Insert date
(j) Insert name of court

I was adjudged bankrupt on (h)   in the (j)

Court No. (k)

(k) Insert number of
bankruptcy
proceedings

(ii) I have not (f) [made a composition with my creditors in satisfaction of my (S.16 debts] or (f) [entered into a scheme of arrangement with creditors] BA 1914)

OR

On (h)   I (f) [made a composition] [entered into a scheme of arrangement] with my creditors.

(iii) I have not entered into a voluntary arrangement

OR

On (h)   I entered into a voluntary arrangement

(iv) I have not been subject to an administration order under Part VI of the County Courts Act 1984

OR

On (h)   an administration order was made against me in the
(j)   county court.

4. A statement of my affairs is filed with this petition.

Date _____

Signature _____

Endorsement

This petition having been presented to the court on _____ it is ordered that the petition shall be heard as follows:—

Date _____

Time _____ hours

Place _____

Complete only if
petition not heard
immediately

PRINTED AND SUPPLIED BY

JORDAN & SONS LIMITED
JORDAN HOUSE
BRUNSWICK PLACE
LONDON N1 6EE
TELEPHONE 01 253 3030
TELEX 261010

Member of
THE LAW SERVICES
ASSOCIATION

JBA27

FORM 16: STATEMENT OF AFFAIRS (DEBTOR'S PETITION)

Rule 6.41   Form 6.28

Statement of Affairs (Debtor's Petition) [1]

Insolvency Act 1986

NOTE:

These details will be the same as those shown at the top of your petition

In the _____

In Bankruptcy   No _____ of 19_____

Re _____

The 'Guidance Notes' Booklet tells you how to complete this form easily and correctly

Show your current financial position by completing all the pages of this form which will then be your Statement of Affairs.

AFFIDAVIT

This Affidavit must be sworn before a Solicitor or Commissioner of Oaths or an officer of the court duly authorised to administer oaths when you have completed the rest of this form

(a) Insert full name and occupation

I (a) _____

_____

(b) Insert full address

of (b) _____

_____

_____

Make oath and say that the several pages exhibited hereto and marked _____ are to the best of my knowledge and belief a full, true and complete statement of my affairs at today's date.

Sworn at _____

Date _____   Signature(s) _____

Before me _____

_____

A Solicitor or Commissioner of Oaths or Duly authorised officer

Before swearing the affidavit, the Solicitor or Commissioner is particularly requested to make sure that the full name, address and description of the deponent are stated, and to initial any crossings-out or other alterations in the printed form. A deficiency in the affidavit in any of the above respects will mean that it will be refused by the court, and will need to be re-sworn.

PRINTED AND SUPPLIED BY

Jordans

JORDAN & SONS LIMITED
JORDAN HOUSE
BRUNSWICK PLACE
LONDON N1 6EE
TELEPHONE 01 253 3030
TELEX 261010

Member of
THE LAW SOCIETY's
ASSOCIATION

JBA28

---

1 See generally paras 10.8.1–10.8.5 in the text.

A

LIST OF SECURED CREDITORS

Is anyone claiming something of yours to clear or reduce their claim?

Tick Box
YES ☐
NO ☐

If '**YES**' give details below:

Name of creditor	Address (with postcode)	Amount owed to creditor £	What of yours is claimed and what is it worth?
1.			
2.			
3.			
4.			

Signature _____

Date _____

PRINTED AND SUPPLIED BY

Jordans
JORDAN & SONS LIMITED
JORDAN HOUSE
BRUNSWICK PLACE
LONDON N1 6EE
TELEPHONE 0 253 3030
TELEX 261010

JBA28A

B

LIST OF UNSECURED CREDITORS

1. No.	2 Name of creditor or claimant	3 Address (with postcode)	4 Amount the creditor says you owe him/her £	5 Amount you think you owe £

PRINTED AND SUPPLIED BY

Jordans
JORDAN & SONS LIMITED
JORDAN HOUSE
BRUNSWICK PLACE
LONDON N1 6EE
TELEPHONE 01 253 3030
TELEX 261010

Member of
THE LAW SERVICES
ASSOCIATION

Signature _____   Date _____

JBA28B

C1

ASSETS

	Tick Box
	Yes No

Do you have any bank accounts or an interest in one?
If **'YES'** state where they are, how much is in them and how much is your share.

_____

_____

_____

_____

_____

Do you have any business bank accounts, including joint accounts?
If **'YES'** state the name of the accounts, where they are
and how much is in them.

Yes   No

_____

_____

_____

Do you have any building society accounts or an interest in one?
If **'YES'** state where they are and how much is in them
and how much is your share.

Yes   No

_____

_____

_____

_____

_____

Signature _____ Date _____

PRINTED AND SUPPLIED BY
Jordans
JORDAN & SONS LIMITED
JORDAN HOUSE
BRUNSWICK PLACE
LONDON N1 6EE
TELEPHONE 01 253 3030
TELEX 261010

Member of
THE LAW SERVICES
ASSOCIATION

JBA28C1

C2
ASSETS

	Tick Box	
	Yes	No

Do you have any other savings?
If '**YES**' give details

_____

_____

_____

_____

| | Yes | No |

Do you use a motor vehicle?
If '**YES**' who owns it and what is it worth?

_____

_____

_____

_____

| | Yes | No |

Have you an interest in any other motor vehicles?
If '**YES**' give details and their value.

_____

_____

_____

_____

PRINTED AND SUPPLIED BY

Jordans
JORDAN & SONS LIMITED
JORDAN HOUSE
BRUNSWICK PLACE
LONDON N1 6EE
TELEPHONE 01 253 3030
TELEX 261010

Member of
THE LAW SOCIETY'S
ASSOCIATION

Signature _____ Date _____

JBA28C2

C3

ASSETS

Now show anything else of yours which may be of value:

£

a) Household furniture and belongings _____ _____

b) Life policies _____ _____

c) Money owed to you _____ _____

d) Stock in trade _____ _____

e) Other property (see Guidance Notes):— _____ _____

TOTAL

Signature _____   Date _____

PRINTED AND SUPPLIED BY

Jordans

JORDAN & SONS LIMITED
JORDAN HOUSE
BRUNSWICK PLACE
LONDON N1 6EE
TELEPHONE 01 253 3030
TELEX 261010

JBA28C3

D

1. State the name, age (if under 18), and relationship to you of your dependants

1 _____   6 _____

2 _____   7 _____

3 _____   8 _____

4 _____   9 _____

5 _____   10 _____

Tick Box
Yes   No
☐   ☐

2. Has distress been levied against you by or on behalf of any creditor?
If 'YES' give details below:—

Name of creditor	Amount of claim £	Date Distress levied	Description and estimated value of property seized
_____	_____	_____	_____
_____	_____	_____	_____
_____	_____	_____	_____
_____	_____	_____	_____
_____	_____	_____	_____
_____	_____	_____	_____
_____	_____	_____	_____
_____	_____	_____	_____

PRINTED AND SUPPLIED BY

Jordans
JORDAN & SONS LIMITED
JORDAN HOUSE
BRUNSWICK PLACE
LONDON N1 6EE
TELEPHONE 01 253 3030
TELEX 261010

Member of
THE LAW SERVICES
ASSOCIATION

JBA28D

Signature _____   Date _____

E

3. At the date you present your bankruptcy petition, is any court judgment or other legal process outstanding against you that has been made by any court in England and Wales?
If **'YES'** give details below:—

Tick Box
Yes ☐ No ☐

Name of creditor	Amount of claim £	Type and date of process issued	Description and estimated value of any property involved
_____	_____	_____	_____
_____	_____	_____	_____
_____	_____	_____	_____
_____	_____	_____	_____
_____	_____	_____	_____
_____	_____	_____	_____
_____	_____	_____	_____
_____	_____	_____	_____

4. At the date you present your bankruptcy petition, is any attachment of earnings order in force against you?
If **'YES'** give details below:—

Tick Box
Yes ☐ No ☐

Name of creditor	Date of order	Court	Amount of instalment payable under order (per month/week) £	Total amount paid under order £	Date order expires (if applicable)
_____	_____	_____	_____	_____	_____
_____	_____	_____	_____	_____	_____
_____	_____	_____	_____	_____	_____

PRINTED AND SUPPLIED BY
Jordans
JORDAN & SONS LIMITED
JORDAN HOUSE
BRUNSWICK PLACE
LONDON N1 6EE
TELEPHONE 01 253 3030
TELEX 261010

Member of
THE LAW SOCIETY'S
ASSOCIATION

JBA28E

Signature _____   Date _____

F

5(a) Have you, before you presented your petition, tried
to come to any agreement with your creditors generally for payment of your debts?

Tick Box
Yes ☐   No ☐

(b) If the answer to 5(a) is 'YES', what terms were offered to the creditors:—

(1) Time for repayment _____

_____

(2) Total pence in £ _____

receivable by creditors _____

(3) When was the offer made? _____

Tick Box
Yes ☐   No ☐

(c) Did the attempt fail because the creditors refused to accept the terms offered?

If 'NO' why did it fail? _____

_____

_____

---

6. Do you think that you will be able to introduce a voluntary arrangement for your
creditors under Part VIII of the Insolvency Act 1986, which is likely to be
acceptable to them?

Tick Box
Yes ☐   No ☐

If 'YES', give brief details _____

_____

_____

PRINTED AND SUPPLIED BY

Jordans

JORDAN & SONS LIMITED
JORDAN HOUSE
BRUNSWICK PLACE
LONDON N1 6EE
TELEPHONE 01 253 3030
TELEX 261010

MEMBER OF
THE LAW SERVICES
ASSOCIATION

JBA28F

Signature _____   Date _____

G

STATEMENT OF MEANS

(List below all items of regular "monthly" income and expenditure)

Items of income	£	Items of expenditure	£

This page shows that I will now be able to pay creditors £ _____ a month.

Signature _____   Date _____

PRINTED AND SUPPLIED BY

Jordans

JORDAN & SONS LIMITED
JORDAN HOUSE
BRUNSWICK PLACE
LONDON N1 6EE
TELEPHONE 01-253 3030
TELEX 261010

JBA28G

FORM 17: STATEMENT OF AFFAIRS (CREDITOR'S PETITION)

Form 6.33

Rule 6.59 Statement of Affairs (Creditor's Petition)[1]
Insolvency Act 1986

NOTE:
These details will be
the same as those
shown at the top of
your petition

In the _____

In Bankruptcy   No _____ of 19 _____

Re _____

The 'Guidance Notes' Booklet tells you how to complete this form easily and correctly

Show your current financial position by completing all the pages of this form which will then be your Statement of Affairs.

Affidavit

This Affidavit must be sworn before a Solicitor or Commissioner of Oaths or an officer of the court duly authorised to administer oaths when you have completed the rest of this form

(a) Insert full name and occupation

I (a) _____

_____

(b) Insert full address

of (b) _____

_____

Make oath and say that the attached pages exhibited hereto and marked _____ are to the best of my knowledge and belief a full, true and complete statement of my affairs as at _____ the date of the bankruptcy order made against me.

Sworn at _____

Date _____   Signature(s) _____

PRINTED AND SUPPLIED BY
Jordans
JORDAN & SONS LIMITED
JORDAN HOUSE
BRUNSWICK PLACE
LONDON N1 6EE
TELEPHONE 01 253 3030
TELEX 261010

Member of
THE LAW SERVICES
ASSOCIATION

JBA33

Before me _____

_____

A Solicitor or Commissioner of Oaths or Duly authorised officer

Before swearing the affidavit the Solicitor or Commissioner is particularly requested to make sure that the full name, address and description of the Deponent are stated, and to initial any crossings-out or other alterations in the printed form. A deficiency in the affidavit in any of the above respects will mean that it is refused by the court, and will need to be re-sworn.

---

1 This can be used for the purposes of Insolvency Rules 1986, r 5.8 with suitable amendment.

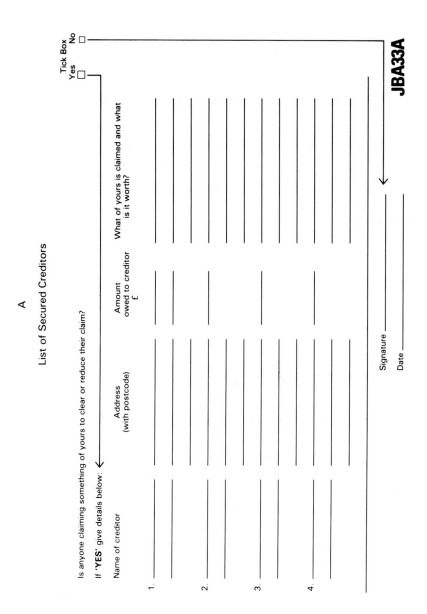

A

List of Secured Creditors

Is anyone claiming something of yours to clear or reduce their claim?

Tick Box
Yes ☐
No ☐

If 'YES' give details below:

Name of creditor	Address (with postcode)	Amount owed to creditor £	What of yours is claimed and what is it worth?
1.			
2.			
3.			
4.			

Signature

Date

JBA33A

B

List of Unsecured Creditors

1 No.	2 Name of creditor or claimant	3 Address (with postcode)	4 Amount the creditor says you owe him/her £	5 Amount you think you owe £

Signature _____   Date _____

JBA33B

C

Assets

Now show anything else of yours which may be of value:

	£
a) Cash at bank or building society _____	_____
b) Household furniture and belongings _____	_____
c) Life policies _____	_____
d) Money owed to you _____	_____
e) Stock in trade _____	_____
f) Motor vehicles _____	_____
g) Other property (see Guidance Notes):— _____	_____
_____	_____
_____	_____
_____	_____
_____	_____
_____	_____
_____	_____
_____	_____
_____	_____
_____	_____
_____	_____
_____	_____
_____	_____
_____	_____
_____	_____
TOTAL	_____

Signature _____   Date _____

JBA33C

FORM 18: ORDER OF APPOINTMENT OF INSOLVENCY PRACTITIONER TO PREPARE A REPORT UNDER SECTION 274(1) OF THE INSOLVENCY ACT 1986

Form 6.29

Rule 6.44   Order of Appointment of Insolvency Practitioner to Prepare a Report Under Section 274(1) of the Insolvency Act 1986[1]

(TITLE)

(a) Insert full name and address of debtor   Upon hearing the petition of (a)

(b) Insert date   the above named debtor, which was presented on (b)

and upon hearing

and upon reading the evidence

(c) Insert name and address of insolvency practitioner to be appointed   It is ordered that (c)

a person who is qualified to act as an insolvency practitioner in relation to the above-named debtor, be appointed to prepare and submit a report to the court by (b)

as to whether the above-named debtor is willing to make a proposal for a voluntary arrangement.

And it is ordered that the court will consider the report on:–

Date _____

Time _____ hours

Place _____

(d) Delete as applicable   (d) [And the debtor is (d) [directed to] [may] attend that hearing]

Dated _____

---

1 See generally paras 10.8.1–10.8.5 in the text.

FORM 19: PROOF OF DEBT—GENERAL FORM

Form 6.37

Rule 6.96

Proof of Debt–General Form

IN BANKRUPTCY

Date of Bankruptcy Order   No

1	Name of Creditor	
2	Address of Creditor	
3	Total amount of claim, including any Value Added Tax and outstanding uncapitalised interest as at the date of the bankruptcy order	£
4	Details of any documents by reference to which the debt can be substantiated. [Note: the official receiver or trustee may call for any document or evidence to substantiate the claim at his discretion]	
5	If the total amount shown above includes Value Added Tax, please show:— (a) amount of Value Added Tax	£
	(b) amount of claim NET of Value Added Tax	£
6	If total amount above includes outstanding uncapitalised interest please state amount	£
7	If you have filled in both box 3 and box 5, please state whether you are claiming the amount shown in box 3 or the amount shown in box 5(b)	
8	Give details of whether the whole or any part of the debt falls within any (and if so which) of the categories of preferential debts under section 386 of, and schedule 6 to, the Insolvency Act 1986 (as read with schedule 3 to the Social Security Pensions Act 1975)	Category Amount(s) claimed as preferential £

9	Particulars of how and when debt incurred	
10	Particulars of any security held, the value of the security, and the date it was given	
11	Signature of creditor or person authorised to act on his behalf	
	Name in BLOCK LETTERS	
	Position with or relation to creditor	

Admitted to vote for

£

Date

Official Receiver/Trustee

Admitted preferentially for

£

Date

Trustee

Admitted non-preferentially for

£

Date

Trustee

PRINTED AND SUPPLIED BY

JORDAN & SONS LIMITED
JORDAN HOUSE
BRUNSWICK PLACE
LONDON N1 6EE
TELEPHONE 01 253 3030
TELEX 261010

JBA37

FORM 20: AFFIDAVIT OF DEBT

Rule 6.96, 6.99   Affidavit of Debt [1]   Form 6.39

IN THE MATTER OF THE INSOLVENCY ACT 1986

(a) Insert full name,   I (a)
address and
description of person
making oath

                         make oath and say:

(b) Delete as   (1) That (b) [I am a creditor of the above-named bankrupt] [I am (c)
applicable

(c) State capacity eg
director, secretary,   of (d)
solicitor etc

(d) Insert full name and
address of creditor

                         a creditor of the above-named bankrupt.

(e) State means of   I have been concerned in this matter (e)
knowledge of matters
sworn to in affidavit

                                                          and am authorised by
                         the creditor to make this affidavit on its/his behalf]

(f) Insert name of   (2) That the said (f)
bankrupt
(g) Insert date   on (g)   the date of the bankruptcy order,
                         was and still is justly and truly indebted (b) [to me] [to the said creditor] in the sum
                         of £   as shown in the proof of debt exhibited hereto marked "A".

                         SWORN at   ⎞
                         this   day of   ⎟
                         19   ⎬
                                 Before me,   ⎟
                                                                     ⎠
                                                  A Solicitor

PRINTED AND SUPPLIED BY

Jordans
JORDAN & SONS LIMITED
JORDAN HOUSE
BRUNSWICK PLACE
LONDON N1 6EE
TELEPHONE 01 253 3030
TELEX 261010

Member of
THE LAW SERVICES
ASSOCIATION

JBA39

---

1 The supervisor may require a creditor to verify his debt by affidavit; if this is desired, it is best to make provision for it in the proposal.

FORM 21: ORIGINATING APPLICATION

Form 7.1

Rule 7.2   Originating Application[1]

IN THE MATTER OF THE INSOLVENCY ACT 1986

Between

Applicant _____

and

Respondent _____

(a) Insert name and address of respondent

Let (a)

attend

before the Judge/Registrar[2] on:—

Date _____

Time _____ hours

Place _____

(b) Insert name of applicant

On the hearing of an application by (b) the applicant for an order in the following terms:—

(c) State the terms of the order to which the applicant claims to be entitled

(c)

The grounds on which the applicant claims to be entitled to the order are:—

(d) Set out grounds or refer to an affidavit in support

(d)

The names and addresses of the persons upon whom it is intended to serve this application are:—

(e) State the names and addresses of the persons intended to be served

(e)

OR

It is not intended to serve any person with this application.

(f) State the applicant's address for service

The applicant's address for service is: (f)

Dated _____

PRINTED AND SUPPLIED BY

Jordans

JORDAN & SONS LIMITED
JORDAN HOUSE
BRUNSWICK PLACE
LONDON N1 6EE
TELEPHONE 01 253 3030
TELEX 261010

Signed: _____

(SOLICITOR FOR THE) APPLICANT

JCP1

If you do not attend, the court may make such order as it thinks fit.

---

1 This is used for an application which is not an application in pending proceedings before the court.

2 Now District Judge.

FORM 22: ORDINARY APPLICATION

Form 7.2

Rule 7.2 Ordinary Application

IN THE MATTER OF THE INSOLVENCY ACT 1986

Between

Applicant _____

and

Respondent _____

Take notice that I intend to apply to the Judge/Registrar[1] on:

Date _____

Time _____ hours

Place _____

(a) State nature and grounds of application

for (a)

Signed: _____

(SOLICITOR FOR THE) APPLICANT

My/Our address for service is:—

(b) Give the name(s) and address(es) of the person(s) (including the respondent) on whom it is intended to serve the application

To: (b)

OR

It is not intended to serve any person with this application

If you do not attend, the court will make such order as it thinks fit

---

1 Now District Judge.

FORM 23: PROXY (COMPANY OR INDIVIDUAL VOLUNTARY ARRANGEMENTS)

Rule 8.1   Insolvency Act 1986   Form 8.1

Proxy (Company or Individual Voluntary Arrangements)

IN BANKRUPTCY

or

IN THE MATTER OF THE INSOLVENCY ACT 1986

Notes to help completion of the form

Please give full name and address for communication

Name of creditor/member _____

Address _____

_____

Please insert name of person (who must be 18 or over) or the "chairman of the meeting" (see note below). If you wish to provide for alternative proxy-holders in the circumstances that your first choice is unable to attend please state the name(s) of the alternatives as well

Name of proxy-holder _____

1 _____

_____

2 _____

_____

3 _____

Please delete words in brackets if the proxy-holder is only to vote as directed ie he has no discretion

I appoint the above person to be my/the creditor's/member's proxy-holder at the meeting of creditors/members to be held on _____ , or at any adjournment of that meeting. The proxy-holder is to propose or vote as instructed below [and in respect of any resolution for which no specific instruction is given, may vote or abstain at his/her discretion].

Voting instructions for resolutions

*Please delete as appropriate

1. For the acceptance/rejection* of the proposed voluntary arrangement [with the following modifications:—]

Any other resolutions which the proxy-holder is to propose or vote in favour of or against should be set out in numbered paragraphs in the space provided below Paragraph 1. If more room is required please use the other side of this form.

_____

_____

_____

_____

_____

_____

This form must be signed

Signature _____ Date _____

Name in CAPITAL LETTERS _____

Only to be completed if the creditor/member has not signed in person

Position with creditor/member or relationship to creditor/member or other authority for signature _____

PRINTED AND SUPPLIED BY

Jordans

JORDAN & SONS LIMITED
JORDAN HOUSE
BRUNSWICK PLACE
LONDON N1 6EE
TELEPHONE 01 253 3030
TELEX 261010

JPR1

Remember: there may be resolutions on the other side of this form.

DRAFT LETTER A: NOMINEE TO DEBTOR

Dear

Your Proposed Voluntary Arrangement

I write to confirm that I am willing to assist you in the preparation of your Proposal for a Voluntary Arrangement under Part VIII of the Insolvency Act 1986.

I confirm that I am a Licensed Insolvency Practitioner.

I confirm my willingness to act as your Nominee and in due course, when the Proposal has been completed, it will be necessary for you to complete a formal Notice to me, pursuant to the Rules.

I have already met with you at length, and obtained sufficient information from you to draft the Proposal, but it is necessary for me to confirm to you some essential matters.

First, whilst I am assisting you in the preparation of the Proposal, this document is nevertheless your Proposal, and you are responsible for its accuracy. I will shortly be letting you have a copy of the draft Proposal. It is important that you go through it in detail and understand it in its entirety. If, when you receive the draft, there are any errors, alterations, amendments or additions that you wish to make, then you should advise me immediately. Furthermore, if there are any points you do not understand, then again, you should contact me at once.

Secondly, it is a mandatory requirement of the Rules that you disclose all your assets and liabilities. You have told me that you have done so, and that the draft Statement of Affairs which has already been prepared is wholly accurate. The importance of a totally accurate disclosure can be demonstrated by giving two examples. If you have omitted any assets, then not only will this almost certainly come to the attention of the creditors in due course, but also this may well constitute what is known as default and may lead to a Bankruptcy Petition being brought against you by either myself as Supervisor, or by any of the creditors. Also, if, in fact, you have not disclosed all your liabilities, then there will be creditors who will not be given notice of the Arrangement. Any creditor not given notice will not be bound by the Arrangement and will be able to take or continue legal proceedings against you, including Bankpruptcy proceedings, notwithstanding the existence of the Voluntary Arrangement.

With the exception of your private residence, none of your assets have been formally valued. The figures for all other assets and liabilities included in the Proposal and supporting documents are figures which you have supplied. This will be made clear in the Proposal. If it subsequently transpires that any of the figures that you have provided are materially wrong, then again, this can constitute default.

Under the terms of the Arrangement, there are a number of continuing obligations placed upon you. I must stress how important your co-operation will be to achieving the success of the Arrangement. If you do not co-operate, and do not comply with my reasonable requirements, then again, this can constitute default.

You have paid me the sum of £. . . . . . and I confirm that this will cover my costs and the legal costs and all disbursements relating to the preparation of the Proposal, the

Application to the Court for the Interim Order, and subsequent legal proceedings thereon, and the calling and holding of the Creditors' Meeting.

As soon as the Proposal and supporting documents have been finalised, an Application will be made to the Court for the Interim Order. We have agreed that Messrs. . . . . will be requested to act as Solicitors in connection with this Application. It will be necessary for you to attend the Hearing of the Application.

If matters go to plan, then I anticipate that the Creditors' Meeting will be held on approximately . . . . It will be necessary for you to attend. I shall take the Chair, but you must be willing to answer all reasonable questions which are put to you by any creditor who attends the Meeting in person. You have informed me that, prior to the holding of the Creditors' Meeting, you are likely to receive £. . . . . . in respect of . . . . We have agreed that these monies must be retained for the purpose of the Arrangement generally and I confirm it is agreed that, as soon as these monies are received, you will pass them to me for me to hold in my firm's Client Account and then, assuming the Proposal is accepted by the Creditors, generally for the purposes of the Arrangement.

Whilst I shall act personally as Nominee, and then, subject to the approval of the Proposal, as Supervisor, I shall generally be assisted on day-to-day matters by my colleagues, ... and . . . . who respectively are Senior Manager and Manager of my firm's Insolvency Department. . . . . is also a licensed Insolvency Practitioner. They have full authority to act on my behalf and, unless you specifically require otherwise, I should be glad if you would contact either of them on any matters or points arising.

I enclose my firm's booklet relating to Individual Voluntary Arrangements, which sets out the basic procedure involved, and the general considerations which are applicable to a Voluntary Arrangement.

I enclose a duplicate copy of this letter which please receipt and return to me to confirm that you have received this letter with its enclosures, and understand the basis upon which I have accepted your instructions.

Yours sincerely

DRAFT LETTER B: NOMINEE TO DEBTOR'S SPOUSE

Dear Madam

I am writing to confirm that I have accepted instructions from your husband . . . . to act as his Nominee for the purpose of a Proposal for a Voluntary Arrangement pursuant to Part VIII of the Insolvency Act 1986.

On the information that your husband has supplied to me, I have formed the view that he is insolvent and, accordingly, the only realistic alternative to a Voluntary Arrangement is Bankruptcy and that is a course of action which he is anxious to avoid. I am sure that you concur with this.

I enclose a copy of your husband's Proposal to his creditors, together with supporting documentation. This Proposal and other documentation will, in due course, be sent to the creditors. I anticipate that a Creditors' Meeting will be held on . . . .

I am writing to you because of the situation relating to your jointly owned property. Your husband values it at £100,000. I understand that there is a Mortgage in favour of . . . . Building Society for £40,000 and a Second Mortgage in favour of . . . . Bank Limited for approximately the same figure. The Proposal envisages that, as soon as the Proposal has been agreed by the creditors, the property will be placed on the open market for sale. It is further proposed that I, if appointed Supervisor, should have the right to determine what Estate Agents and Solicitors should be instructed. Anticipated costs of sale are £3,000, so there is a likely equity available on sale of £17,000. The Proposal envisages that one half of that sum, namely £8,500 will be made available for the Voluntary Arrangement, and that the other half will be paid to you.

I am bound to bring four matters to your attention.

First, you are not, as a matter of law, bound to agree to a sale, but I understand that you do so agree.

Secondly, by agreeing to a sale, it is likely that, in the event of your not having arranged alternative accommodation, your Local Authority will consider that you have voluntarily rendered yourself homeless, and will not be under an obligation to provide you and your family with alternative accommodation.

Thirdly, in the event of your husband having a Bankruptcy Order made against him, it is unlikely that any Trustee in Bankruptcy would seek to enforce a sale of the property for at least twelve months after the date of his appointment.

Fourthly, on the facts available to me, it seems that the whole of the liability to . . . . Bank is in respect of your husband's business, in which you are not a Partner and played no part. I understand that at all material times you have had your own independent employment as a . . . . You should, therefore, understand that it is open to you to argue that the whole of the liability to the Bank should be set against your husband's interest in the property. This would result in your receiving, on sale, more than £8,500 and your husband and his creditors receiving nothing.

I understand from your husband that you are aware of all these points, but nevertheless, to assist with the Voluntary Arrangement, are prepared to proceed on the basis as set out above. I need to be satisfied that you do understand the position, and that you are aware of your rights and the alternative courses of action open to you.

I should also make it clear that, if my understanding of your position is not correct, then it is possible that the proposal will be accepted by the creditors on a faulty basis. This could well lead to subsequent Bankruptcy proceedings being brought against your husband, notwithstanding the approval of the Voluntary Arrangement.

I have raised with you matters of importance and some matters which are technical in their nature and involve not uncomplicated legal points. You will understand that I am assisting your husband and not you, and I cannot offer you advice as such. I do, however, strongly urge you to take your own wholly independent legal advice as to your position as regards the Voluntary Arrangement, with specific reference to the question of the house.

I understand that you are proposing to consult Messrs. . . . . who are your Solicitors. Will you please arrange to see them as quickly as possible and show them the enclosed Proposal and supporting documents and, of course, this letter?

I should be glad to hear from you or your Solicitors within the next . . . . . . days that you confirm and agree the basis upon which the house is to be dealt with in the context of the Voluntary Arrangement and that you specifically agree that I may have the conduct of the sale and that you agree that on completion you will give voluntary possession of the property.

Your husband knows, of course, that I am writing to you in this way, and I am today sending him, by separate post, a copy of this letter.

Yours faithfully

DRAFT LETTER C: NOMINEE TO CREDITOR TAKING PROCEEDINGS

Dear Sir

Re: _____

Following my telephone conversation today with your Mr. . . . ., I am writing to confirm that I am assisting the above-named in connection with his proposed Voluntary Arrangement.

I confirm that an Interim Order was made by the . . . . County Court on . . . . and I enclose a sealed copy.

   You will, of course, be aware that, as a result of the Interim Order being made, s 252(2) of the Insolvency Act 1986 provides that whilst the Interim Order is in force:

(*a*) no Bankruptcy Petition relating to the debtor may be presented or proceeded with; and

(*b*) no other proceedings and no execution or other legal process may be commenced or continued against the debtor or his property, except with the leave of the Court.

On behalf of your Client, ..., you have served on . . . . a Statutory Demand. You were proposing to present a Bankruptcy Petition. I confirm that it is now agreed that you will desist from so doing.

I should be glad to have your immediate confirmation by return of post.

OR:

Your Client has obtained a judgment against Mr. . . . . and you have made application to . . . . Court for a Charging Order Nisi. This Application was due to be heard on . . . . It is confirmed that you will not be proceeding with this Application and on . . . . you will ask the District Judge to adjourn the Application, pending the decision of the Creditors' Meeting to be held on . . . . to consider the Voluntary Arrangement.

You have specifically confirmed that you will not be asking the . . . . Court for leave to pursue the Application for a Charging Order Nisi.

I enclose a copy of a letter which I have written to the Court.

Yours faithfully

DRAFT LETTER D: NOMINEE TO PREFERENTIAL CREDITOR

Dear Sir

Re: _____

I am writing to confirm that I am acting as Nominee in respect of . . . . of . . . . and I enclose a copy of the Proposal and other supporting documents.

An Interim Order was made on . . . . and you will see from the documentation herewith that the Creditors' Meeting is to be held at . . . . on . . . . at . . . . . . o'clock.

On the basis of the information supplied by Mr. . . . ., your total claim is for £. . . . . ., of which £. . . . . . is preferential and £. . . . . . unsecured.

I should be glad to have your early agreement as to these figures and division between preferential and unsecured claims. If you have any other claims against the debtor, then I shall be glad to have details of these as quickly as possible.

I understand that Returns for . . . . and . . . . are still outstanding. You will see that the Proposal specifically contains provision for these Returns to be completed and submitted within . . . . months of the Creditors' Meeting.

Please confirm that this will be acceptable.

If, in fact, there are any other outstanding Returns, will you please advise me immediately so that, if necessary, the appropriate amendment can be made to the Proposal at the Creditors' Meeting.

Yours faithfully

DRAFT LETTER E: NOMINEE TO THIRD PARTY WILLING TO INJECT FUNDS

Dear Sir

Re: _____

I confirm that I am assisting your above-named . . . . in connection with his Proposal for a Voluntary Arrangement pursuant to Part VIII of the Insolvency Act 1986.

I understand that you are aware of your . . . .'s financial difficulties and are willing to assist him.

I further understand that in the event of the creditors accepting the Proposal with the consequential effect that Bankruptcy proceedings will not be taken against your . . . ., then you are willing to make available the sum of £. . . . . . for the general purposes of the Arrangement.

I enclose a copy of the Proposal and supporting documents, and would specifically draw your attention to . . . . and . . . ., the latter demonstrating that, as a result of the payment you are prepared to make, there will be an enhanced dividend to the unsecured creditors.

I am writing to confirm:

1. You are under no obligation whatsoever as a matter of law to make this payment;

2. The sum of £. . . . . . has already been paid to me and is being held by me in an interest bearing Account. If the Arrangement is approved by the creditors, then this sum and accrued interest will be made available for the general purposes of the Arrangement. If the Arrangement is rejected by the creditors, then the sum with accrued interest will be returned to you;

OR

3. Within . . . . . . days of the approval of the Arrangement by creditors, you will let me have the sum of £. . . . . . for the general purposes of the Arrangement.

I understand that you have taken your own legal advice. If, in fact, you have not done so, then I advise you to do so immediately.

Your assistance in this respect is, I know, greatly appreciated by your . . . . and will certainly also be appreciated by the creditors.

Yours faithfully

DRAFT LETTER F: NOMINEE TO COURT TO HEAR CHARGING ORDER

Dear Sir

Case No. . . . . . .
Re: . . . .
Application by . . . . for Charging Order Nisi
to be heard on . . . . . . at . . . . . . o'clock

I am acting as Nominee in respect of . . . . and I understand that the Plaintiff in the above action, ..., is making an Application to be heard by the District Judge on . . . . at . . . . for a Charging Order Nisi.

An Interim Order was made by the . . . . County Court on . . . . and I enclose a sealed copy.

Messrs. . . . . act for the Plaintiff and, in view of the provisions of s 252 of the Insolvency Act 1986, it is agreed that they will not proceed with their Client's Application, but on the Hearing, will seek an Adjournment to the first open date after . . . ., that being the day on which the Creditors' Meeting is to be held.

I should be glad if you would kindly place this letter before the District Judge. In the circumstances, the debtor will not be represented at the Hearing.

I have, of course, sent a copy of this letter to Messrs. . . . .

Yours faithfully

Appendix 3

EXTRACTS FROM INSOLVENCY ACT 1986

Moratorium for insolvent debtor

252   Interim order of court

(1) In the circumstances specified below, the court may in the case of a debtor (being an individual) make an interim order under this section.

(2) An interim order has the effect that, during the period for which it is in force—
   (*a*)   no bankruptcy petition relating to the debtor may be presented or proceeded with, and
   (*b*)   no other proceedings, and no execution or other legal process, may be commenced or continued against the debtor or his property except with the leave of the court.

253   Application for interim order

(1) Application to the court for an interim order may be made where the debtor intends to make a proposal to his creditors for a composition in satisfaction of his debts or a scheme of arrangement of his affairs (from here on referred to, in either case, as a "voluntary arrangement").

(2) The proposal must provide for some person ("the nominee") to act in relation to the voluntary arrangement either as trustee or otherwise for the purpose of supervising its implementation.

(3) Subject as follows, the application may be made—
   (*a*)   if the debtor is an undischarged bankrupt, by the debtor, the trustee of his estate, or the official receiver, and
   (*b*)   in any other case, by the debtor.

(4) An application shall not be made under subsection (3)(*a*) unless the debtor has given notice of his proposal (that is, the proposal to his creditors for a voluntary arrangement) to the official receiver and, if there is one, the trustee of his estate.

(5) An application shall not be made while a bankruptcy petition presented by the debtor is pending, if the court has, under section 273 below, appointed an insolvency practitioner to inquire into the debtor's affairs and report.

254   Effect of application

(1) At any time when an application under section 253 for an interim order is pending, the court may stay any action, execution or other legal process against the property or person of the debtor.

(2) Any court in which proceedings are pending against an individual may, on proof that an application under that section has been made in respect of that individual, either stay the proceedings or allow them to continue on such terms as it thinks fit.

255   Cases in which interim order can be made

(1) The court shall not make an interim order on an application under section 253 unless it is satisfied—

(a)   that the debtor intends to make such a proposal as is mentioned in that section;
(b)   that on the day of the making of the application the debtor was an undischarged bankrupt or was able to petition for his own bankruptcy;
(c)   that no previous application has been made by the debtor for an interim order in the period of 12 months ending with that day; and
(d)   that the nominee under the debtor's proposal to his creditors is a person who is for the time being qualified to act as an insolvency practitioner in relation to the debtor, and is willing to act in relation to the proposal.

(2) The court may make an order if it thinks that it would be appropriate to do so for the purpose of facilitating the consideration and implementation of the debtor's proposal.

(3) Where the debtor is an undischarged bankrupt, the interim order may contain provision as to the conduct of the bankruptcy, and the administration of the bankrupt's estate, during the period for which the order is in force.

(4) Subject as follows, the provision contained in an interim order by virtue of subsection (3) may include provision staying proceedings in the bankruptcy or modifying any provision in this Group of Parts, and any provision of the rules in their application to the debtor's bankruptcy.

(5) An interim order shall not, in relation to a bankrupt, make provision relaxing or removing any of the requirements of provisions in this Group of Parts, or of the rules, unless the court is satisfied that that provision is unlikely to result in any significant diminution in, or in the value of, the debtor's estate for the purposes of the bankruptcy.

(6) Subject to the following provisions of this Part, an interim order made on an application under section 253 ceases to have effect at the end of the period of 14 days beginning with the day after the making of the order.

256   Nominee's report on debtor's proposal

(1) Where an interim order has been made on an application under section 253, the nominee shall, before the order ceases to have effect, submit a report to the court stating—

(a)   whether, in his opinion, a meeting of the debtor's creditors should be summoned to consider the debtor's proposal, and (*b*)   if in his opinion such a meeting should be summoned, the date on which, and time and place at which, he proposes the meeting should be held.

(2) For the purpose of enabling the nominee to prepare his report the debtor shall submit to the nominee—

(*a*)   a document setting out the terms of the voluntary arrangement which the debtor is proposing, and

(*b*)   a statement of his affairs containing—

(i)   such particulars of his creditors and of his debts and other liabilities and of his assets as may be prescribed, and

(ii)   such other information as may be prescribed.

(3) The court may, on an application made by the debtor in a case where the nominee has failed to submit the report required by this section, do one or both of the following, namely—

(*a*)   direct that the nominee shall be replaced as such by another person qualified to act as an insolvency practitioner in relation to the debtor;

(*b*)   direct that the interim order shall continue, or (if it has ceased to have effect) be renewed, for such further period as the court may specify in the direction.

(4) The court may, on the application of the nominee, extend the period for which the interim order has effect so as to enable the nominee to have more time to prepare his report.

(5) If the court is satisfied on receiving the nominee's report that a meeting of the debtor's creditors should be summoned to consider the debtor's proposal, the court shall direct that the period for which the interim order has effect shall be extended, for such further period as it may specify in the direction, for the purpose of enabling the debtor's proposal to be considered by his creditors in accordance with the following provisions of this Part.

(6) The court may discharge the interim order if it is satisfied, on the application of the nominee—

(*a*)   that the debtor has failed to comply with his obligations under subsection (2), or

(*b*)   that for any other reason it would be inappropriate for a meeting of the debtor's creditors to be summoned to consider the debtor's proposal.

257   Summoning of creditors' meeting

(1) Where it has been reported to the court under section 256 that a meeting of the debtor's creditors should be summoned, the nominee (or his replacement under section 256(3)(*a*)) shall, unless the court otherwise directs, summon that meeting for the time, date and place proposed in his report.

(2) The persons to be summoned to the meeting are every creditor of the debtor of whose claim and address the person summoning the meeting is aware.

(3) For this purpose the creditors of a debtor who is an undischarged bankrupt include–

(*a*)   every person who is a creditor of the bankrupt in respect of a bankruptcy debt, and

(*b*)   every person who would be such a creditor if the bankruptcy had commenced on the day on which notice of the meeting is given.

Consideration and implementation of debtor's proposal

258   Decisions of creditors' meeting

(1) A creditors' meeting summoned under section 257 shall decide whether to approve the proposed voluntary arrangement.

(2) The meeting may approve the proposed voluntary arrangement with modifications, but shall not do so unless the debtor consents to each modification.

(3) The modifications subject to which the proposed voluntary arrangement may be approved may include one conferring the functions proposed to be conferred on the nominee on another person qualified to act as an insolvency practitioner in relation to the debtor.

But they shall not include any modification by virtue of which the proposal ceases to be a proposal such as is mentioned in section 253.

(4) The meeting shall not approve any proposal or modification which affects the right of a secured creditor of the debtor to enforce his security, except with the concurrence of the creditor concerned.

(5) Subject as follows, the meeting shall not approve any proposal or modification under which—

   (*a*)   any preferential debt of the debtor is to be paid otherwise than in priority to such of his debts as are not preferential debts, or

   (*b*)   a preferential creditor of the debtor is to be paid an amount in respect of a preferential debt that bears to that debt a smaller proportion than is borne to another preferential debt by the amount that is to be paid in respect of that other debt.

However, the meeting may approve such a proposal or modification with the concurrence of the preferential creditor concerned.

(6) Subject as above, the meeting shall be conducted in accordance with the rules.

(7) In this section "preferential debt" has the meaning given by section 386 in Part XII; and "preferential creditor" is to be construed accordingly.

259   Report of decisions to court

(1) After the conclusion in accordance with the rules of the meeting summoned under section 257, the chairman of the meeting shall report the result of it to the court and, immediately after so reporting, shall give notice of the result of the meeting to such persons as may be prescribed.

(2) If the report is that the meeting has declined (with or without modifications) to approve the debtor's proposal, the court may discharge any interim order which is in force in relation to the debtor.

260   Effect of approval

(1) This section has effect where the meeting summoned under section 257 approves the proposed voluntary arrangement (with or without modifications).

(2) The approved arrangement—

   (*a*)   takes effect as if made by the debtor at the meeting, and (*b*)   binds every person who in accordance with the rules had notice of, and was entitled to vote at, the meeting (whether or not he was present or represented at it) as if he were a party to the arrangement.

(3) The Deeds of Arrangement Act 1914 does not apply to the approved voluntary arrangement.

(4) Any interim order in force in relation to the debtor immediately before the end of the period of 28 days beginning with the day on which the report with respect to the creditors' meeting was made to the court under section 259 ceases to have effect at the end of that period.

This subsection applies except to such extent as the court may direct for the purposes of any application under section 262 below.

(5) Where proceedings on a bankruptcy petition have been stayed by an interim order which ceases to have effect under subsection (4), that petition is deemed, unless the court otherwise orders, to have been dismissed.

261   Effect where debtor an undischarged bankrupt

(1) Subject as follows, where the creditors' meeting summoned under section 257 approves the proposed voluntary arrangement (with or without modifications) and the debtor is an undischarged bankrupt, the court may do one or both of the following, namely—

(*a*)   annul the bankruptcy order by which he was adjudged bankrupt;
(*b*)   give such directions with respect to the conduct of the bankruptcy and the administration of the bankrupt's estate as it thinks appropriate for facilitating the implementation of the approved voluntary arrangement.

(2) The court shall not annul a bankruptcy order under subsection (1)—

(*a*)   at any time before the end of the period of 28 days beginning with the day on which the report of the creditors' meeting was made to the court under section 259, or
(*b*)   at any time when an application under section 262 below, or an appeal in respect of such an application, is pending or at any time in the period within which such an appeal may be brought.

262   Challenge of meeting's decision

(1) Subject to this section, an application to the court may be made, by any of the persons specified below, on one or both of the following grounds, namely—

(*a*)   that a voluntary arrangement approved by a creditors' meeting summoned under section 257 unfairly prejudices the interests of a creditor of the debtor;
(*b*)   that there has been some material irregularity at or in relation to such a meeting.

(2) The persons who may apply under this section are—

(*a*)   the debtor;
(*b*)   a person entitled, in accordance with the rules, to vote at the creditors' meeting;
(*c*)   the nominee (or his replacement under section 256(3)(*a*) or 258(3)); and
(*d*)   if the debtor is an undischarged bankrupt, the trustee of his estate or the official receiver.

(3) An application under this section shall not be made after the end of the period of 28 days beginning with the day on which the report of the creditors' meeting was made to the court under section 259.

(4) Where on an application under this section the court is satisfied as to either of the grounds mentioned in subsection (1), it may do one or both of the following, namely—

    (*a*)   revoke or suspend any approval given by the meeting;

    (*b*)   give a direction to any person for the summoning of a further meeting of the debtor's creditors to consider any revised proposal he may make or, in a case falling within subsection (1)(*b*), to reconsider his original proposal.

(5) Where at any time after giving a direction under subsection (4)(*b*) for the summoning of a meeting to consider a revised proposal the court is satisfied that the debtor does not intend to submit such a proposal, the court shall revoke the direction and revoke or suspend any approval given at the previous meeting.

(6) Where the court gives a direction under subsection (4)(*b*), it may also give a direction continuing or, as the case may require, renewing, for such period as may be specified in the direction, the effect in relation to the debtor of any interim order.

(7) In any case where the court, on an application made under this section with respect to a creditors' meeting, gives a direction under subsection (4)(*b*) or revokes or suspends an approval under subsection (4)(*a*) or (5), the court may give such supplemental directions as it thinks fit and, in particular, directions with respect to—

    (*a*)   things done since the meeting under any voluntary arrangement approved by the meeting, and

    (*b*)   such things done since the meeting as could not have been done if an interim order had been in force in relation to the debtor when they were done.

(8) Except in pursuance of the preceding provisions of this section, an approval given at a creditors' meeting summoned under section 257 is not invalidated by any irregularity at or in relation to the meeting.

263   Implementation and supervision of approved voluntary arrangement

(1) This section applies where a voluntary arrangement approved by a creditors' meeting summoned under section 257 has taken effect.

(2) The person who is for the time being carrying out, in relation to the voluntary arrangement, the functions conferred by virtue of the approval on the nominee (or his replacement under section 256(3)(*a*) or 258(3)) shall be known as the supervisor of the voluntary arrangement.

(3) If the debtor, any of his creditors or any other person is dissatisfied by any act, omission or decision of the supervisor, he may apply to the court; and on such an application the court may—

    (*a*)   confirm, reverse or modify any act or decision of the supervisor,

    (*b*)   give him directions, or

    (*c*)   make such other order as it thinks fit.

(4) The supervisor may apply to the court for directions in relation to any particular matter arising under the voluntary arrangement.

(5) The court may, whenever—

    (*a*)   it is expedient to appoint a person to carry out the functions of the supervisor, and

    (*b*)   it is inexpedient, difficult or impracticable for an appointment to be made without the assistance of the court,

make an order appointing a person who is qualified to act as an insolvency practitioner in relation to the debtor, either in substitution for the existing supervisor or to fill a vacancy.

This is without prejudice to section 41(2) of the Trustee Act 1925 (power of court to appoint trustees of deeds of arrangement).

(6) The power conferred by subsection (5) is exercisable so as to increase the number of persons exercising the functions of the supervisor or, where there is more than one person exercising those functions, so as to replace one or more of those persons.

PART IX

BANKRUPTCY

CHAPTER I

BANKRUPTCY PETITIONS; BANKRUPTCY ORDERS

Preliminary

264 Who may present a bankruptcy petition

(1) A petition for a bankruptcy order to be made against an individual may be presented to the court in accordance with the following provisions of this Part—
   (a)   by one of the individual's creditors or jointly by more than one of them,
   (b)   by the individual himself,
   (c)   by the supervisor of, or any person (other than the individual) who is for the time being bound by, a voluntary arrangement proposed by the individual and approved under Part VIII, or
   (d)   where a criminal bankruptcy order has been made against the individual, by the Official Petitioner or by any person specified in the order in pursuance of section 39(3)(b) of the Powers of Criminal Courts Act 1973.

(2) Subject to those provisions, the court may make a bankruptcy order on any such petition.

Debtor's petition

272 Grounds of debtor's petition

(1) A debtor's petition may be presented to the court only on the grounds that the debtor is unable to pay his debts.

(2) The petition shall be accompanied by a statement of the debtor's affairs containing—
   (a)   such particulars of the debtor's creditors and of his debts and other liabilities and of his assets as may be prescribed, and
   (b)   such other information as may be prescribed.

273 Appointment of insolvency practitioner by the court

(1) Subject to the next section, on the hearing of a debtor's petition the court shall not make a bankruptcy order if it appears to the court—
   (a)   that if a bankruptcy order were made the aggregate amount of the bankruptcy debts, so far as unsecured, would be less than the small bankruptcies level,
   (b)   that if a bankruptcy order were made, the value of the bankrupt's estate would be equal to or more than the minimum amount,

   (*c*)   that within the period of 5 years ending with the presentation of the petition the debtor has neither been adjudged bankrupt nor made a composition with his creditors in satisfaction of his debts or a scheme of arrangement of his affairs, and

   (*d*)   that it would be appropriate to appoint a person to prepare a report under section 274.

"The minimum amount" and "the small bankruptcies level" mean such amounts as may for the time being be prescribed for the purposes of this section.

(2) Where on the hearing of the petition, it appears to the court as mentioned in subsection (1), the court shall appoint a person who is qualified to act as an insolvency practitioner in relation to the debtor—

   (*a*)   to prepare a report under the next section, and

   (*b*)   subject to section 258(3) in Part VIII, to act in relation to any voluntary arrangement to which the report relates either as trustee or otherwise for the purpose of supervising its implementation.

274　Action on report of insolvency practitioner

(1) A person appointed under section 273 shall inquire into the debtor's affairs and, within such period as the court may direct, shall submit a report to the court stating whether the debtor is willing, for the purposes of Part VIII, to make a proposal for a voluntary arrangement.

(2) A report which states that the debtor is willing as above mentioned shall also state—

   (*a*)   whether, in the opinion of the person making the report, a meeting of the debtor's creditors should be summoned to consider the proposal, and

   (*b*)   if in that person's opinion such a meeting should be summoned, the date on which, and time and place at which, he proposes the meeting should be held.

(3) On considering a report under this section the court may—

   (*a*)   without any application, make an interim order under section 252, if it thinks that it is appropriate to do so for the purpose of facilitating the consideration and implementation of the debtor's proposal, or

   (*b*)   if it thinks it would be inappropriate to make such an order, make a bankruptcy order.

(4) An interim order made by virtue of this section ceases to have effect at the end of such period as the court may specify for the purpose of enabling the debtor's proposal to be considered by his creditors in accordance with the applicable provisions of Part VIII.

(5) Where it has been reported to the court under this section that a meeting of the debtor's creditors should be summoned, the person making the report shall, unless the court otherwise directs, summon that meeting for the time, date and place proposed in his report.

The meeting is then deemed to have been summoned under section 257 in Part VIII, and subsections (2) and (3) of that section, and sections 258 to 263 apply accordingly.

275　Summary administration

(1) Where on the hearing of a debtor's petition the court makes a bankruptcy order and the case is as specified in the next subsection, the court shall, if it appears to it appropriate to do so, issue a certificate for the summary administration of the bankrupt's estate.

(2) That case is where it appears to the court—
- (*a*) that if a bankruptcy order were made the aggregate amount of the bankruptcy debts so far as unsecured would be less than the small bankruptcies level (within the meaning given by section 273), and
- (*b*) that within the period of 5 years ending with the presentation of the petition the debtor has neither been adjudged bankrupt nor made a composition with his creditors in satisfaction of his debts or a scheme of arrangement of his affairs,

whether the bankruptcy order is made because it does not appear to the court as mentioned in section 273(1)(*b*) or (*d*), or it is made because the court thinks it would be inappropriate to make an interim order under section 252.

(3) The court may at any time revoke a certificate issued under this section if it appears to it that, on any grounds existing at the time the certificate was issued, the certificate ought not to have been issued.

Other cases for special consideration

276 Default in connection with voluntary arrangement

(1) The court shall not make a bankruptcy order on a petition under section 264(1)(*c*) (supervisor of, or person bound by, voluntary arrangement proposed and approved) unless it is satisfied—
- (*a*) that the debtor has failed to comply with his obligations under the voluntary arrangement, or
- (*b*) that information which was false or misleading in any material particular or which contained material omissions—
  - (i) was contained in any statement of affairs or other document supplied by the debtor under Part VIII to any person, or
  - (ii) was otherwise made available by the debtor to his creditors at or in connection with a meeting summoned under that Part, or
- (*c*) that the debtor has failed to do all such things as may for the purposes of the voluntary arrangement have been reasonably required of him by the supervisor of the arrangement.

(2) Where a bankruptcy order is made on a petition under section 264(1)(*c*), any expenses properly incurred as expenses of the administration of the voluntary arrangement in question shall be a first charge on the bankrupt's estate.

282 Court's power to annul bankruptcy order

(1) The court may annul a bankruptcy order if it at any time appears to the court—
- (*a*) that, on any grounds existing at the time the order was made, the order ought not to have been made, or
- (*b*) that, to the extent required by the rules, the bankruptcy debts and the expenses of the bankruptcy have all, since the making of the order, been either paid or secured for to the satisfaction of the court.

(2) The court may annul a bankruptcy order made against an individual on a petition under paragraph (*a*), (*b*) or (*c*) of section 264(1) if it at any time appears to the court, on an application by the Official Petitioner—
- (*a*) that the petition was pending at a time when a criminal bankruptcy order was made against the individual or was presented after such an order was so made, and

(*b*)   no appeal is pending (within the meaning of section 277) against the individual's conviction of any offence by virtue of which the criminal bankruptcy order was made;

and the court shall annual a bankruptcy order made on a petition under section 264(1)(*d*) if it at any time appears to the court that the criminal bankruptcy order on which the petition was based has been rescinded in consequence of an appeal.

(3)   The court may annul a bankruptcy order whether or not the bankrupt has been discharged from the bankruptcy.

(4)   Where the court annuls a bankruptcy order (whether under this section or under section 261 in Part VIII)—

(*a*)   any sale or other disposition of property, payment made or other thing duly done, under any provision in this Group of Parts, by or under the authority of the official receiver or a trustee of the bankrupt's estate or by the court is valid, but

(*b*)   if any of the bankrupt's estate is then vested, under any such provision, in such a trustee, it shall vest in such person as the court may appoint or, in default of any such appointment, revert to the bankrupt on such terms (if any) as the court may direct;

and the court may include in its order such supplemental provisions as may be authorised by the rules.

(5)   In determining for the purposes of section 279 whether a person was an undischarged bankrupt at any time, any time when he was a bankrupt by virtue of an order that was subsequently annulled is to be disregarded.

CHAPTER II

PROTECTION OF BANKRUPT'S ESTATE AND INVESTIGATION OF HIS AFFAIRS

283   Definition of bankrupt's estate

(1)   Subject as follows, a bankrupt's estate for the purposes of any of this Group of Parts comprises—

(*a*)   all property belonging to or vested in the bankrupt at the commencement of the bankruptcy, and

(*b*)   any property which by virtue of any of the following provisions of this Part is comprised in that estate or is treated as falling within the preceding paragraph.

(2)   Subsection (1) does not apply to—

(*a*)   such tools, books, vehicles and other items of equipment as are necessary to the bankrupt for use personally by him in his employment, business or vocation;

(*b*)   such clothing, bedding, furniture, household equipment and provisions as are necessary for satisfying the basic domestic needs of the bankrupt and his family.

This subsection is subject to section 308 in Chapter IV (certain excluded property reclaimable by trustee).

(3)   Subsection (1) does not apply to—

(*a*)   property held by the bankrupt on trust for any other person, or

(*b*)   the right of nomination to a vacant ecclesiastical benefice.

(4)   References in any of this Group of Parts to property, in relation to a bankrupt, include references to any power exercisable by him over or in respect of property except

in so far as the power is exercisable over or in respect of property not for the time being comprised in the bankrupt's estate and—

    (*a*)   is so exercisable at a time after either the official receiver has had his release in respect of that estate under section 299(2) in Chapter III or a meeting summoned by the trustee of that estate under section 331 in Chapter IV has been held, or

    (*b*)   cannot be so exercised for the benefit of the bankrupt;

and a power exercisable over or in respect of property is deemed for the purposes of any of this Group of Parts to vest in the person entitled to exercise it at the time of the transaction or event by virtue of which it is exercisable by that person (whether or not it becomes so exercisable at that time).

(5) For the purposes of any such provision in this Group of Parts, property comprised in a bankrupt's estate is so comprised subject to the rights of any person other than the bankrupt (whether as a secured creditor of the bankrupt or otherwise) in relation thereto, but disregarding—

    (*a*)   any rights in relation to which a statement such as is required by section 269(1)(*a*) was made in the petition on which the bankrupt was adjudged bankrupt, and

    (*b*)   any rights which have been otherwise given up in accordance with the rules.

(6) This section has effect subject to the provisions of any enactment not contained in this Act under which any property is to be excluded from a bankrupt's estate.

284 Restrictions on dispositions of property

(1) Where a person is adjudged bankrupt, any disposition of property made by that person in the period to which this section applies is void except to the extent that it is or was made with the consent of the court, or is or was subsequently ratified by the court.

(2) Subsection (1) applies to a payment (whether in cash or otherwise) as it applies to a disposition of property and, accordingly, where any payment is void by virtue of that subsection, the person paid shall hold the sum paid for the bankrupt as part of his estate.

(3) This section applies to the period beginning with the day of the presentation of the petition for the bankruptcy order and ending with the vesting, under Chapter IV of this Part, of the bankrupt's estate in a trustee.

(4) The preceding provisions of this section do not give a remedy against any person—

    (*a*)   in respect of any property or payment which he received before the commencement of the bankruptcy in good faith, for value and without notice that the petition had been presented, or

    (*b*)   in respect of any interest in property which derives from an interest in respect of which there is, by virtue of this subsection, no remedy.

(5) Where after the commencement of his bankruptcy the bankrupt has incurred a debt to a banker or other person by reason of the making of a payment which is void under this section, that debt is deemed for the purposes of any of this Group of Parts to have been incurred before the commencement of the bankruptcy unless—

    (*a*)   that banker or person had notice of the bankruptcy before the debt was incurred, or

    (*b*)   it is not reasonably practicable for the amount of the payment to be recovered from the person to whom it was made.

(6) A disposition of property is void under this section notwithstanding that the property is not or, as the case may be, would not be comprised in the bankrupt's estate; but nothing in this section affects any disposition made by a person of property held by him on trust for any other person.

285   Restriction on proceedings and remedies

(1) At any time when proceedings on a bankruptcy petition are pending or an individual has been adjudged bankrupt the court may stay any action, execution or other legal process against the property or person of the debtor or, as the case may be, of the bankrupt.

(2) Any court in which proceedings are pending against any individual may, on proof that a bankruptcy petition has been presented in respect of that individual or that he is an undischarged bankrupt, either stay the proceedings or allow them to continue on such terms as it thinks fit.

SCHEDULE 1

Power of Administrator or Administrative Receiver

1. Power to take possession of, collect and get in the property of the company and, for that purpose, to take such proceedings as may seem to him expedient.

2. Power to sell or otherwise dispose of the property of the company by public auction or private contract or, in Scotland, to sell, feu, hire out or otherwise dispose of the property of the company by public roup or private bargain.

3. Power to raise or borrow money and grant security therefor over the property of the company.

4. Power to appoint a solicitor or accountant or other professionally qualified person to assist him in the performance of his functions.

5. Power to bring or defend any action or other legal proceedings in the name and on behalf of the company.

6. Power to refer to arbitration any question affecting the company.

7. Power to effect and maintain insurances in respect of the business and property of the company.

8. Power to use the company's seal.

9. Power to do all acts and to execute in the name and on behalf of the company any deed, receipt or other document.

10. Power to draw, accept, make and endorse any bill of exchange or promissory note in the name and on behalf of the company.

11. Power to appoint any agent to do any business which he is unable to do himself or which can more conveniently be done by an agent and power to employ and dismiss employees.

12. Power to do all such things (including the carrying out of works) as may be necessary for the realisation of the property of the company.

13. Power to make any payment which is necessary or incidental to the performance of his functions.

14. Power to carry on the business of the company.

15. Power to establish subsidiaries of the company.

16. Power to transfer to subsidiaries of the company the whole or any part of the business and property of the company.

17. Power to grant or accept a surrender of a lease or tenancy of any of the property of the company, and to take a lease or tenancy of any property required or convenient for the business of the company.

18. Power to make any arrangement or compromise on behalf of the company.

19. Power to call up any uncalled capital of the company.

20. Power to rank and claim in the bankruptcy, insolvency, sequestration or liquidation of any person indebted to the company and to receive dividends, and to accede to trust deeds for the creditors of any such person.

21. Power to present or defend a petition for the winding up of the company.

22. Power to change the situation of the company's registered office.

23. Power to do all other things incidental to the exercise of the foregoing powers.

SCHEDULE 5

Powers of Trustee in Bankruptcy

Part I

Powers Exercisable with Sanction

1. Power to carry on any business of the bankrupt so far as may be necessary for winding it up beneficially and so far as the trustee is able to do so without contravening any requirement imposed by or under any enactment.

2. Power to bring, institute or defend any action or legal proceedings relating to the property comprised in the bankrupt's estate.

3. Power to accept as the consideration for the sale of any property comprised in the bankrupt's estate a sum of money payable at a future time subject to such stipulations as to security or otherwise as the creditors' committee or the court thinks fit.

4. Power to mortgage or pledge any part of the property comprised in the bankrupt's estate for the purpose of raising money for the payment of his debts.

5. Power, where any right, option or other power forms part of the bankrupt's estate, to make payments or incur liabilities with a view to obtaining, for the benefit of the creditors, any property which is the subject of the right, option or power.

6. Power to refer to arbitration, or compromise on such terms as may be agreed on, any debts, claims or liabilities subsisting or supposed to subsist between the bankrupt and any person who may have incurred any liability to the bankrupt.

7. Power to make such compromise or other arrangement as may be thought expedient with creditors, or persons claiming to be creditors, in respect of bankruptcy debts.

8. Power to make such compromise or other arrangement as may be thought expedient with respect to any claim arising out of or incidental to the bankrupt's estate made or capable of being made on the trustee by any person or by the trustee on any person.

Part II

General Powers

9. Power to sell any part of the property for the time being comprised in the bankrupt's estate, including the goodwill and book debts of any business.

10. Power to give receipts for any money received by him, being receipts which effectually discharge the person paying the money from all responsibility in respect of its application.

11. Power to prove, rank, claim and draw a dividend in respect of such debts due to the bankrupt as are comprised in his estate.

12. Power to exercise in relation to any property comprised in the bankrupt's estate any powers the capacity to exercise which is vested in him under Parts VIII to XI of this Act.

13. Power to deal with any property comprised in the estate to which the bankrupt is beneficially entitled as tenant in tail in the same manner as the bankrupt might have dealt with it.

Part III

Ancillary Powers

14. For the purposes of, or in connection with, the exercise of any of his powers under Parts VIII to XI of this Act, the trustee may, by his official name—
    (a)   hold property of every description,
    (b)   make contracts,
    (c)   sue and be sued,
    (d)   enter into engagements binding on himself and, in respect of the bankrupt's estate, on his successors in office,
    (e)   employ an agent,
    (f)   execute any power of attorney, deed or other instrument;
and he may do any other act which is necessary or expedient for the purposes of or in connection with the exercise of those powers.

SCHEDULE 6

THE CATEGORIES OF PREFERENTIAL DEBTS

Category 1: Debts due to Inland Revenue

1. Sums due at the relevant date from the debtor on account of deductions of income tax from emoluments paid during the period of 12 months next before that date.

The deductions here referred to are those which the debtor was liable to make under section 204 of the Income and Corporation Taxes Act 1970 (pay as you earn), less the amount of the repayments of income tax which the debtor was liable to make during that period.

2. Sums due at the relevant date from the debtor in respect of such deductions as are required to be made by the debtor for that period under section 69 of the Finance (No. 2) Act 1975 (sub-contractors in the construction industry).

Category 2: Debts due to Customs and Excise

3. Any value added tax which is referable to the period of 6 months next before the relevant date (which period is referred to below as "the 6-month period").

For the purposes of this paragraph—

(a)   where the whole of the prescribed accounting period to which any value added tax is attributable falls within the 6-month period, the whole amount of that tax is referable to that period; and

(b)   in any other case the amount of any value added tax which is referable to the 6-month period is the proportion of the tax which is equal to such proportion (if any) of the accounting reference period in question as falls within the 6-month period;

and in sub-paragraph (a) "prescribed" means prescribed by regulations under the Value Added Tax Act 1983.

4. The amount of any car tax which is due at the relevant date from the debtor and which became due within a period of 12 months next before that date.

5. Any amount which is due—

(a)   by way of general betting duty or bingo duty, or

(b)   under section 12(1) of the Betting and Gaming Duties Act 1981 (general betting duty and pool betting duty recoverable from agent collecting stakes), or

(c)   under section 14 of, or Schedule 2 to, that Act (gaming licence duty),

from the debtor at the relevant date and which became due within the period of 12 months next before that date.

Category 3: Social security contributions

6. All sums which on the relevant date are due from the debtor on account of Class 1 or Class 2 contributions under the Social Security Act 1975 or the Social Security (Northern Ireland) Act 1975 and which became due from the debtor in the 12 months next before the relevant date.

7. All sums which on the relevant date have been assessed on and are due from the debtor on account of Class 4 contributions under either of those Acts of 1975, being sums which—

(*a*)   are due to the Commissioners of Inland Revenue (rather than to the Secretary of State or a Northern Ireland department), and

(*b*)   are assessed on the debtor up to 5th April next before the relevant date,

but not exceeding, in the whole, any one year's assessment.

Category 4: Contributions to occupational pension schemes, etc.

8. Any sum which is owed by the debtor and is a sum to which Schedule 3 to the Social Security Pensions Act 1975 applies (contributions to occupational pension schemes and state scheme premiums).

Category 5: Remuneration, etc., of employees

9. So much of any amount which —

(*a*)   is owed by the debtor to a person who is or has been an employee of the debtor, and

(*b*)   is payable by way of remuneration in respect of the whole or any part of the period of 4 months next before the relevant date,

as does not exceed so much as may be prescribed by order made by the Secretary of State.

10. An amount owed by way of accrued holiday remuneration, in respect of any period of employment before the relevant date, to a person whose employment by the debtor has been terminated, whether before, on or after that date.

11. So much of any sum owed in respect of money advanced for the purpose as has been applied for the payment of a debt which, if it had not been paid, would have been a debt falling within paragraph 9 and 10.

12. So much of any amount which—

(*a*)   is ordered (whether before or after the relevant date) to be paid by the debtor under the Reserve Forces (Safeguard of Employment) Act 1985, and

(*b*)   is so ordered in respect of a default made by the debtor before that date in the discharge of his obligations under that Act,

as does not exceed such amount as may be prescribed by order made by the Secretary of State.

Interpretation for Category 5

13.—(1) For the purposes of paragraphs 9 to 12, a sum is payable by the debtor to a person by way of remuneration in respect of any period if—

(*a*)   it is paid as wages or salary (whether payable for time or for piece work or earned wholly or partly by way of commission) in respect of services rendered to the debtor in that period, or

(*b*)   it is an amount falling within the following sub-paragraph and is payable by the debtor in respect of that period.

(2) An amount falls within this sub-paragraph if it is—

(*a*)   a guarantee payment under section 12(1) of the Employment Protection (Consolidation) Act 1978 (employee without work to do for a day or part of a day);

(*b*)   remuneration on suspension on medical grounds under section 19 of that Act;

(*c*)   any payment for time off under section 27(3) (trade union duties), 31(3) (looking for work, etc.) or 31A(4) (ante-natal care) of that Act; or (*d*) remuneration under a protective award made by an industrial tribunal under section 101 of the Employment Protection Act 1975 (redundancy dismissal with compensation).

14.—(1) This paragraph relates to a case in which a person's employment has been terminated by or in consequence of his employer going into liquidation or being adjudged bankrupt or (his employer being a company not in liquidation) by or in consequence of—

(*a*) a receiver being appointed as mentioned in section 40 of this Act (debenture-holders secured by floating charge), or

(*b*) the appointment of a receiver under section 53(6) or 54(5) of this Act (Scottish company with property subject to floating charge), or

(*c*) the taking of possession by debenture-holders (so secured), as mentioned in section 196 of the Companies Act.

(2) For the purposes of paragraphs 9 to 12, holiday remuneration is deemed to have accrued to that persion in respect of any period of employment if, by virtue of his contract of employment or of any enactment that remuneration would have accrued in respect of that period if his employment had continued until he became entitled to be allowed the holiday.

(3) The reference in sub-paragraph (2) to any enactment includes an order or direction made under an enactment.

15. Without prejudice to paragraphs 13 and 14—

(*a*) any remuneration payable by the debtor to a person in respect of a period of holiday or of absence from work through sickness or other good cause is deemed to be wages or (as the case may be) salary in respect of services rendered to the debtor in that period, and

(*b*) references here and in those paragraphs to remuneration in respect of a period of holiday include any sums which, if they had been paid, would have been treated for the purposes of the enactments relating to social security as earnings in respect of that period.

Orders

16. An order under paragraph 9 or 12—

(*a*) may contain such transitional provisions as may appear to the Secretary of State necessary or expedient;

(*b*) shall be made by statutory instrument subject to annulment in pursuance of a resolution of either House of Parliament.

Appendix 4

EXTRACTS FROM INSOLVENCY RULES 1986

Note: amendments made to these provisions by the Insolvency (Amendment) Rules 1987 are shown in square brackets.

THE SECOND GROUP OF PARTS

INDIVIDUAL INSOLVENCY; BANKRUPTCY

PART 5

INDIVIDUAL VOLUNTARY ARRANGEMENTS

5.1 Introductory

(1) The Rules in this Part apply where a debtor, with a view to an application for an interim order under Part VIII of the Act, makes a proposal to his creditors for a voluntary arrangement, that is to say, a composition in satisfaction of his debts or a scheme of arrangement of his affairs.

(2) The Rules apply whether the debtor is an undischarged bankrupt ("Case 1"), or he is not ("Case 2").

SECTION A: THE DEBTOR'S PROPOSAL

5.2 Preparation of proposal

The debtor shall prepare for the intended nominee a proposal on which (with or without amendments to be made under Rule 5.3(3) below) to make his report to the court under section 256.

5.3 Contents of proposal

(1) The debtor's proposal shall provide a short explanation why, in his opinion, a voluntary arrangement under Part VIII is desirable, and give reasons why his creditors may be expected to concur with such an arrangement.

(2) The following matters shall be stated, or otherwise dealt with, in the proposal—
    (a)   the following matters, so far as within the debtor's immediate knowledge—
        (i)   his assets, with an estimate of their respective values,

229

       (ii)   the extent (if any) to which the assets are charged in favour of creditors,

       (iii) the extent (if any) to which particular assets are to be excluded from the voluntary arrangement;

(*b*)   particulars of any property, other than assets of the debtor himself, which is proposed to be included in the arrangement, the source of such property and the terms on which it is to be made available for inclusion;

(*c*)   the nature and amount of the debtor's liabilities (so far as within his immediate knowledge), the manner in which they are proposed to be met, modified, postponed or otherwise dealt with by means of the arrangement and (in particular)—

       (i)   how it is proposed to deal with preferential creditors (defined in section 258(7)) and creditors who are, or claim to be, secured,

       (ii)   how associates of the debtor (being creditors of his) are proposed to be treated under the arrangement, and

       (iii) in Case 1 whether, to the debtor's knowledge, claims have been made under section 339 (transactions at an undervalue), section 340 (preferences) or section 343 (extortionate credit transactions), or there are circumstances giving rise to the possibility of such claims, and in Case 2 whether there are circumstances which would give rise to the possibility of such claims in the event that he should be adjudged bankrupt,

and, where any such circumstances are present, whether, and if so how, it is proposed under the voluntary arrangement to make provision for wholly or partly indemnifying the insolvent estate in respect of such claims;

(*d*)   whether any, and if so what, guarantees have been given of the debtor's debts by other persons, specifying which (if any) of the guarantors are associates of his;

(*e*)   the proposed duration of the voluntary arrangement;

(*f*)   the proposed dates of distributions to creditors, with estimates of their amounts;

(*g*)   the amount proposed to be paid to the nominee (as such) by way of remuneration and expenses;

(*h*)   the manner in which it is proposed that the supervisor of the arrangement should be remunerated, and his expenses defrayed;

(*j*)   whether, for the purposes of the arrangement, any guarantees are to be offered by any persons other than the debtor, and whether (if so) any security is to be given or sought;

(*k*)   the manner in which funds held for the purposes of the arrangement are to be banked, invested or otherwise dealt with pending distribution to creditors;

(*l*)   the manner in which funds held for the purpose of payment to creditors, and not so paid on the termination of the arrangement, are to be dealt with;

(*m*) if the debtor has any business, the manner in which it is proposed to be conducted during the course of the arrangement;

(*n*)   details of any further credit facilities which it is intended to arrange for the debtor, and how the debts so arising are to be paid;

(*o*)   the functions which are to be undertaken by the supervisor of the arrangement;

(*p*)   the name, address and qualification of the person proposed as supervisor of the voluntary arrangement, and confirmation that he is (so far as the debtor is aware) qualified to act as an insolvency practitioner in relation to him.

(3) With the agreement in writing of the nominee, the debtor's proposal may be amended at any time up to the delivery of the former's report to the court under section 256.

5.4 Notice to intended nominee

(1) The debtor shall give to the intended nominee written notice of his proposal.

(2) The notice, accompanied by a copy of the proposal, shall be delivered either to the nominee himself, or to a person authorised to take delivery of documents on his behalf.

(3) If the intended nominee agrees to act, he shall cause a copy of the notice to be endorsed to the effect that it has been received by him on a specified date.

(4) The copy of the notice so endorsed shall be returned by the nominee forthwith to the debtor at an address specified by him in the notice for that purpose.

(5) Where (in Case 1) the debtor gives notice of his proposal to the official receiver and (if any) the trustee, the notice must contain the name and address of the insolvency practitioner who has agreed to act as nominee.

5.5 Application for interim order

(1) An application to the court for an interim order under Part VIII of the Act shall be accompanied by an affidavit of the following matters—
  (a) the reasons for making the application;
  (b) particulars of any execution or other legal process which, to the debtor's knowledge, has been commenced against him;
  (c) that he is an undischarged bankrupt or (as the case may be) that he is able to petition for his own bankruptcy;
  (d) that no previous application for an interim order has been made by or in respect of the debtor in the period of 12 months ending with the date of the affidavit; and
  (e) that the nominee under the proposal (naming him) is a person who is qualified to act as an insolvency practitioner in relation to the debtor, and is willing to act in relation to the proposal.

(2) A copy of the notice to the intended nominee under Rule 5.4, endorsed to the effect that he agrees so to act, [and a copy of the debtor's proposal given to the nominee under that Rule] shall be exhibited to the affidavit.

(3) On receiving the application and affidavit, the court shall fix a venue for the hearing of the application.

(4) The applicant shall give at least 2 days' notice of the hearing—
  (a) in Case 1, to the bankrupt, the official receiver and the trustee (whichever of those three is not himself the applicant),
  (b) in Case 2, to any creditor who (to the debtor's knowledge) has presented a bankruptcy petition against him, and
  (c) in either case, to the nominee who has agreed to act in relation to the debtor's proposal.

[Court in which application to be made

5.5A—(1) Except in the case of a bankrupt, an application to the court under Part VIII of the Act shall be made to a court in which the debtor would be entitled to present his own petition in bankruptcy under Rule 6.40.

(2) The application shall contain sufficient information to establish that it is brought in the appropriate court.

(3) In the case of a bankrupt such an application shall be made to the court having the conduct of his bankruptcy and shall be filed with those bankruptcy proceedings.]

5.6   Hearing of the application

(1) Any of the persons who have been given notice under Rule 5.5(4) may appear or be represented at the hearing of the application.

(2) The court, in deciding whether to make an interim order on the application, shall take into account any representations made by or on behalf of any of those persons (in particular, whether an order should be made containing such provision as is referred to in section 255(3) and (4)).

(3) If the court makes an interim order, it shall fix a venue for consideration of the nominee's report. Subject to the following paragraph, the date for that consideration shall be not later than that on which the interim order ceases to have effect under section 255(6)).

(4) If under section 256(4) an extension of time is granted for filing the nominee's report, the court shall, unless there appear to be good reasons against it, correspondingly extend the period for which the interim order has effect.

5.7   Action to follow making of order

(1) Where an interim order is made, at least 2 sealed copies of the order shall be sent by the court forthwith to the person who applied for it; and that person shall serve one of the copies on the nominee under the debtor's proposal.

(2) The applicant shall also forthwith give notice of the making of the order to any person who was given notice of the hearing pursuant to Rule 5.5(4) and was not present or represented at it.

5.8   Statement of affairs

(1) In Case 1, if the debtor has already delivered a statement of affairs under section 272 (debtor's petition) or 288 (creditor's petition), he need not deliver a further statement unless so required by the nominee, with a view to supplementing or amplifying the former one.

(2) In Case 2, the debtor shall, within 7 days after his proposal is delivered to the nominee, or within such longer time as the latter may allow, deliver to the nominee a statement of his (the debtor's) affairs.

(3) The statement shall comprise the following particulars (supplementing or amplifying, so far as is necessary for clarifying the state of the debtor's affairs, those already given in his proposal)—

    (a) a list of his assets, divided into such categories as are appropriate for easy identification, with estimated values assigned to each category;

    (b) in the case of any property on which a claim against the debtor is wholly or partly secured, particulars of the claim and its amount, and of how and when the security was created;

    (c) the names and addresses of the debtor's preferential creditors (defined in section 258(7)), with the amounts of their respective claims;

    (d) the names and addresses of the debtor's unsecured creditors, with the amounts of their respective claims;

(e)   particulars of any debts owed by or to the debtor to or by persons who are associates of his;

(f)   such other particulars (if any) as the nominee may in writing require to be furnished for the purposes of making his report to the court on the debtor's proposal.

(4) The statement of affairs shall be made up to a date not earlier than 2 weeks before the date of the notice to the nominee under Rule 5.4.

However, the nominee may allow an extension of that period to the nearest practicable date (not earlier than 2 months before the date of the notice under Rule 5.4); and if he does so, he shall give his reasons in his report to the court on the debtor's proposal.

(5) The statement shall be certified by the debtor as correct, to the best of his knowledge and belief.

5.9   Additional disclosure for assistance of nominee

(1) If it appears to the nominee that he cannot properly prepare his report on the basis of information in the debtor's proposal and statement of affairs, he may call on the debtor to provide him with—

(a)   further and better particulars as to the circumstances in which, and the reasons why, he is insolvent or (as the case may be) threatened with insolvency;

(b)   particulars of any previous proposals which have been made by him under Part VIII of the Act;

(c)   any further information with respect to his affairs which the nominee thinks necessary for the purposes of his report.

(2) The nominee may call on the debtor to inform him whether and in what circumstances he has at any time—

(a)   been concerned in the affairs of any company (whether or not incorporated in England and Wales) which has become insolvent, or

(b)   been adjudged bankrupt, or entered into an arrangement with his creditors.

(3) For the purpose of enabling the nominee to consider the debtor's proposal and prepare his report on it, the latter must give him access to his accounts and records.

5.10   Nominee's report on the proposal

(1) The nominee's report shall be delivered by him to the court not less than 2 days before the interim order ceases to have effect.

(2) With his report the nominee shall deliver—

(a)   a copy of the debtor's proposal (with amendments, if any, authorised under Rule 5.3(3)); and

(b)   a copy or summary of any statement of affairs provided by the debtor.

(3) If the nominee makes known his opinion that a meeting of the debtor's creditors should be summoned under section 257, his report shall have annexed to it his comments on the debtor's proposal.

If his opinion is otherwise, he shall give his reasons for that opinion.

(4) The court shall cause the nominee's report to be endorsed with the date on which it is filed in court. Any creditor of the debtor is entitled, at all reasonable times on any business day, to inspect the file.

(5) In Case 1, the nominee shall send to the official receiver and (if any) the trustee—

(*a*)   a copy of the debtor's proposal,

(*b*)   a copy of his (the nominee's) report and his comments accompanying it (if any), and

(*c*)   a copy or summary of the debtor's statement of affairs.

In Case 2, the nominee shall send a copy of each of those documents to any person who has presented a bankruptcy petition against the debtor.

5.11   Replacement of nominee

Where the debtor intends to apply to the court under section 256(3) for the nominee to be replaced, he shall give to the nominee at least 7 days' notice of his application.

SECTION B: ACTION ON THE PROPOSAL; CREDITORS' MEETING

5.12   Consideration of nominee's report

(1) At the hearing by the court to consider the nominee's report, any of the persons who have been given notice under Rule 5.5(4) may appear or be represented.

(2) Rule 5.7 applies to any order made by the court at the hearing.

5.13   Summoning of creditors' meeting

(1) If in his report the nominee states that in his opinion a meeting of creditors should be summoned to consider the debtor's proposal, the date on which the meeting is to be held shall be not less than 14 [. . .] days from that on which the nominee's report is filed in court under Rule 5.10 [, nor more than 28 days from that on which the report is considered by the court under Rule 5.12].

(2) Notices calling the meeting shall be sent by the nominee, at least 14 days before the day fixed for it to be held, to all the creditors specified in the debtor's statement of affairs, and any other creditors of whom the nominee is otherwise aware.

(3) Each notice sent under this Rule shall specify the court to which the nominee's report on the debtor's proposal has been delivered and shall state the effect of Rule 5.18(1), (3) and (4) (requisite majorities); and with it there shall be sent—

(*a*)   a copy of the proposal,

(*b*)   a copy of the statement of affairs or, if the nominee thinks fit, a summary of it (the summary to include a list of the creditors and the amounts of their debts), and

(*c*)   the nominee's comments on the proposal.

5.14   Creditors' meeting: supplementary

(1) Subject as follows, in fixing the venue for the creditors' meeting, the nominee shall have regard to the convenience of creditors.

(2) The meeting shall be summoned for commencement between 10.00 and 16.00 hours on a business day.

(3) With every notice summoning the meeting there shall be sent out forms of proxy.

5.15   The chairman at the meeting

(1) Subject as follows, the nominee shall be chairman of the creditors' meeting.

(2) If for any reason the nominee is unable to attend, he may nominate another person to act as chairman in his place; but a person so nominated must be either—

    (*a*) a person qualified to act as an insolvency practitioner in relation to the debtor, or

    (*b*) an employee of the nominee or his firm who is experienced in insolvency matters.

5.16 The chairman as proxy-holder

The chairman shall not by virtue of any proxy held by him vote to increase or reduce the amount of the remuneration or expenses of the nominee or the supervisor of the proposed arrangement, unless the proxy specifically directs him to vote in that way.

5.17 Voting rights

(1) Subject as follows, every creditor who was given notice of the creditors' meeting is entitled to vote at the meeting or any adjournment of it.

(2) In Case 1, votes are calculated according to the amount of the creditor's debt as at the date of the bankruptcy order, and in Case 2 according to the amount of the debt as at the date of the meeting.

(3) A creditor shall not vote in respect of a debt for an unliquidated amount, or any debt whose value is not ascertained, except where the chairman agrees to put upon the debt an estimated minimum value for the purpose of entitlement to vote.

(4) The chairman has power to admit or reject a creditor's claim for the purpose of his entitlement to vote, and the power is exercisable with respect to the whole or any part of the claim.

(5) The chairman's decision on entitlement to vote is subject to appeal to the court by any creditor, or by the debtor.

(6) If the chairman is in doubt whether a claim should be admitted or rejected, he shall mark it as objected to and allow the creditor to vote, subject to his vote being subsequently declared invalid if the objection to the claim is sustained.

(7) If on an appeal the chairman's decision is reversed or varied, or a creditor's vote is declared invalid, the court may order another meeting to be summoned, or make such other order as it thinks just.

    The court's power to make an order under this paragraph is exercisable only if it considers that the matter is such as to give rise to unfair prejudice or a material irregularity.

(8) An application to the court by way of appeal under this Rule against the chairman's decision shall not be made after the end of the period of 28 days beginning with the day on which the chairman's report to the court is made under section 259.

(9) The chairman is not personally liable for any costs incurred by any person in respect of an appeal under this Rule.

5.18 Requisite majorities

(1) Subject as follows, at the creditors' meeting for any resolution to pass approving any proposal or modification there must be a majority in excess of three-quarters in

value of the creditors present in person or by proxy and voting on the resolution.

(2) The same applies in respect of any other resolution proposed at the meeting, but substituting one-half for three-quarters.

(3) In the following cases there is to be left out of account a creditor's vote in respect of any claim or part of a claim—
  (*a*)   where written notice of the claim was not given, either at the meeting or before it, to the chairman or the nominee;
  (*b*)   where the claim or part is secured;
  (*c*)   where the claim is in respect of a debt wholly or partly on, or secured by, a current bill of exchange or promissory note, unless the creditor is willing—
     (i)   to treat the liability to him on the bill or note of every person who is liable on it antecedently to the debtor, and against whom a bankruptcy order has not been made (or, in the case of a company, which has not gone into liquidation), as a security in his hands, and
     (ii)   to estimate the value of the security and (for the purpose of entitlement to vote, but not of any distribution under the arrangement) to deduct it from his claim.

(4) Any resolution is invalid if those voting against it include more than half in value of the creditors, counting in these latter only those—
  (*a*)   to whom notice of the meeting was sent;
  (*b*)   whose votes are not to be left out of account under paragraph (3); and
  (*c*)   who are not, to the best of the chairman's belief, associates of the debtor.

(5) It is for the chairman of the meeting to decide whether under this Rule—
  (*a*)   a vote is to be left out of account in accordance with paragraph (3), or
  (*b*)   a person is an associate of the debtor for the purposes of paragraph (4)(*c*);
and in relation to the second of these two cases the chairman is entitled to rely on the information provided by the debtor's statement of affairs or otherwise in accordance with this Part of the Rules.

(6) If the chairman uses a proxy contrary to Rule 5.16, his vote with that proxy does not count towards any majority under this Rule.

(7) Paragraphs (5) to (9) of Rule 5.17 apply as regards an appeal against the decision of the chairman under this Rule.

5.19   Proceedings to obtain agreement on the proposal

(1) On the day on which the creditors' meeting is held, it may from time to time be adjourned.

(2) If on that day the requisite majority for the approval of the voluntary arrangement (with or without modifications) has not been obtained, the chairman may, and shall if it is so resolved, adjourn the meeting for not more than 14 days.

(3) If there are subsequently further adjournments, the final adjournment shall not be to a day later than 14 days after that on which the meeting was originally held.

(4) If the meeting is adjourned under paragraph (2), notice of the fact shall be given by the chairman forthwith to the court.

(5) If following any final adjournment of the meeting the proposal (with or without modifications) is not agreed to, it is deemed rejected.

Section C: Implementation of the Arrangement

5.20   Resolutions to follow approval

(1) If the voluntary arrangement is approved (with or without modifications), a resolution may be taken by the creditors, where two or more insolvency practitioners are appointed to act as supervisor, on the question whether acts to be done in connection with the arrangement may be done by any one of them, or must be done by both or all.

(2) If at the creditors' meeting a resolution is moved for the appointment of some person other than the nominee to be supervisor of the arrangement, there must be produced to the chairman, at or before the meeting—
- (*a*)   that person's written consent to act (unless he is present and then and there signifies his consent), and
- (*b*)   his written confirmation that he is qualified to act as an insolvency practitioner in relation to the debtor.

5.21   Hand-over of property etc to supervisor

(1) Forthwith after the approval of the voluntary arrangement, the debtor in Case 2, and the official receiver or trustee in Case 1, shall do all that is required for putting the supervisor into possession of the assets included in the arrangement.

(2) On taking possession of the assets in Case 1, the supervisor shall discharge any balance due to the official receiver and (if other) the trustee by way of remuneration or on account of—
- (*a*)   fees, costs, charges and expenses properly incurred and payable under the Act or the Rules, and
- (*b*)   any advances made in respect of the insolvent estate, together with interest on such advances at the rate specified in section 17 of the Judgments Act 1838 at the date of the bankruptcy order.

(3) Alternatively in Case 1, the supervisor must, before taking possession, give the official receiver or the trustee a written undertaking to discharge any such balance out of the first realisation of assets.

(4) The official receiver and (if other) the trustee has in Case 1 a charge on the assets included in the voluntary arrangement in respect of any sums due as above until they have been discharged, subject only to the deduction from realisations by the supervisor of the proper costs and expenses of realisation.

Any sums due to the official receiver take priority over those due to a trustee.

(5) The supervisor shall from time to time out of the realisation of assets discharge all guarantees properly given by the official receiver or the trustee for the benefit of the estate, and shall pay all their expenses.

5.22   Report of creditors' meeting

(1) A report of the creditors' meeting shall be prepared by the chairman of the meeting.

(2) The report shall—
- (*a*)   state whether the proposal for a voluntary arrangement was approved or rejected and, if approved, with what (if any) modifications;
- (*b*)   set out the resolutions which were taken at the meeting, and the decision on each one;

(*c*)   list the creditors (with their respective values) who were present or represented at the meeting, and how they voted on each resolution; and

(*d*)   include such further information (if any) as the chairman thinks it appropriate to make known to the court.

(3)   A copy of the chairman's report shall, within 4 days of the meeting being held, be filed in court; and the court shall cause that copy to be endorsed with the date of filing.

(4)   The persons to whom notice of the result is to be given, under section 259(1), are all those who were sent notice of the meeting under this Part of the Rules [and, in Case 1, the official receiver and (if any) the trustee].

The notice shall be sent immediately after a copy of the chairman's report is filed in court under paragraph (3).

5.23   Register of voluntary arrangements

(1)   The Secretary of State shall maintain a register of individual voluntary arrangements, and shall enter in it all such matters as are reported to him in pursuance of Rules 5.24, 5.25 and 5.29.

(2)   The register shall be open to public inspection.

5.24   Reports to Secretary of State

(1)   Immediately after the chairman of the creditors' meeting has filed in court a report that the meeting has approved the voluntary arrangement, he shall report to the Secretary of State the following details of the arrangement—

(*a*)   the name and address of the debtor;

(*b*)   the date on which the arrangement was approved by the creditors;

(*c*)   the name and address of the supervisor; and

(*d*)   the court in which the chairman's report has been filed.

(2)   A person who is appointed to act as supervisor of an individual voluntary arrangement (whether in the first instance or by way of replacement of another person previously appointed) shall forthwith give written notice to the Secretary of State of his appointment.

If he vacates office as supervisor, he shall forthwith give written notice of that fact also to the Secretary of State.

5.25   Revocation or suspension of the arrangement

(1)   This Rule applies where the court makes an order of revocation or suspension under section 262.

(2)   The person who applied for the order shall serve sealed copies of it—

(*a*)   in Case 1, on the debtor, the official receiver and the trustee;

(*b*)   in Case 2, on the debtor; and

(*c*)   in either case on the supervisor of the voluntary arrangement.

(3)   If the order includes a direction by the court under section 262(4)(*b*) for any further creditors' meeting to be summoned, notice shall also be given (by the person who applied for the order) to whoever is, in accordance with the direction, required to summon the meeting.

(4)   The debtor (in Case 2) and the [trustee, or if there is no trustee, the official receiver] (in Case 1) shall—

(a) forthwith after receiving a copy of the court's order, give notice of it to all persons who were sent notice of the creditors' meeting which approved the voluntary arrangement or who, not having been sent that notice, appear to be affected by the order;

(b) within 7 days of their receiving a copy of the order (or within such longer period as the court may allow), give notice to the court whether it is intended to make a revised proposal to creditors, or to invite re-consideration of the original proposal.

(5) The person on whose application the order of revocation or suspension was made shall, within 7 days after the making of the order, give written notice of it to the Secretary of State.

5.26 Supervisor's accounts and reports

(1) Where the voluntary arrangement authorises or requires the supervisor—

(a) to carry on the debtor's business or to trade on his behalf or in his name, or

(b) to realise assets of the debtor or (in Case 1) belonging to the estate, or

(c) otherwise to administer or dispose of any funds of the debtor or the estate,

he shall keep accounts and records of his acts and dealings in and in connection with the arrangement, including in particular records of all receipts and payments of money.

(2) The supervisor shall, not less often than once in every 12 months beginning with the date of his appointment, prepare an abstract of such receipts and payments, and send copies of it, accompanied by his comments on the progress and efficacy of the arrangement, to—

(a) the court,

(b) the debtor, and

(c) all those of the debtor's creditors who are bound by the arrangement.

If in any period of 12 months he has made no payments and had no receipts, he shall at the end of that period send a statement to that effect to all who are specified in sub-paragraphs (a) to (c) above.

(3) An abstract provided under paragraph (2) shall relate to a period beginning with the date of the supervisor's appointment or (as the case may be) the day following the end of the last period for which an abstract was prepared under this Rule; and copies of the abstract shall be sent out, as required by paragraph (2), within the 2 months following the end of the period to which the abstract relates.

(4) If the supervisor is not authorised as mentioned in paragraph (1), he shall, not less often than once in every 12 months beginning with the date of his appointment, send to all those specified in paragraph (2)(a) to (c) a report on the progress and efficacy of the voluntary arrangement.

(5) The court may, on application by the supervisor, vary the dates on which the obligation to send abstracts or reports arises.

5.27 Production of accounts and records to Secretary of State

(1) The Secretary of State may at any time during the course of the voluntary arrangement or after its completion require the supervisor to produce for inspection—

(a) his records and accounts in respect of the arrangement, and

(b) copies of abstracts and reports prepared in compliance with Rule 5.26.

(2) The Secretary of State may require production either at the premises of the supervisor or elsewhere; and it is the duty of the supervisor to comply with any requirement imposed on him under this Rule.

(3) The Secretary of State may cause any accounts and records produced to him under this Rule to be audited; and the supervisor shall give to the Secretary of State such further information and assistance as he needs for the purposes of his audit.

5.28   Fees, costs, charges and expenses

The fees, costs, charges and expenses that may be incurred for any purposes of the voluntary arrangement are—
- (*a*)   any disbursements made by the nominee prior to the approval of the arrangement, and any remuneration for his services as such agreed between himself and the debtor, the official receiver or the trustee;
- (*b*)   any fees, costs, charges or expenses which—
    - (i)   are sanctioned by the terms of the arrangement, or
    - (ii)   would be payable, or correspond to those which would be payable, in the debtor's bankruptcy.

5.29   Completion of the arrangement

(1) Not more than 28 days after the final completion of the voluntary arrangement, the supervisor shall send to all creditors of the debtor who are bound by the arrangement, and to the debtor, a notice that the arrangement has been fully implemented.

(2) With the notice there shall be sent to each of those persons a copy of a report by the supervisor summarising all receipts and payments made by him in pursuance of the arrangement, and explaining any difference in the actual implementation of it as compared with the proposal as approved by the creditors' meeting.

(3) The supervisor shall, within the 28 days mentioned above, send to the Secretary of State and to the court a copy of the notice under paragraph (1), together with a copy of the report under paragraph (2).

(4) The court may, on application by the supervisor, extend the period of 28 days under paragraphs (1) and (3).

Section D: General

5.30   False representations, etc.

(1) The debtor commits an offence if he makes any false representation or commits any other fraud for the purpose of obtaining the approval of his creditors to a proposal for a voluntary arrangement under Part VIII of the Act.

(2) A person guilty of an offence under this Rule is liable to imprisonment or a fine, or both.

SCHEDULE 5

PUNISHMENT OF OFFENCES UNDER THE RULES

Note: In the fourth and fifth columns of this Schedule, "the statutory maximum" means the prescribed sum under section 32 of the Magistrates' Courts Act 1980 (c.43).

Rule creating offence.	General nature of offence.	Mode of prosecution.	Punishment.	Daily default fine (where applicable).
In Part 1, Rule 1.30.	False representation or fraud for purpose of obtaining members' or creditors' consent to proposal for voluntary arrangement.	1. On indictment.	7 years or a fine, or both.	
		2. Summary.	6 months or the statutory maximum, or both.	
In Part 2, Rule 2.52(4).	Administrator failing to send notification as to progress of administration.	Summary.	One-fifth of the statutory maximum.	One-fiftieth of the statutory maximum.
In Part 3, Rule 3.32(5).	Administrative receiver failing to send notification as to progress of receivership.	Summary.	One-fifth of the statutory maximum.	One-fiftieth of the statutory maximum.
In Part 5, Rule 5.30.	False representation or fraud for purpose of obtaining creditors' consent to proposal for voluntary arrangement.	1. On indictment.	7 years or a fine, or both.	
		2. Summary.	6 months or the statutory maximum, or both.	
In Part 12, Rule 12.18.	False representation of status for purpose of inspecting documents.	1. On indictment.	2 years or a fine, or both.	
		2. Summary.	6 months or the statutory maximum, or both.	

Appendix 5

SOCIETY OF PRACTITIONERS OF INSOLVENCY GUIDELINES

STATEMENT OF INSOLVENCY PRACTICE 3
(reproduced by kind permission of the Society of Practitioners of Insolvency Limited)
Individual Voluntary Arrangements

Introduction

1. This statement of insolvency practice is one of a series issued by the Council of the Society with a view to harmonising the approach of members to questions of insolvency practice. It should be read in conjunction with the Explanatory Foreword to the Statements of Insolvency Practice.

2. The statement has been prepared for the sole use of members in dealing with individual voluntary arrangements for debtors in England and Wales. Members are reminded that SPI Statements of Insolvency Practice are for the purpose of guidance only and may not be relied upon as definitive statements. No liability attaches to the Council or anyone involved in the preparation or publication of statements of insolvency practice.

3. The Insolvency Act 1986 (IA 1986) and associated Rules set out a procedure which enables a debtor to make a proposal for a voluntary arrangement (IVA) with his creditors. The Rules (The Insolvency Rules 1986) specify two types of debtor
   "Case 1": an undischarged bankrupt;
   "Case 2": not an undischarged bankrupt.

4. The guidance which follows is intended to given an overview of the practical steps to be taken when a member is contacted to consider, and possibly administer, such an arrangement. The relevant legislation is contained in sections 252–263 (inclusive) of the IA 1986 and rules 5.1–5.30 (inclusive) of the Rules, as amended by the Insolvency (Amendment) Rules 1987.

Basis of the Arrangement

5. The terms of the voluntary arrangement will be contained in the debtor's proposal, as modified, which is eventually approved by the creditors. A comprehensive and accurately drafted proposal is therefore fundamental to the arrangement. In view of the importance of the proposal the member should, where the circumstances are complex, consider whether it should be approved by a lawyer. The contents of the proposal are given further consideration in paragraph 14.

6. In dealing with an IVA the member should bear in mind his duty to ensure a fair balance between the interests of the debtor, his creditors and any other parties involved.

Initial Contact with the Debtor

7. The member's first contact with the debtor may arise in one of five different ways, as follows:

   (a) the matter is referred to him by the court under section 273 IA 1986;
   (b) the matter is referred to him by the Official Receiver (OR);
   (c) the member is acting as the debtor's trustee in bankruptcy and considers that an IVA may be appropriate;
   (d) the debtor submits a proposal for an IVA to the member without prior contact;
   (e) the debtor consults the member about his financial situation generally and is advised that an IVA may be appropriate.

   (Note that an application to the court for an Interim Order (IO) may not be made while a bankruptcy petition presented by the debtor is pending if the court has, under Section 273 IA 1986, appointed an IP to enquire into the debtor's affairs.)

8. In any of these instances, the debtor should be told at the initial interview of the member's requirements to maintain independence. Consideration should be given to the need for separate representation for the debtor's spouse or family, and any third parties who may be involved in providing funds.

9. In instances where the assets are not already protected by a bankruptcy order or by the presentation of a debtor's petition the member should give consideration to the need for early action to protect the assets. This would involve the preparation of an estimated statement of affairs and an embryonic proposal so as to be able to make a quick application for an IO and any other Orders that may be desirable according to the nature of the assets. This statement of affairs can be amended and the proposal modified following the member's further enquiries into the position.

10. The member should consider the likely costs, including legal costs, of obtaining approval for an IVA, and make suitable arrangements for their payment. These arrangements could include third party guarantees.

11. When considering an application for an IO the court needs to be satisfied that:

    (a) the debor intends to make a proposal to his creditors;
    (b) the debtor was an undischarged bankrupt or could have petitioned for his own bankruptcy when he applied for the IO;
    (c) the debtor has made no previous application for an IO within the previous 12 months; and
    (d) the nominee is qualified to act as an insolvency practitioner in relation to the debtor, and is willing so to act.

    Therefore it is necessary for the member to establish that the above requirements are satisfied, both in relation to the debtor and his own position, and to consider any possible ethical restrictions (see appropriate RPB ethical guidance notes).

Statement of Affairs and Obtaining Additional Information

12. An accurate statement of affairs and a detailed assessment of the debtor's situation should be produced before the proposal is drafted. If this is not possible, this work

should be undertaken after an application has been made for an IO or after it has been granted. The member should detail the nature and amount of all the debtor's assets and liabilities. His approach should cover the points listed below:

(a) Creditors

The member should obtain details of all known or possible liabilities including:

(i)   guarantee liabilities;

(ii)   claims for breach of contract, including claims in respect of faulty and incomplete work and hire purchase and leasing agreements;

(iii)   creditors who are "associates" (as defined in section 435 IA 1986);

(iv)   guarantors of the debtor's debts, including associates;

(v)   unsecured creditors

He should also:

(vi)   identify preferential creditors and try to establish whether they are likely to be paid in full;

(vii)   identify any creditors who have commenced execution or any other legal process;

(viii)   consider the possibility of early informal discussions with the key creditors to establish their views. These creditors will include any petitioning creditors and government bodies which might have preferential claims;

(ix)   establish whether associates may consider withdrawing or deferring their claims;

(x)   identify secured creditors (both partially and fully secured).

(b) Assets

If the debtor owns a business, the member should consider the manner in which that business is to be dealt with. Points to be borne in mind are:

(i)   whether the debtor should continue trading, and if so, on what terms;

(ii)   the implications of ROT claims;

(iii)   what should happen if, despite all efforts, further losses are incurred, and

(iv)   the probable requirements of certain creditors (eg. HMC&E, Inland Revenue and statutory undertakings) with regard to submission of future returns and payments;

(v)   the most beneficial time for the debtor to cease trading bearing in mind work in progress, tax implications, and the beneficial realisation of stock and other assets;

(vi)   immediate cash requirements of the debtor's business;

(vii)   insurance, rent and other ongoing costs;

(viii)   credit requirements/availability for his business;

(ix)   the cash flow forecast.

If the debtor's business is to be continued a "business plan" should be produced to justify this decision.

(c) General

The member should enquire as to:

(i)   possible transactions at an undervalue (sections 339 and 423 IA 1986);

(ii)   payments which may be preferences (section 340 IA 1986);

(With regard to the above points, (i) and (ii), the member should consider whether outside monies should be injected to compensate creditors for the right to pursue such matters, which would exist in a bankruptcy.)

(iii)   liabilities which may be extortionate credit transactions, both those outstanding and paid (section 343 IA 1986);

(iv)   form an opinion of whether the debtor is credible and making a full disclosure. The member should explain the consequences of making false representations;

(v)   whether the debtor has been involved in any previous business failure, either individual or corporate, and if so the details of that failure and the debtor's responsibility for it;

(vi)   the timetable for the IVA;

(vii)   sums owed to the debtor by his associates, details of which should be included in the statement of affairs.

It should be noted that a Case 1 debtor who has delivered a statement of affairs under Section 273 or Section 288 need not deliver a further statement unless so required by the nominee.

Consideration of Alternative Arrangements

13. Throughout his consideration of the above factors the member should be forming his opinion of the appropriate method of dealing with the debtor's affairs. Although this will be partly a subjective review of the factors already referred to, the member should take into account:

(a) the debtor's attitude;

(b) the likelihood of the debtor adhering to the proposal;

(c) the extent of the control over the assets exercised by the debtor as opposed to the supervisor of the proposal (bear in mind that in an IVA the assets do not vest by law in the supervisor);

(d) the removal/absence of the restrictions imposed upon bankrupts.

The Proposal

14. In theory, the proposal will be submitted to the proposed nominee by the debtor prior to the application for an IO. However, in practice, the proposal will normally be drafted by the proposed nominee or the debtor's solicitor. It may then be amended by agreement between the nominee and the debtor at any time up to the presentation of the nominee's report to the court. After that time further modifications may only be proposed by creditors and any modifications made must have the consent of the debtor. In view of the importance of the contents of the proposal the member should, prior to submitting his report to the court, satisfy himself that the proposal, as modified, is drafted in such a way that the terms of the IVA can be clearly understood and that the arrangement is likely to proceed to a successful conclusion.

15. The proposal should include sections covering the following:

(a) the background to the arrangement, including details of the circumstances in which the debtor has become insolvent and of his relevant personal circumstances;

(b) the statement of affairs, which should include details of both business assets and liabilities and also personal assets and liabilities;

   (c) the actual financial proposal to be put to the creditors. This section should include:

       (i) details of assets to be realised for the benefit of creditors and details of those which are to be excluded from the proposal, together with the reasons for the exclusion and whether alternatives are to be suggested;

       (ii) the debtor's proposal regarding future income over a specific period;

      (iii) whether third party funds are to be injected;

      (iv) the debtor's specific proposals with regard to any interest he may have in his dwelling house;

       (v) details of creditors to be included in the arrangement. It is important that every creditor or potential creditor including preferential creditors who will invariably form part of the arrangement should be considered, to minimise the possibility of some creditors not being bound by the terms of the IVA. Secured creditors should also be included if they are to form part of the proposal. If they are not, they should be provided with a copy of the proposal, since if this adversely affects such a creditor's security, their consent must be obtained. The date to which claims are to be calculated should be stated together with details of the arrangement with regard to, if appropriate, secured creditors and hire purchase or leasing agreements;

   (d) the intentions with regard to any business operated by the debtor stating in particular whether the business is to be continued, and if so, the extent to which, if any, the supervisor shall exercise any degree of control over the business. If the supervisor is not to exercise any degree of control, consideration should be given to specifically stating this in the proposal;

   (e) the powers, duties and responsibilities of the supervisor. This will need to deal with the question of admission or rejection of claims and the basis on which the supervisor is to report to creditors;

   (f) miscellaneous matters which under the Act or Rules need to be included.

16. Other matters which the member shall consider in relation to the contents of the proposal:

   (a) whether a committee of creditors is to be appointed and if so what will be its powers, duties and responsibilities;

   (b) what will happen to surplus funds arising, for example, from more beneficial trading than was originally envisaged, when the IVA is concluded;

   (c) confirmation that when the terms of the IVA have been successfully completed the creditors will no longer be entitled to pursue the debtor for the balance of their claim;

   (d) what will happen to unclaimed dividends or unpresented cheques when the IVA is concluded;

   (e) how to deal with creditors who have not made claims;

   (f) in the event of the arrangement not being successfully completed, and a bankruptcy ensuing, clarification of the amounts for which the creditors will be entitled to claim;

   (g) the proposals with regard to maintenance orders or attachment of earnings orders in favour of the debtor's wife, and with regard to fines;

   (h) in view of the fact that the assets do not automatically vest in the supervisor it may be advisable for the proposal to provide for such vesting or for the supervisor to be granted a charge over assets, or to be given some other suitable form of security or for a declaration of trust or power of attorney to be executed;

    (i) the attitude to be adopted with regard to contingent creditors;

    (j) the situation with regard to overseas creditors;

    (k) the circumstances in which the supervisor is to present a petition for a bankruptcy order;

    (l) the situation with regard to tax liabilities arising on disposal of the debtor's assets, or the future income of or gifts to the debtor from a third party, that are applied towards the payment of creditors' claims;

    (m) the approach to be adopted in respect of inadvertently omitted creditors;

    (n) the inclusion of power for the supervisor or any creditors' committee to be able to determine that an IVA has no future and petition for bankruptcy and authority to retain and use funds from the IVA for such costs.

The Interim Order

17. Before he can apply to the court for an IO the debtor must give written notice of his proposal to the intended nominee, and this must be acknowledged by the latter. Both the application for the Interim Order and the notice to the intended nominee must be accompanied by a copy of the proposal. A copy of the endorsed notice should be returned to the debtor and a further copy will be exhibited with an affidavit, which is to accompany his application to court for the IO. The affidavit must state the following:

    (a) the reason for application;

    (b) details of any execution or legal process which has been commenced against the debtor;

    (c) that the debtor is an undischarged bankrupt or able to petition for his own bankruptcy;

    (d) that no previous application for an IO has been made in the previous 12 months;

    (e) that the nominee is qualified to act as an insolvency practitioner and is prepared to act in relation to the proposal.

The affidavit and application for the IO will be filed in court and the court will fix an appointment for hearing the application. The nominee, or his authorised representative, is entitled to attend the hearing and may wish to do so in order to express his views on the length of time needed to prepare his report and comments.

18. The applicant (which in Case 1 can be the debtor, trustee, or OR) must give at least two days' notice of the hearing to the nominee. In addition, in Case 1 notice must be given to the debtor, trustee, or OR (whichever of these is not the applicant) and in Case 2, to any creditor who has presented a bankruptcy petition against the debtor.

19. The IO has the effect that, during the period for which it is in force, no bankruptcy petition relating to the debtor may be presented or proceeded with, nor may any other proceedings, execution or legal process be commenced or continued against the debtor or his property, except with the leave of the court.

20. In Case 1 the debtor, trustee or OR may apply for the IO but in Case 2 only the debtor may make an application. In Case 1, notice of the proposal must be given to the OR and trustee (if applicable) before the application is made to the court. Generally an IO will cease to have effect after 14 days from the day following the making of the Order, although, on good reason being shown, an extension may be granted by the court.

The Nominee's Report

21. The nominee's report to the court must be filed not less than two days before the IO ceases to have effect. In this report the nominee must state whether in his opinion a meeting of creditors should be convened to consider the proposal and, if so, propose the location and timing of such meeting.

22. To the report should be attached a copy of the debtor's proposal (as modified) and of the statement of affairs. If the nominee's opinion is that a meeting of creditors should not be summoned he must give reasons for his opinion. The report and enclosures should be filed in court and will be endorsed with the filing date. In Case 1 the nominee must send to the OR a copy of the proposal, together with his comments and the statement of affairs. In Case 2 these items should be sent to any person who has presented a petition for a bankruptcy order.

23. It may be possible, with the approval of the court, for the nominee's report and his comments on the statement of affairs to be considered along with the application for an IO. Combining the two hearings in this way may result in an overall saving of both time and costs. If such approval is given, the nominee should request an extension of the IO to cover the period of the meeting, a fourteen day adjournment and the four days for delivering the report of the chairman of the meeting of creditors.

The Nominee's Comments

24. If the nominee reports that a meeting of creditors should be held he is required to set out his comments on the proposal and to annex them to his report to the court. The matters upon which the nominee will wish to comment will vary from case to case but where applicable they should include:

   (a) the extent to which the nominee has investigated the debtor's circumstances;
   (b) the basis upon which assets have been valued;
   (c) the extent to which the nominee considers that reliance can be placed upon the debtor's estimate of the liabilities to be included in the IVA;
   (d) information on the attitude adopted by the debtor with particular reference to instances where he has failed to cooperate with the nominee;
   (e) the result of any discussions between the nominee and secured creditors or other interested parties upon whose cooperation the performance of the IVA will depend;
   (f) details of any previous history of failures in which the debtor has been involved in so far as they are known to the nominee;
   (g) an estimate of the result for the creditors if the IVA is approved, explaining why it is more beneficial for creditors than any alternative insolvency proceeding;
   (h) the likely effect of the proposal's rejection by the creditors;
   (i) details of any claims which have come to his attention which might be capable of being pursued by a trustee in bankruptcy but not by the supervisor, or which a trustee in bankruptcy would be in a better position to pursue.

The Meeting of Creditors

25. Having reported to the court that a meeting of creditors should be held, the nominee must then convene such a meeting, which must take place not less than 14 days after his report has been filed in court and within 28 days of its consideration by the court. 14 days' notice of the meeting must be given to the creditors. The following points must be adhered to:

(a) The venue must be fixed with regard to the convenience of the creditors.

(b) The meeting is to be held between 10.00 and 16.00 hrs on a business day.

(c) The chairman of the meeting will be the nominee or another insolvency practitioner or an experienced member of the nominee's staff. Unless a proxy held by the chairman specifically directs him to vote in relation to an increase or decrease in the amount of the nominee's/supervisor's remuneration and expenses as proposed in the IVA, he shall not do so.

(d) Notice of the meeting must be sent to:

   (i)   Case 1: every person who is a creditor of the bankrupt or would have been a creditor if the bankruptcy had commenced on the date of the notice;

   (ii) Case 2: all creditors specified in the debtor's statement of affairs and any other creditors of whom the nominee has knowledge.

(e) The notice of the meeting should enclose:

   (i)   a copy of the proposal, as modified;

   (ii)   the statement of affairs or a summary (including a full list of creditors and the amounts due);

   (iii) the nominee's comments on the proposal;

   (iv)   a proxy form;

   (v)   details of the rules regarding the requisite majorities at the meeting, as set out in Rule 5.18.

26. Before the meeting the nominee should take the following steps:

(a) record all proxies received, and details of claims;

(b) complete the meeting record as far as possible detailing the names and voting value of creditors;

(c) note all resolutions in advance and discuss with the debtor modifications suggested by creditors prior to the meeting;

(d) review the proposal in the light of creditors' responses and possible changes in circumstances;

(e) prepare a brief report for presentation at the meeting, summarising the debtor's proposal and outlining the likely effects of acceptance and rejection;

(f) consider voting rights and requisite majority (see Rules 5.17 and 5.18).

27. The chairman must decide the amount for which creditors are to be allowed to vote. Proxies to be used at the meeting may be lodged at any time, even during the course of the meeting.

28. After the chairman has presented his report to the meeting he should allow creditors an opportunity to make comments, ask questions or propose modifications to the debtor's proposal. The nominee should try to ensure that the debtor attends the meeting in order to answer questions and to give consideration to proposed modifications. If the debtor is not in attendance and modifications are proposed, the meeting will have to be adjourned (Section 258 IA 1986).

29. If modifications are proposed by a creditor the chairman should give careful consideration to the manner in which he will use specific instructions given to him by creditors to vote for either the acceptance or the rejection of the original proposal. If the particular words in the proxy form have not been deleted so as to entitle the proxy holder to vote only as directed, the proxy holder is entitled to vote or abstain on any modification at his discretion.

30. However, the chairman should bear in mind that, if a creditor is aggrieved that a vote on proposed modifications has been taken and a decision reached which might have been different if creditors represented by proxy had been present at the meeting or had been given the opportunity of amending their proxy, the aggrieved creditor may challenge the decision by an application to the Court under Section 262 IA 1986. Therefore the chairman may wish to consider an adjournment or suspension of the meeting to give him an opportunity to explain the circumstances to the creditor or creditors from whom he holds a proxy and to obtain their further instructions. The general requirements regarding proxies and company representation are set out in rules 8.1–8.7.

31. At the meeting the creditors will consider whether to approve the proposed IVA, with or without modifications. Each such modification must have the consent of the debtor and cannot include any proposal which would affect the right of a secured creditor to enforce his security, unless that particular creditor concurs. It is recommended that any such consent from debtor or creditor be obtained in writing. In addition, unless the creditor concerned agrees, the meeting may not approve an amendment where a preferential creditor is to receive either a smaller proportion of its debts than the other creditors in that class or settlement other than in priority to non-preferential debts.

32. The proposed modifications may include the conferring of the proposed functions of the supervisor on a qualified insolvency practitioner other than the nominee.

33. If a majority for approval of the IVA is not obtained the chairman may adjourn the meeting, and must adjourn if it is so resolved. The maximum period for adjournment is 14 days from the original meeting date, but within this period there can be more than one adjournment. The chairman must give notice to court that the meeting is adjourned and should consider the need to apply for an extension of the IO.

Administration Following the Meeting of Creditors

34. The chairman must report the result of the meeting to the court, to be filed within four days of the meeting. This report will state whether the IVA was approved or rejected and list any modifications made to it. It will also detail the resolutions taken at the meeting, the decisions reached, and list the creditors present or represented at the meeting together with how they voted. If the debtor comes under Case 1, the court, on receipt of the chairman's report, may decide either to annul the bankruptcy order or to give directions for the conduct of the bankruptcy.

35. The chairman must also give creditors notice of the outcome of the meeting. The notice should be accompanied by a VAT Bad Debt Relief claim form (but bear in mind the provisions of S.11 FA 1990). If an IVA is approved it binds every person who received notice of it. If the debtor was bankrupt the court may annul the bankruptcy order or give appropriate directions to implement the proposal.

36. After filing his report of the meeting with the court, the chairman must report to the Secretary of State, giving details of:

(a) the name and address of the debtor;
(b) the date the IVA was approved by creditors;
(c) the name and address of the supervisor;
(d) details of the court in which the report was filed; and
(e) the appropriate registration fee (Note: where he replaced another insolvency practitioner previously appointed, the supervisor must also give written notice

of his appointment to the Secretary of State accompanied by the appropriate registration fee).

37. Once these formalities have been completed, the proposal should be implemented. It may be necessary to give undertakings to the OR or trustee (if appropriate) regarding their costs. The nominee (or other person proposed) is now the "supervisor" and he may apply to the court for directions if necessary.

38. An application may be made to the court that the IVA is unfairly prejudicial to a creditor or the debtor, or that there was a material irregularity at the meeting. The debtor, creditor, nominee, trustee or OR may make this application within 28 days from the date the report of the meeting was filed with the court. The court may revoke or suspend the approval given at the meeting or direct the party to summon a further meeting to revise the proposal. The supervisor should consider obtaining legal advice if the meeting's decision is challenged.

39. If the debtor fails to comply with any part of his proposals a supervisor should consider bankruptcy proceedings under section 246(1)(c) IA 1986. The proposal may also provide for the supervisor to be given power to determine that an IVA has no future (see para 16).

40. The supervisor should maintain accounts of his receipts and payments and records of all his acts and dealings (Rule 5.26). At least once every twelve months, from the date of his appointment, he must prepare copies of an abstract of his receipts and payments, together with his comments as to the progress of the administration. These are to be filed with the court and sent to the debtor and to the creditors bound by the proposal. The Secretary of State may require sight of the records and accounts at any time during or after the IVA.

41. The fees to be charged are those which were sanctioned in the terms of the proposal.

42. At the end of the arrangement the supervisor shall prepare a summary of all his receipts and payments and a report explaining any differences from the original proposal. This shall be sent, together with a notice that the IVA has been fully implemented, to all creditors, the debtor, the court and the Secretary of State within 28 days following the completion of the IVA.

INDEX

References are to page numbers. *Italic* references indicate materials contained in the Appendices.

Abstract of receipts   27, 80, *252*
Accounting period
  effect of interim order on   118, 120
Accounts
  debtor's   16, 37, 38, 54
  supervisor's   27, 79–81
Adjournment
  creditors' meeting, of   61, 63, 64
  interim order hearing, of   103
Adjudication, order of   2
Administration order   2
Administrator (of estate)   49
Advertisement
  claims, for   39
  stay of (bankruptcy)   48
Affidavit
  bankruptcy petition, supporting   95
  debt, of   *199*
  interim order application, with   46, 99, *166*
After-acquired property   33, *138, 158*
Agreement, *see* Arrangement; Contract; Scheme of arrangement
Amendment of proposal   15, 18, 21, 28, 36, 61, *250–1*
Annulment of bankruptcy order   100, 101, 102–3
Appeal
  jurisdiction for   7
Approval of proposal   3, 15, 18, 21, 61, 69–70
  challenge to, *see* Creditors' meeting
  effect   70–1, 100, *136*
Arrangement
  see also Proposal
  amendment of   15, 18, 28, 36, *146*
    time for   28
  approval, *see* Approval of proposal
  bankruptcy petition, effect on   106
  binding effect   3, 70
  challenge to   72–6, 93
  completion   96–7, *137, 141, 252*
  deed, of   1, 2
  duration, *see* Duration
  failure of   93 *et seq*, 96, *141*
  flow chart   5
  frustration   97
  old law   2

scheme of, *see* Scheme of arrangement
  setting aside   97, 106
Asset(s)
  after-acquired   10, 33, *138, 158*
  annulment of bankruptcy order, and   102
  beneficial ownership of   34
  book debts, *see* Book debts
  capital gains tax   120
  concealment   47
  contingent   16
  disclosure   16, 17, *125, 130*
  distribution by deed of arrangement   1
  excluded   18, 19, 28–9, 91, *150*
  extent of   16
  jointly owned   31, 86, 111
  particulars of, to nominee   54
  property, *see* Dwellinghouse; Freehold; Leasehold; Matrimonial home
  proposal, in   16, 17, *125, 130*
  details in   28–9
  exclusion from   18, 19, 28–9, 91
  prospective   16
  protection of   *244*
  realisation   23, 86
    below estimate   17, 21, 22, 39
    costs of   17, 19
    supervisor, by   79, 84, 86
    time for   23, 86
    trustee's powers   11
  recovery   12
  sale   12, 87
  securities   31, *157*
  supervisor to hold   27, 86, 102
  third party, of   19, 20
  title to   29, 86, 87, 88
  trust, held in   34, *147, 148, 161*
  VAT on disposal   118
  value   16, 17, 21, 22
  work in progress, *see* Work in progress
Associate   20, 22, 67
  spouse as   21, 116

Bank account
  funds realised, for   25, *143–4*
Bankruptcy
  act of   1, 2
  after-acquired property   33

Bankruptcy *continued*
  alternative to
    pre-1986 Act 2
    voluntary arrangement, as   1, 10
  approval of arrangement, effect on   100,
      105
  assets, exclusion of   18, 29
  conversion into voluntary arrangement   1,
      48, 110
  creditors   102, 107–8
  debtor, of
    existing, *see* Undischarged bankrupt
    supervening   70, 93 *et seq*, 105, 106
  deed of arrangement and   1, 2
  disposal of assets   34, 105
  estate
    definition of, in   18, 111
    supervening bankruptcy, in   107, 108
  existing, *see* Undischarged bankrupt
  income payments order   11, 33
  joint assets   31
  jurisdiction   3, 7
  matrimonial home, and   113–4
  old procedure   1, 2
  order   1, 5, 10, 45, 50, 64
    annulment of   100, 101, 102–3
    court's power to make   93–4
    effect on arrangement   106
    made subsequently   70, 93 *et seq*, 105,
        106 *et seq*
  partnership, *see* Partnership
  petition
    categories of petitioner   93
    creditor, by   1, 2, 93 *et seq*, 105 *et seq*
    debtor, by   46, 105, 108–10, *180–1*
    dismissal of   71–2, 104
    disposal of assets, after   34
    evidence for   95
    form of   95, *178–9, 180–1*
    interim order, and   43, 45
    pending   103–4
    procedure   95–6
    revival of   72
    stay of   48, 71
    supervisor, by   93, 105
    termination of arrangement, by   93 *et*
        seq, 105 *et seq*
  preferential creditors   102, 107–8
  principles applied   38
  stay of advertisement   48
  stay of proceedings   48, 71, 100
  supervening   70, 93 *et seq*, 105, 106
  trustee, *see* Trustee in bankruptcy
  voluntary arrangement compared   10, 11,
      12, 18
Beneficial interest
  see also Trust

asset, in, disclosure   16, 29, 31, *148*
  spouse's, in debtor's home   114, 115
Book debt   23, 30, 87, *156*
  avoidance of assignment   38
Breach of covenant   17, 30, 89
Business
  see also Work in progress
  assets   18, 19, 29
  debtor's ongoing   10, 25–6, 37–8,
      138–9
    contracts of employment   91
    default in payments   91
    justification for   90
    liabilities   91
    losses, tax and   120
    profits, tax and   38
    supervisor's role   79, 90–1
    VAT, and   118, *139*

Capital gains tax
  liability at date of interim order   120
  roll-over relief   119–20
Certificate of compliance   41
Chairman
  creditors' meeting, of   3, 62–63, *249–52*
    appeal procedure   65
    powers   66
    report by   57, 68, 174
    report to Secretary of State, by   69, *176*
    voting rights, and   64–6
Challenge to arrangement   72–6, 93
Charge   18, 32, 86
  matrimonial home, on   115–16
Child
  associate, as   21
  matrimonial proceedings, and   112
Claims
  see also Creditor; Debt
  admissibility   66
  advertisement of   39
  agreement of   39–40, 85, *142*
  contingent   40, *152*
  debtor's   88
  disputed   40, 60, 66, 85, *152*
  non-provable   40
  notice of   66–7
  preferential, *see* Preferential creditor
  provable   116
  quantification of, by nominee   24, 63, 64
  unliquidated   64–5, 66
  unsatisfied   38
  voting at creditors' meeting, and   64–6
Companies Court   13
Company
  insolvency practitioner, as   4
  voluntary arrangements   8

Composition with creditors, *see* Scheme of
    arrangement
'Concertina order' 57, *170*
Contract
    employment, of 91
    meaning 4
    voluntary arrangement as 4, 106
Costs
    see also Expenses
    administrative 12
    application for interim order, of 12, 24,
        244
    realisation of asset, of 17
County court
    jurisdiction 7
Court
    administration order, and 2
    annulment of bankruptcy order by 100,
        101
    appeals 7
    challenge to decision of creditors' meeting,
        powers 77
    consent to disposal of asset by
        bankrupt 34, 105
    county, jurisdiction 7
    directions 27, 35, 101
    function in voluntary arrangements 3,
        4
    High, jurisdiction 7
    interim order 3, 8, 43
        powers in connection with 45, 47, 78
    nominee's report, delivery to 28
    payment into 25
    supervisor
        application by, to 27, 35, 82
        appointment of, by 41, 83
        fees of, approval 4
        powers in relation to 81–2
Credit facilities 26, 90, *156*
Creditor(s)
    agreement with
        pre-1986 Act 2
        see also Arrangement; Scheme of
            arrangement
    challenge to decision of creditors'
        meeting 76
    claims, *see* Claims
    committee, *see* Creditors' committee
    composition with, under 1914 Act 2
    'debtor's creditors' 60
    deed of arrangement, assent to 1
    disappears 25
    dissenting minority 3
    fraud on 83, 97
    identity of 20
    Inland Revenue as 117, 120
    meeting of, *see* Creditors' meeting

moratorium with 3, 43, 50
    pre-1986 Act 2
not bound by arrangement 39, 70–1,
    105
notice to 47, 96
    meeting, of 60, 70–1
omission from arrangement 29
particulars of, to nominee 54
payment 23, 24, *143*
    see also Dividend
petition for bankruptcy of debtor, by 93,
    103–4, 106, *192–5*
preferential, *see* Preferential creditor
proposal, and 10, 16, 17
scheme of arrangement, *see* Scheme of
    arrangement
secured, *see* Secured creditor
spouse as 112, 116
supervening bankruptcy, and 107–8
tax on release of debt 120–1
undischarged bankrupt, of 102
unfair prejudice 72, 73–5
voting rights 64–7
Creditors' committee 24, 35, 36, 39
    supervisor, and 84–5
Creditors' meeting
    adjournment 61, 63, 64, *251*
    agreement of claims, at 40
    approval of proposal 3, 15, 18, 21, 61,
        69–70
        challenge to 73 *et seq*, 93
        effect of 70
        majority for 66–67
    amendment of proposal at, *see* Proposal
    chairman, *see* Chairman
    challenge to decision 72–6, 93
        applicants 72, 76–7
    conduct of 62
    convening of
        nominee, by 60, *249*
        supervisor, by 36–7, 39
    date of 23, 54, 59
    debtor's attendance 61
    debtor's bankruptcy petition, on 110
    majority 64, 66–7
    nominee's report, and 54, 55, 56, 59
    notice of 60, 70–1, *172, 173, 249*
        form of 60
    order for 59
    preliminary matters 60, *250*
    proxy
        form 60
        voting by 63–4
    purpose 61
    rejection of proposal 68
        challenge to 73
    resolution 68

Creditors' meeting *continued*
  resolution *continued*
    validity   67
    time   59, *249*
    venue   59, *249*
    voting rights   64–7

Date
  creditors' meeting, of   23, 54, 59
  distribution to creditors, for   24
  dividends, for   24
  preferential debt, for   107
Death
  debtor, of   49, 56, 67–8, 72, *144*
  supervisor, of   62, *145*
Debt
  see also Claim; Creditor; Liabilities
  affidavit of   *199*
  bad debt relief (VAT)   118–19
  contingent   40, *152*
  credit, arising from   26
  guarantor of   22, 23
  matrimonial home, secured on   115–16
  preferential, *see* Preferential creditor
  priority of payment   25
  proof of   38, 39–40
    form for   60, *197–8*
  provable   116
  unliquidated   64–5
Debtor
  accounts   16, 37, 38, 54
  affidavit by   46, 99
  assets of, *see* Asset(s)
  associate of   20, 21, 22, 67, 116
  bankrupt, *see* Bankruptcy; Undischarged
    bankrupt
  business of, during arrangement, *see*
    Business
  challenge to decision of creditors'
    meeting   76
  co-operation by   12, 85
    failure of   95
  credit facilities   26
  creditors' meeting, attendance   61
  criminal liability   97
  death of   49, 56, 67–8, 72, *144*
  default by   17, 19, 26, 35, 39, 85, 93 *et seq, 252*
    see also Default; Offence
  defrauding creditor   83, 97, 106
  duties   85, 94–5
  entry into arrangement   3, 5, 8
    see also Arrangement
  examination on oath   11
  good faith of   12, 97
  income for domestic needs   33
  individual   8, 9

interim order, application for   3, 7, 8, 45,
    99, *248*
  nominee's help, with   9
liabilities, *see* Liabilities
misleading, etc, information by   94, 97
obligations   37, 85, *137–8*
  failure to comply   94
partnership as   13
personal circumstances of   111–12
petition for own bankruptcy   46, 105,
    108–10
  ground for   108
  statement of affairs   108
proposal for voluntary arrangement, *see*
    Proposal
records   54
responsibility   12, 37, 85, 94
statement of affairs   54, 55, 60, 102,
    182–191, 244
  bankruptcy petition, with   108
  undischarged bankrupt, as, *see*
    Undischarged bankrupt
  wrongdoing by   38–39, *140–1*
Deed of arrangement   1, 2, 71
Default
  debtor, of   17, 19, 26, 35, 39, 85, 93 *et seq*
    opportunity to explain   95
  matrimonial matters, and   113, 115
  nominee, of   56
  petition for bankruptcy, for   93, 105, *137*
  procedure on   95–6
Defrauding of creditor   83, 97, 106
Disclaimer   11, 30, 89
Disclosure   35, 38–9
  assets, of   16, 17, *125, 130*
  effect of non-disclosure   94–5
  legal proceedings, of   46
Distribution   24, 25, *155*
  see also Dividend
  uncollected   25
Distribution of property in specie   11, 38
Dividend   25, 38
  date of payment   24
  payment of final   23, 24
  VAT on   119
Document
  proposal for arrangement, as   3, 15
Domestic needs
  debtor's, income for   33
Duration
  interim order, of, *see* Interim order
  voluntary arrangement, of   23, *137*
    extension   23, 35, *137, 155*
Duty of care
  nominee, of   9
  supervisor   84, *147*
Dwellinghouse   90

Dwellinghouse *continued*
  matrimonial home, *see* Matrimonial home
  title 29
  valuation 17, 29
  voluntary homelessness 115

Employee
  contract 91
  PAYE, and 120
Equipment
  value, in proposal 17
Evidence
  bankruptcy petition, for 95
Execution
  interim order, and 43, 45
Expenses
  debtor's income, deducted from 33
  nominee, of 24
  tax liability, and 121
Extortionate credit transaction 11, 20, *127*

Failure of arrangement 93 *et seq*, 96, *141*
Fees
  DTI 99
  nominee's 9, 24, 63
  official receiver's 102
  supervisor's 12, 24, 26, 41, 63
    drawings on account 40
  trustee in bankruptcy's 102
Firm
  voluntary arrangements 8
Forfeiture 30, 43, *152*
Fraud of creditor 83, 97, 106
Freehold *125, 126*
  charge on 32
  sale 87, 89–90
  valuation of 29, *149*
Funds
  administration of, by supervisor 79
  banking and investment 25
  payment into court 25

Guarantor 22, 23, 25, *156*

HM Customs and Excise 37, 38, 62, 90, 117
  et seq
  specialist team 118
High Court
  jurisdiction 7
Home, *see* Dwellinghouse; Matrimonial home
Husband
  see also Spouse
  joint applications 9

Income 33
  after-acquired *159*
  tax on 120
Individual
  meaning 8, 9
Information
  false etc, by debtor 94, 97
Inland Revenue 38, 62, 90, 117 *et seq*
  debtor's history 117
  Enforcement Office 117, 120, 121
Insolvency administration order 49
Insolvency practitioner(s)
  chairman of creditors' meeting 63
  debtor, initial interview with *244*
  nominee, as 4, 9, 28
  fees *252*
  report by, on debtor's bankruptcy
    petition 109–10, *196*
  rivalry between 62
  Society of, guidelines *243–52*
  supervisor, as 3, 4, 28, 61, 62
Intended nominee, *see* Nominee
Interest (money)
  credit facilities, on 26
  creditor's right to 40
Interim order *169*
  accounting period, effect on 118, 120
  affidavit in support 46, 99, *166, 248*
  application for 3, 7, 8, 9, 15, 43, 44–5,
    99, *248*
    bankruptcy petition pending,
      where 104
    circumstances 13
    costs 12, 24
    effect 45, 168
    form *165*
    legal proceedings, disclosure of 46
    requirements for *244*
  conditions for 46
  copy to creditor in litigation 60
  court's power 43
  debtor's bankruptcy petition, made
    on 110
  discharge 50, 56
  duration 50, 71
    extension 50, 56, 57, 71, 78, *171, 177*
  effect 43, 71, 104
    creditors, on 50
  form 50
  hearing 47–8
    adjournment 103
    attendance at 51, 103
    notice of 47, *248*
  made without hearing 47
  nominee's report, court's consideration
    of 55, 103
  one-stage order 57, *170*

Interim order *continued*
  practice direction   51
  purpose of   43
  service   47, 49, 50, 103, *248*
  undischarged bankrupt, wording for   99,
    100
Investment
  funds realised, of   25

Joint ownership
  see also Matrimonial home
  assets   31, 86, 111
  freehold of
    sale   87, 89
    valuation   29, *149*
  leasehold
    sale   89
    valuation   *149*
Jurisdiction   3, 7

Land charges   32, 72, 104
Land Registry   32
Landlord   17, 21, 30, 62, 89
Leasehold
  assignment   89
  charge on   32, 89
  covenant   17, 30, 89
  disclaimer, and   11, 30, 89
  forfeiture   30, 43, *152*
  rent arrears   17, 30, 89
  sale of   17, 30, 87
  surrender   *152*
  valuation   17, 30, 89, *149*
Legal aid   12, 13, 31, 37, 88
Legal proceedings   37, 43, 87–9
  application for interim order, and   46
  costs of   88
  stay of   45
Liabilities   17, 26
  debtor's business, of   91
  particulars of, to nominee   54
  proposal, in   20, 21, 28–9, *126, 130, 131*
    omission   29
  secured   20, *151*
  statement of, *see* Statement of affairs
  tax, *see* Taxation
Liability
  debtor's criminal   97
  nominee's   9
  supervisor, of   84, 89, *127, 147, 160*
Lien   18, 32
Life policy   *158*
  value, in proposal   17, 32, *158*
Litigation, *see* Legal proceedings

Material irregularity   72, 74, 75–6
Material omission   94
Matrimonial home   19, 111
  bankruptcy, and   113
  beneficial interest in   114, 115
  charge on, to secure debt   115–16
  effect of arrangement on   114–15
  joint ownership   113, 115
  sale   114–16
  sole ownership by debtor   113, 115
  third party rights   113–14, *157*
  voluntary homelessness   115
Matrimonial proceedings   89, 111
  effect of interim order   112–13
Minor
  see also Child
  occupation of matrimonial home by   113
Misleading information   94
Misrepresentation   97
Modifications to proposal   15, 18, 21, 28, 36,
    61, *146, 250–1*
Moratorium with creditors   3, 43, 50
  pre-1986 Act   2
Mortgage   18
Motor vehicle
  exclusion from proposal   32
  value, in proposal   17, 32, *158*

National insurance contributions   33
Nominee   3, 4, 9, 12
  chairman of creditors' meeting, as   62–3
  challenge to decision of creditors'
    meeting   76
  debtor's duty to inform of bankruptcy
    etc   102
  duty of care   9
  expenses   24
  fees   9, 24, 63
  intended   9, 12, 16, 20, 53
    agreement to act   44
    charges etc, and   32
    leaseholds, and   30
    notice of proposal to   44, 46, *167*
  liability   9
  liaison with official receiver/trustee   49,
    102
  official receiver as   4
  powers   54
  proposal
    amendment of, agreement to   28
    comments on   *249*
    details in   *127*
    preparation of, by   9, 15, 27
  qualification   28, 46
    see also Insolvency practitioner(s)
  quantification of claims   24

Nominee *continued*
  replacement 56
    supervisor, as 61, 62
  report of 3, 12, 28, *133–5, 249*
    copies 55
    court's consideration of 55, 57, 103
    extension of interim order for 50
    form 54
    inspection 55
    particulars for 54
    purpose 54
    submission to court 53
  supervisor, as 4, 28, 61, 62, 81
  tax returns, and 38
  third party to debtor/creditor contract,
    as 4
  vacancy in office 56
Notice
  interim order hearing, of 47, 49, 100, 101,
    248
  claim, of 66–7
  completion of arrangement, of 96
  creditors' meeting, of 60, 70–1, *172,
    173*
    constructive or implied 70
  proposal, of 44, 46, *167*

Offence
  debtor, by 97
Official receiver 4, 11
  appearance at hearings 103
  chairman's report, copy to 68
  challenge to decision of creditors'
    meeting 76
  fees 102
  interim order
    appearance at hearing 47, 49, 103
    application for, by 45, 99
    notice of, to 47, 49, 100, 101, *248*
  notice of proposal, to 44
Order
  adjudication, of 2
  administration 2
  interim, *see* Interim order
  receiving 1

PAYE 90, 120
Partner
  disqualification 13
  insolvency petition against 13
  interim order application by 8, 9
Partnership
  petition against 13
  unregistered company, as 13, 14
  voluntary arrangements 8, 9, 13, 14

  winding up of 13, 14
Payment, *see* Dividend
Pension policy 32
Personal representatives 49, *144*
Petition for bankruptcy, *see* Bankruptcy
Plant
  value of, in proposal 17
Power of attorney 37, 86, *147, 161*
Preferences 11, 38, *154*
  voidable 106, *127*
Preferential creditor
  categories 21
  debtor undischarged bankrupt 102
  HM Customs and Excise, as 117
  Inland Revenue, as 117
  proposal, in 20, 21, 25, 61, *151–2*
  rights of 21, 61, 117
  supervening bankruptcy, in 107–8
Procedure
  bankruptcy petition for default, for 95–6
  voluntary arrangement, for 3, 8
    flow chart 5
Profits 38
Proof of debt 38, 39–40
  form for 60, *197–8*
Property
  see also Asset(s); Dwellinghouse;
    Matrimonial home
  annulment of bankruptcy, after 102–3
  bankruptcy, meaning in 18
  disposal of
    debtor, by, after bankruptcy
      petition 34, 105
    supervisor, by 84, 105
  encumbrance on 32
  freehold, *see* Freehold
  leasehold, *see* Leasehold
  other than assets, in proposal 19
Proposal 3–5
  accuracy 94–5, *243*
  amendments to 15, 18, 21, 28, 36, 61, *146,
    250–1*
    time for 28
  approval, *see* Approval of proposal
  assets, *see* Asset(s)
  bankruptcy
    principles 38
    supervening, provision for 107
  business, ongoing 26
    see also Business
  charges 32
  completion of arrangement 97
  contents 10, 15, 16 *et seq*, 84, *125 et seq,
    246–7*
  copy of 46, 60
  credit facilities 26
  creditor not bound, inclusion in 39

Proposal *continued*
　debtor's obligations　37
　　failure to comply　94
　default provisions　35, 39, 95, 96
　　see also Default
　desirability for　10, 16
　disclosure, warranty of　35
　draft clauses　*147–61*
　duration of arrangement　23, 35, *137*
　failure of arrangement　96, *141*
　false or misleading information in　94–5
　implementation　*252*
　　debtor's duties　85
　　supervisor's duties　84 *et seq*
　income　33
　interest (money)　40
　liabilities, *see* Liabilities
　matrimonial proceedings, and　112, 115
　modifications to　15, 18, 21, 28, 36, 61,
　　146, 250–1
　nominee, and, *see* Nominee
　nominee's report on, *see* Nominee
　preferential creditor　20, 21, 25, 61,
　　151–2
　preparation　9, 15, 16 *et seq*
　property other than assets　19
　rejection　68
　revised　77–8
　secured creditor　20–1, 61
　standard conditions　34, 60, *136–46*
　supervisor's fees, and　24
　　see also Supervisor
　taxation, and　117, 119, 120
　trust, debtor's declaration　34, 35, *138*
　voidable transactions, *see* Extortionate
　　credit transaction; Preferences;
　　Transaction at undervalue
　written document　3, 15
Proxy
　creditors' meeting
　　form　60, *202*
　　voting by　63–4

Receiving order
　abolition　1
Records
　debtor's　54
　supervisor's　27, 79–81
Register
　individual voluntary arrangements, of　69
Remuneration
　see also Costs; Fees
　nominee, of　9, 24, 63
　professional adviser, of　24
　supervisor, of　12, 24, 63
Rent arrears　17, 30, 89

Report
　see also Records
　chairman of creditors' meeting, of, *see*
　　Chairman
　insolvency practitioner, by, on debtor's
　　bankruptcy petition　109–10, *196*
　nominee, of, *see* Nominee
　Secretary of State, to　69, *176*
　supervisor's　79–81, 96, *175*
Reservation of title　18, *150*
Resolution of creditors' meeting　68
　validity　67
Returns
　tax　38
　VAT　119

Scheme of arrangement　44
　composition with creditors compared　44
　under 1914 Act　2
　voluntary arrangement, as　44
Secretary of State
　notice to by supervisor　69, *176*
　report to by chairman　69, *176*
Secured creditor
　exercise of right of sale by　90
　meaning　17, 18
　notice of claim　67
　notice of creditors' meeting to　60
　proposal, in　20–1, 61
　servicing of debt of　89–90
　supervening bankruptcy, and　107–8
Securities　31, *157*
Security　25
Service
　see also Notice
　interim order hearing, of　47, 49
　　when pending bankruptcy petition　103
　'concertina order', and　57
Set-off　31, 38
　VAT, of　118
Shares　31, *157*
Solicitor
　fees　24
Spouse
　see also Matrimonial home; Matrimonial
　　proceedings
　associate, as　21, 116
　contribution of asset by　19
　creditor, as　112, 116
　debtor separated from　89
　gift to　21, 22
　'joint application' by　9, 112
　position of　111–12
Standard conditions　34, 60, *136–46, 159*
Statement of affairs　54, 55, 60, 102, *244*
　bankruptcy petition, with　108

Statement of affairs *continued*
  creditors' petition *192–5*
  debtor's petition *182–91*
Stay of action 45, *168*
Stay of bankruptcy proceedings 48, 71, 100
Stock in trade 19, 91, *150*
Stocks 31
Supervisor 3, 4, 17
  accounts 27, 79–81, *252*
  advertising for claims by 39
  affidavit by 95
  appointment 41, 83
  assets
    after-acquired 33
    capital gains tax on 120
    holding of 27, 86, 102
    trustee of, as 34, 35, *138*
  bank account 25, *143–4*
  claims, and 39–40, 85, *142*
  completion of arrangement, duties 96,
    252
  court
    directions from 27, 35, 82, 84, *142*
    powers on application from debtor
      etc 81–2
  creditors
    advice from *142*
    certificate of compliance to 41
    duty to inform 84–5
    notice of completion of arrangement
      to 96
  creditors' meeting, convening of 36–7
  death 62, *145*
  debtor, contact with 85, 86, 95
  dividends, responsibility for 25
  duties 27, 35, 84
  expenses 24, *143–4*
  fees 12, 24, 26, 41, 63
    drawings on account 40
  grievance against 81–2, 85
  insolvency practitioner as 3, 4, 28, 61, 62
  joint 62
  liability 84, *127, 147, 160*
  leaseholds, and 89
  moratorium with creditors pre-1986 Act,
    of 2
  negligence *147*
  nominee, in place of 61, 62
  notice of appointment, to Secretary of
    State 69, *176*
  official receiver as 4
  PAYE, and 120
  petition for bankruptcy of debtor, by 93,
    105
  power of attorney 37, 86, *147, 161*
  powers 11, 21, 27, 32, 35, 84, *140, 147,*
    159–60

qualification 28
records 27, 79–81
removal 83
report 79–81, 96, *175*
resignation 41
responsibilities 27, 35
role 27, 35, 79
taxation, and 119, 120
third party to debtor/creditor contract,
  as 4
trustee, as 27, 44
undertaking by, to official
  receiver/trustee 102
VAT, and 118–19
vacancy in office 41, 69, 83, *145*

Taxation 33, 38, 91, 117 *et seq*
  bad debts 118–19, 121
  capital gains tax roll-over relief 119–20
  deduction, creditor and 120–1
  outstanding accounts 120
  provable liability, as 119
  VAT, *see* VAT
Taxation authorities, *see* HM Customs and
  Excise; Inland Revenue
Termination of arrangement 93 *et seq*, 96,
  144–5
Third party
  assets of 19–20, 25
  debtor/creditor contract, to 4
  guarantor, as 25, *155*
  matrimonial home, and, *see* Matrimonial
    home
  obligations 19–20, *139–40, 151*
Time limit
  see also Duration
  amendment of proposal, for 28
  appeal against chairman's decision,
    for 65
  challenge of decision of creditors' meeting,
    for 77
Title
  assets, to 86
  freehold, to 29
Trade, *see* Business
Trading accounts 16, 37, 38, 54
  VAT, for 118
Transaction at undervalue 11, 20, 21, 22,
  38, 106, *127, 153*
Trust
  assets held in 34, *147, 148, 161*
  interests in 16, 29
Trustee
  see also Trustee in bankruptcy
  assets held by debtor as 16
  deed of arrangement, of 1

Trustee *continued*
  moratorium with creditors pre-1986 Act,
      of 2
  scheme of arrangement, under 44
  supervisor as 27, 44
Trustee in bankruptcy
  after-acquired property 33
  appearance at hearings 103
  appointment 108
  chairman's report, copy to 68
  challenge to decision of creditors'
      meeting 76
  fees 102
  interim order
    appearance at hearing 47, 49, 103
    application for, by 45, 99
    notice of, to 47, 49, 100, 101, *248*
  notice of proposal to 44
  powers 11, 21

Undertaking
  supervisor's to official
      receiver/trustee 102
Undervalue, *see* Transaction at undervalue
Undischarged bankrupt
  annulment of order 100, 101, 102–3
  assets 102
  bankruptcy to continue 99 *et seq,*
      154–5
  creditors of 102
  debtor as 99 *et seq*
    declaration by 99
    interim order, and 13, 45, 46, 48, 99,
        100, 103
    legal aid 12
    meaning of 'creditors' 60
  flow chart 5

property hand-over 102
Unfair prejudice 72, 73–5

VAT 37, 38, 90, 91, 117
  bad debt relief 118–19
  debtor's registration 119
  returns 119
  supervisor's position 118
Valuation
  assets, of, in proposal 16, 17, 22
  book debts 30
  copy of, to creditor 60
  creditor's right to complain 17
  dwellinghouse 17, 29
  freehold 29, *149*
  leasehold 17, 30, 89, *149*
  life policy 17, 32
  motor vehicles 17, 32
  plant 17
  securities 31
  work in progress 31
Vehicle
  exclusion from proposal 32
  value, in proposal 17, 32, *158*
Voidable transaction, *see* Extortionate credit
      transaction; Preferences; Transaction at
      undervalue
Vote
  creditors' meeting, at 63, 64–7
  proxy, by 60, 63–4

Warranty 35, *136*
Wife
  see also Spouse
  joint applications 9
Work in progress 19, 23, 26, 87
  value 31